DOODLE EASY LANDSCAPES WITH JUST A PEN

DRAW *the* GREAT OUTDOORS!

HARRISON
HOW

PAGE STREET
PUBLISHING CO.

PAGE STREET
PUBLISHING CO.

First published in 2024 by
Page Street Publishing Co.
27 Congress Street, Suite 1511
Salem, MA 01970
www.pagestreetpublishing.com

Distributed by Macmillan, sales in Canada by The Canadian Manda Group.

28 27 26 25 24 1 2 3 4 5

ISBN-13: 979-8-8900-313-2-7

Library of Congress Control Number: 2023949691

Edited by Alexandra Murphy
Book design by Emma Hardy for Page Street Publishing Co.
Cover and Illustrations by Harrison How

Printed and bound in the United States of America

trustees

Page Street Publishing protects our planet by donating to nonprofits like The Trustees, which focuses on local land conservation.

Dear Grandma Bobbie,

I love you more than words can say. You have been an inspiration to me my entire life. Your tenacity and resilience have taught me so much about how to face life's challenges with courage.

I will never forget how you supported me by sending newspaper clippings of the week's best comics. I'm so grateful for every card you've sent my way! You have shown me that no matter what life throws your way, you can always find a way to smile and do something kind for others.

Thank you for being such a strong role model for me. I am so grateful to have you in my life.

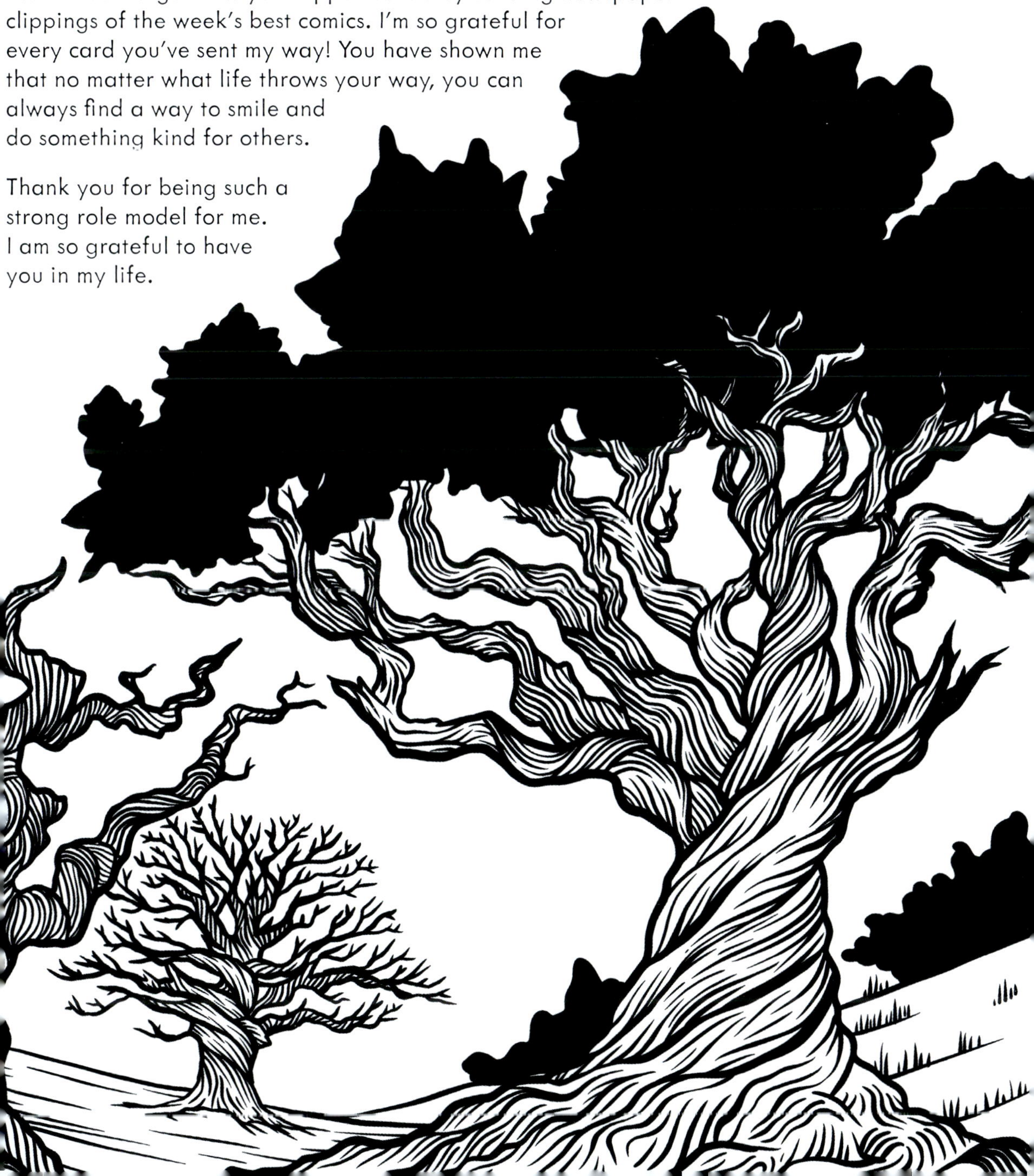

CONTENTS

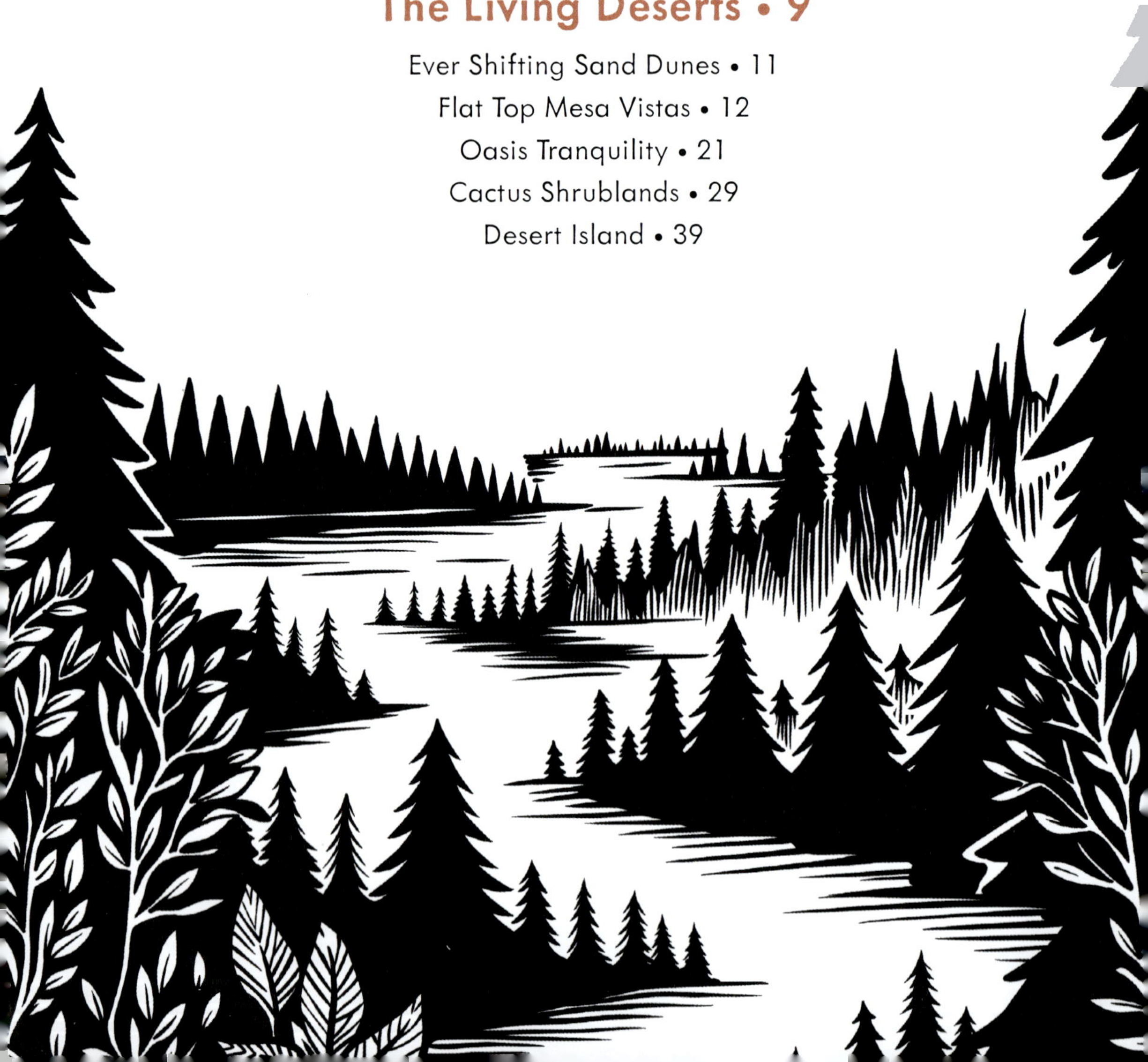

The Mountains Are Calling • 49

Spirited Arboreal Places • 81

Shifting Coastal Seascapes • 111

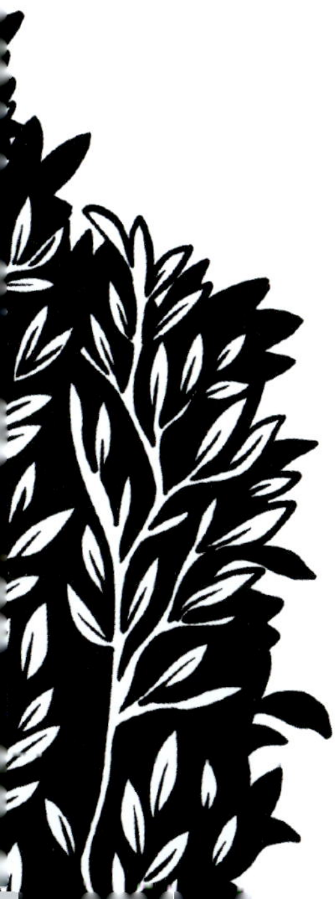

INTRODUCTION

Welcome, fellow art enthusiasts and nature lovers, to the enchanting realm of *Draw the Great Outdoors!*, where creativity and mindfulness converge to unveil the wonders of the natural world. Embark on an immersive journey of artistic exploration, where you'll discover the transformative power of drawing nature and the joy of capturing its beauty on paper.

This comprehensive guide is designed to cater to drawing enthusiasts of all skill levels, from budding beginners to seasoned artists seeking new inspiration. Whether you're drawn to the intricate details of a thorny cactus or the grandeur of a snow-capped mountain range, this book will gently guide you through the process of capturing nature's unique landscapes.

As you progress through the book, you'll unlock a treasure trove of resources.

The book's content is meticulously structured to progressively build your artistic confidence. You'll begin each scene by doodling fundamental elements, like plants and rocks, before progressing to astounding scenes that incorporate these building blocks. Some scenes even stand alone, showcasing how seemingly simple elements can coalesce over time into a captivating composition. This approach aims to empower you to learn not only the "building blocks" of nature but also how to creatively combine them to create your own unique landscapes.

It's important to note that my personal art process is dynamic and adapts to the specific scene I'm depicting. While this book provides step-by-step guidance through detailed specific tutorials, my individual creative process doesn't always follow such a structured approach. However, by understanding how to draw these landscapes, you'll be equipped to approach drawing many places with confidence and creativity. I'm here to empower you to embark on your own artistic journey through the wonders of the natural world.

Drawing nature is not merely an artistic pursuit; it's an act of mindfulness that fosters a deeper connection with the natural world. As you observe the intricate details of a leaf, the gentle sway of a tree branch or the mesmerizing flow of a river, you'll find yourself immersed in the present moment, slowing down and appreciating the beauty that surrounds you.

Studies have shown that immersing yourself in the act of drawing nature can be like hitting the reset button on your mind and body. Think reduced stress and anxiety, replaced by a sense of calm focus. Feel your creativity and problem-solving skills blossom as you engage with the intricate details and diverse forms found in the natural world. Imagine sharpening your concentration as you meticulously capture the essence of a scene on paper.

Drawing has had a profound impact on my emotional well-being, fostering a deeper connection with and appreciation for the beauty that surrounds us.

So, grab your drawing tools and prepare to embark on a journey that's as good for your soul as it is for your artistic expression. This book is your guide, offering not just simple tips and techniques, but also a window into the transformative power of drawing nature. Let's get started, and together we'll unlock the magic of the great outdoors, one mindful line at a time.

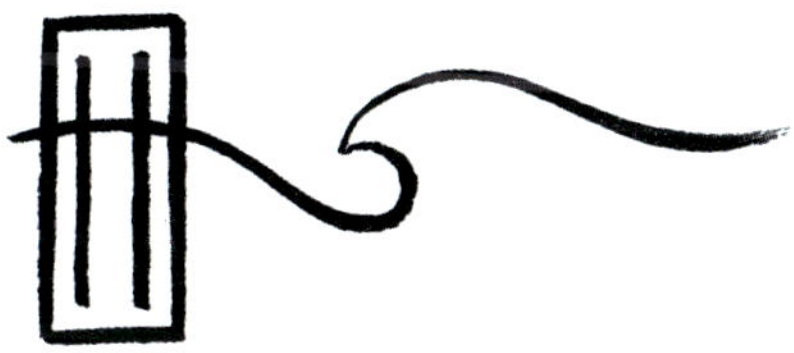

Tip: All drawing mediums can work with this book! However, I believe that drawing with pen helps build confidence most quickly, due to its permanence. Permanent pens, markers and inks allow us to learn how to adjust and overcome the mistakes in a drawing. That being said, drawing digitally is another top notch medium that can allow the gift of an easy undo. Whatever you choose, commit and take time to develop a relationship with your mediums to allow for a greater focus on the art itself.

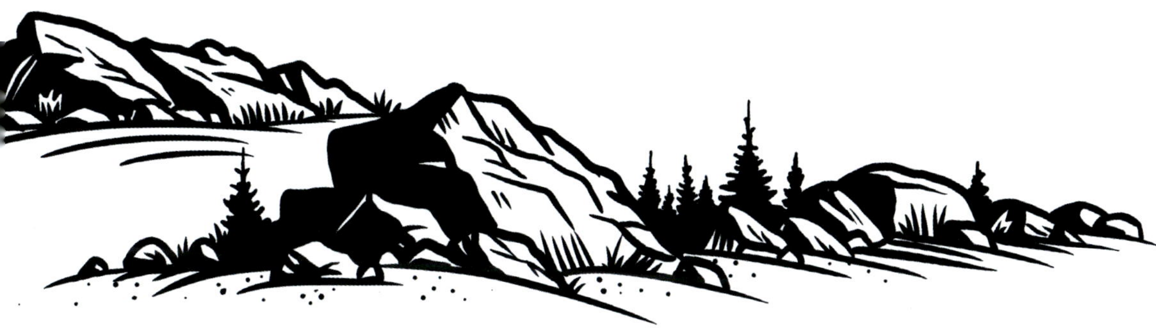

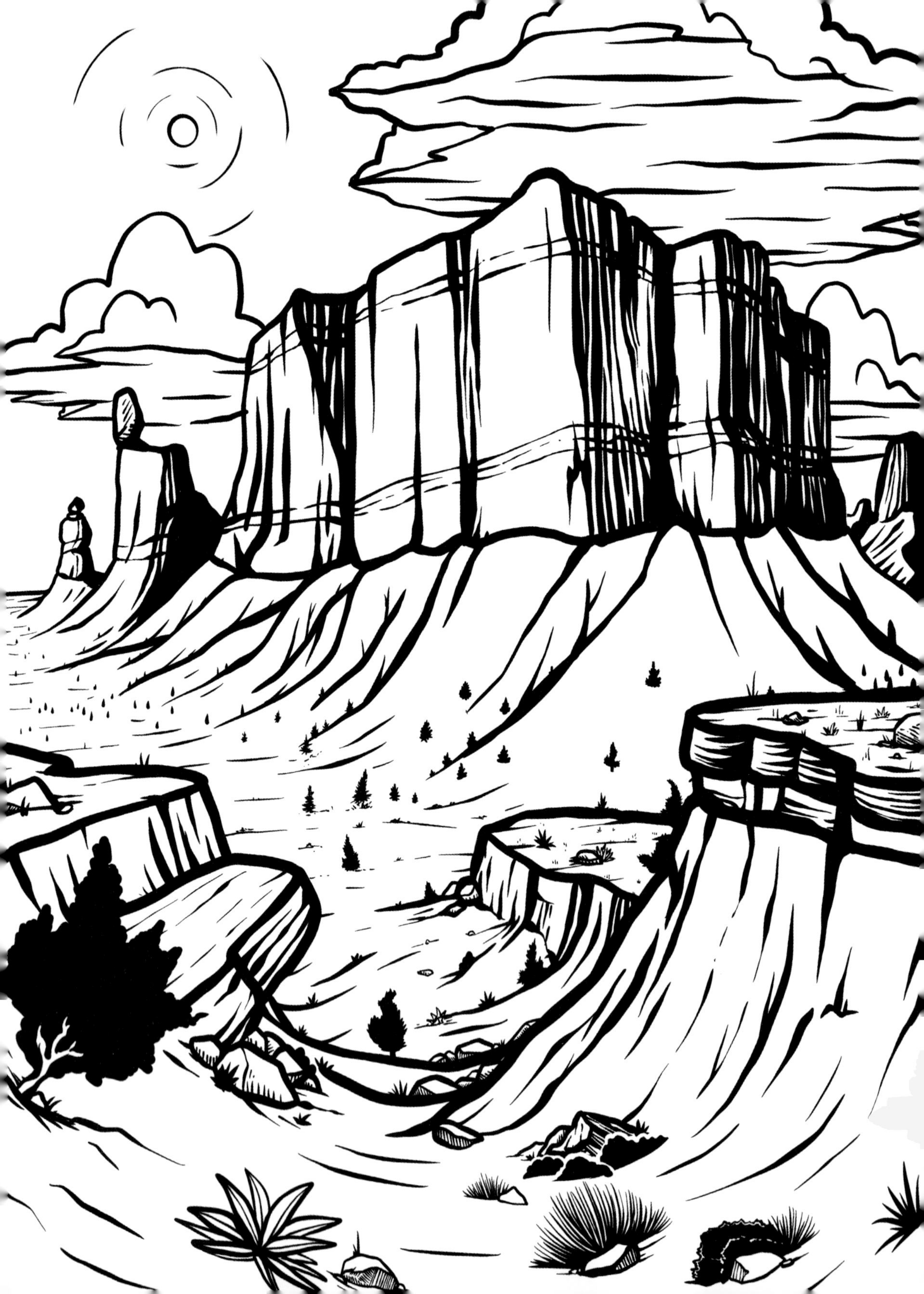

THE LIVING DESERTS

The deserts of our planet stretch across vast expanses; their landscapes are painted in hues of rock, dirt and sand. Under the relentless gaze of the sun, these arid lands seem devoid of life, their surfaces parched and barren. Yet beneath this stark exterior lies an intricate web of life, adapted to the harsh conditions of the desert.

It's a land of hidden wonders, waiting to be discovered. Hardy succulents cling tenaciously to the terrain, their plump leaves storing precious moisture like tiny water balloons. The pointed cacti stand with rows of spines in the scorching sun. We'll delve into majestic Flat Top Mesa Vistas (page 12) and see how easy they are to draw. We will explore the diverse ecosystems of Cactus Shrublands (page 29) and learn to grasp the essence of these complex landscapes on paper. Scattered amidst the desert's vastness, we'll discover Oasis Tranquility (page 21), providing a life-giving haven where lush vegetation thrives, offering a stark contrast to the surrounding aridity.

But why start in the desert? The desert, despite its challenges, is a place where beauty thrives in unexpected ways. It's a testament to the power of adaptation, resilience and the sheer tenacity of life. And I can't wait to guide you, step by step, as you learn to translate this unique beauty onto the page. We will learn about stacking compositions, adding depth, using a variety of line weights and so much more.

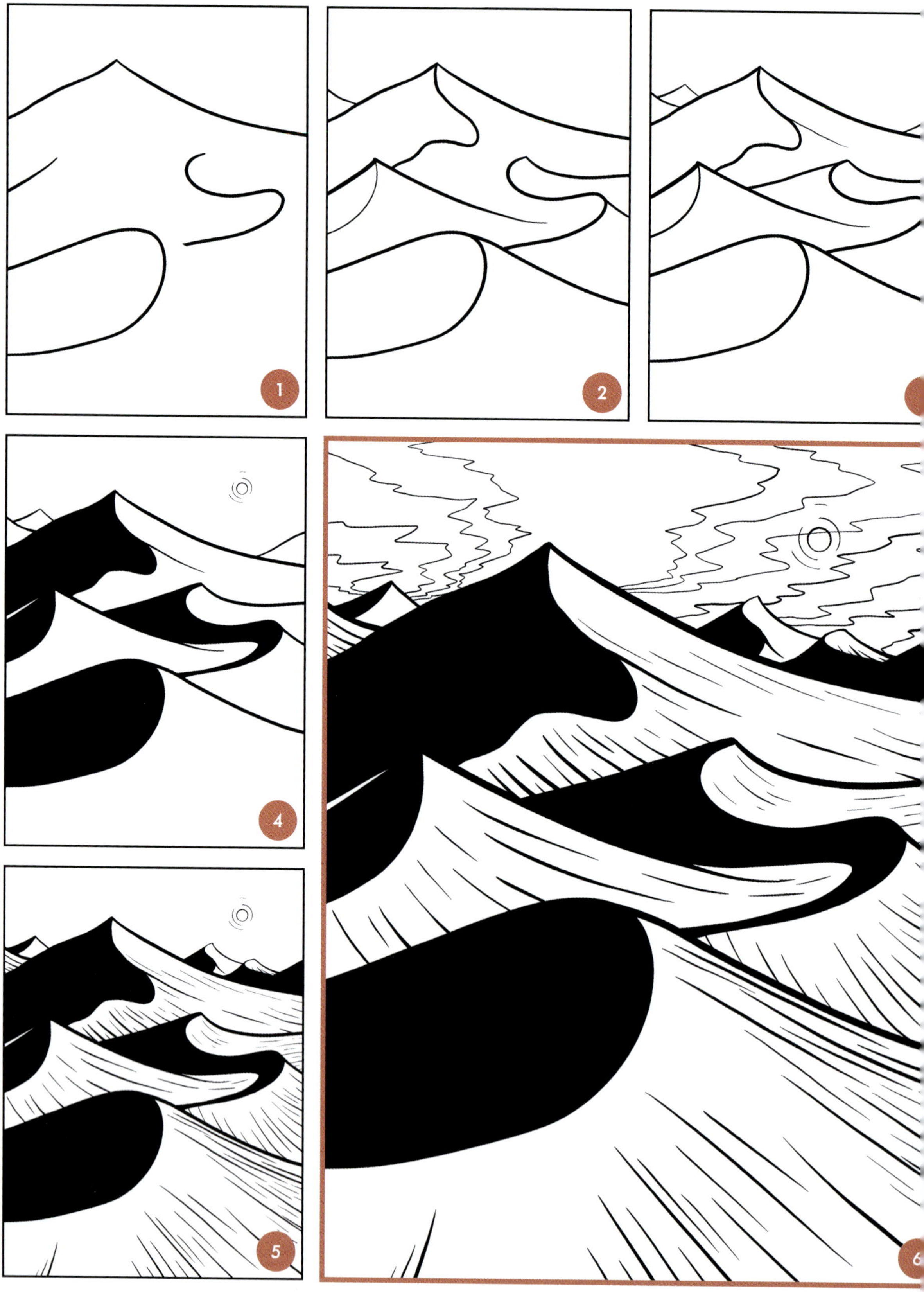
1
2
4
5

1. Ever Shifting Sand Dunes

The desert wind whispers secrets as it sculpts the sand into hypnotizing dunes, their shapes ever-shifting under the sun's gaze. Let's create their dance with simple lines, creating a sense of movement and vastness in our very first drawing. No need for complex details yet—just pure desert magic and an immediate artistic win! So, grab your pencil and prepare to be surprised by the simplicity of drawing these iconic landscapes.

1. Start with a curvy, asymmetrical S shape on the right side of the frame. Make the top curve slightly shorter and wider than the bottom one. Add a similar bigger S shape on the left, but let it run out of frame. Above these shapes, make an upside-down V that connects the sides of the frame.

2. Begin to lay in your dune shapes! From each high point of the S shapes, draw a sloping line to the right side, that curves parallel to your top V shape. From the pointy peaks of the dunes, add some curvy ridgelines and draw another dune hidden in the background on the top left.

3. Complete the front dunes. Add a slope from the point of the first S shape toward the left until it hits the other dune. From the curve of the big dune in the back, add a small slope. Then add some simple dunes in the background with more upside-down Vs or dashes.

4. Draw a blazing hot sun with a small circle in the sky then add a few arcs circling randomly for some extra heat waves. For the shadows, shade in the left sides of the main dunes following the S-like curves you created.

5. Build the background by shading the left of the small dune, then repeat all these steps with another layer of dune shapes in the top right of the frame. Add some sandy texture to the middle-ground dunes with dashes that follow their natural slopes. For the dune in the foreground, add slanting dashes that begin slightly lower than its slope and connect them to the bottom of the frame.

6. To complete this landscape with even more heat, draw some dehydrated cirrus clouds by using squiggles back and forth from the top of the page to the horizon.

2. Flat Top Mesa Vistas

Perched atop mesas, flat-topped plateaus offer breathtaking vistas of the surrounding landscape. These expansive views, stretching towards the horizon, provide a sense of vastness and grandeur. Before we embark on capturing the breathtaking vistas from a flat-topped mesa, let's equip ourselves with some essential artistic tools! Fear not, fellow artists, for these tools are far simpler than they might seem. We'll be learning how to break down these majestic formations into basic shapes, allowing you to confidently translate their grandeur onto paper.

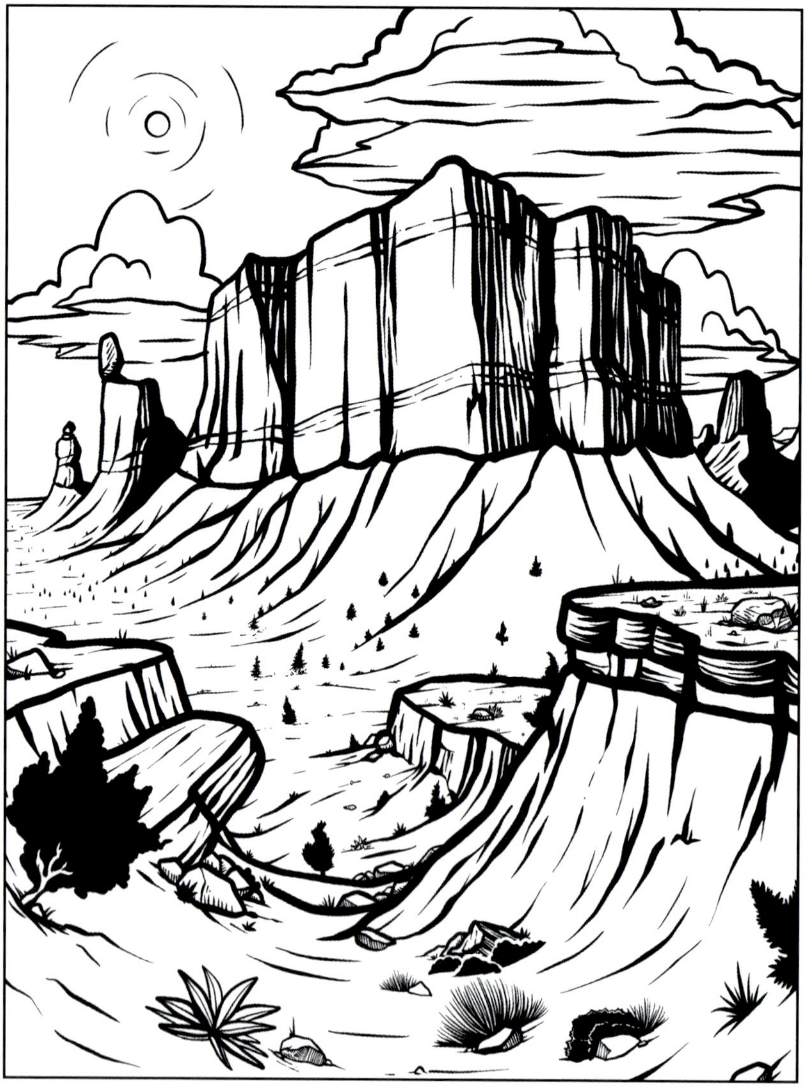

Rocks

Solid in their simplicity, rocks are a strong staple for many of our landscape drawings. They might seem daunting at first, but like many natural wonders, rocks can be simplified into basic shapes. This little tutorial will show you how to transform a couple of jagged ovals into a convincing pile of rocks, building the foundation for your future landscape drawings.

1

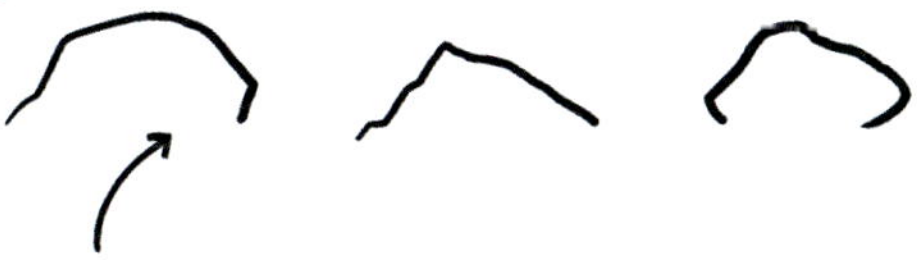

Start with a couple jagged half-circle shapes in a line.

2

Add a small pebble or two underneath the rocks.

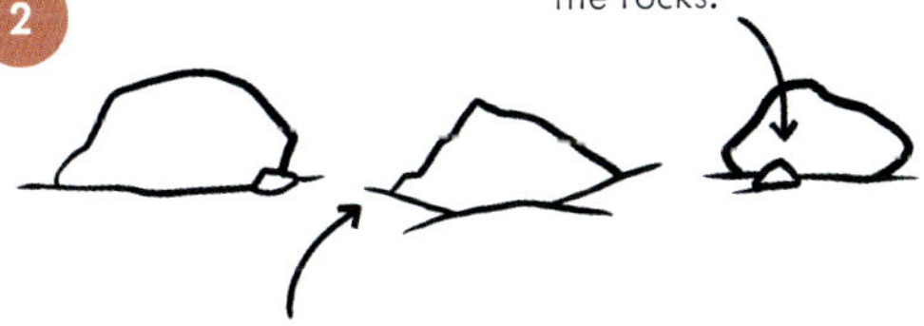

Draw the ground they're resting on with a few horizontal strokes. For a half-buried look, have one small line across the bottom with a few diagonal strokes on each side.

3

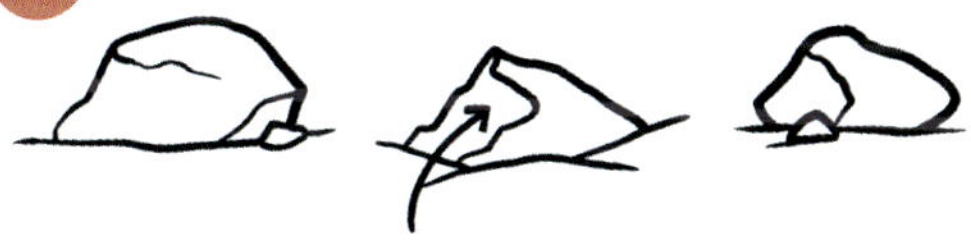

Add jagged diagonal strokes across the center of your rocks.

4

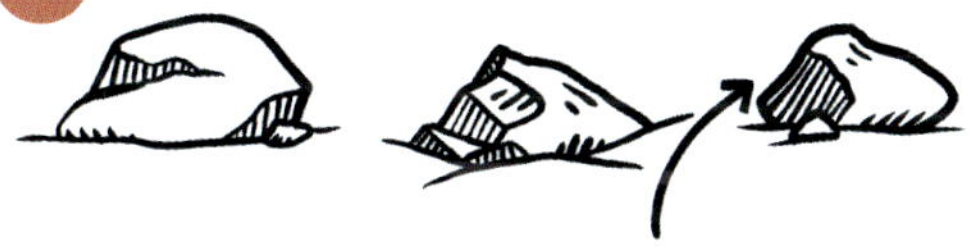

Shade your rocks with diagonal dashes on the bottom and along the opposite side of your light source (in this example, the sun is at the top right).

Desert Chaparral

Short, stout bushes, despite their spiky nature, can be drawn using a series of layered shapes, transforming them into a spiky haven of shade and protection for small creatures in your landscapes.

Draw a cloud-like shape with a flat bottom and squiggly roundish top.

1

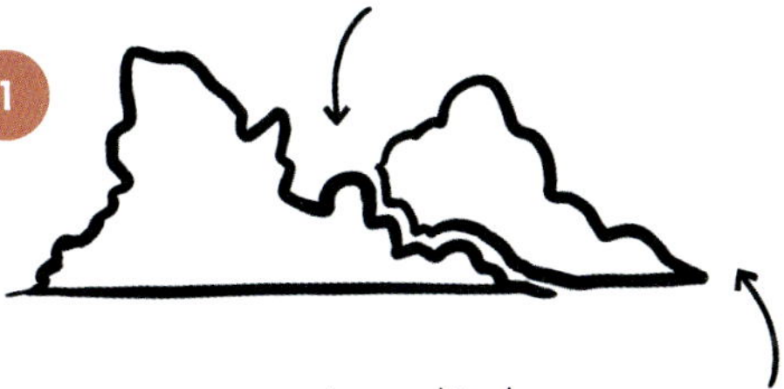

Layer this shape as many times as you like to create a fuller bush.

2

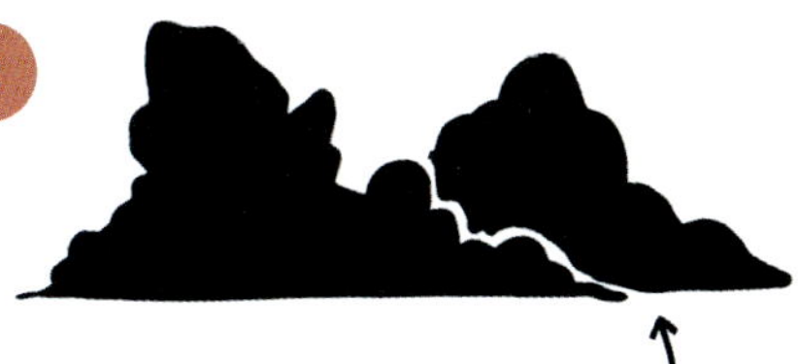

Shade in your bushes, leaving a light outline between your layers.

Juniper Trees

Despite their potentially rugged appearance, junipers are super simple to draw. This tutorial will show you how to break down a juniper tree into basic shapes, layer by layer, until you have a convincing shrub tree to add to your landscape drawings.

1

Make a gnarled trunk by drawing two lines that come up from the ground and branch out at the top.

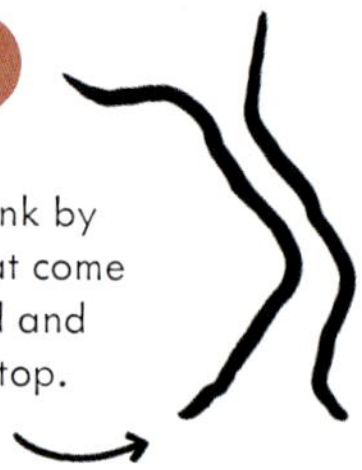

2

Add branches with sporadic V shapes from the top of the trunk.

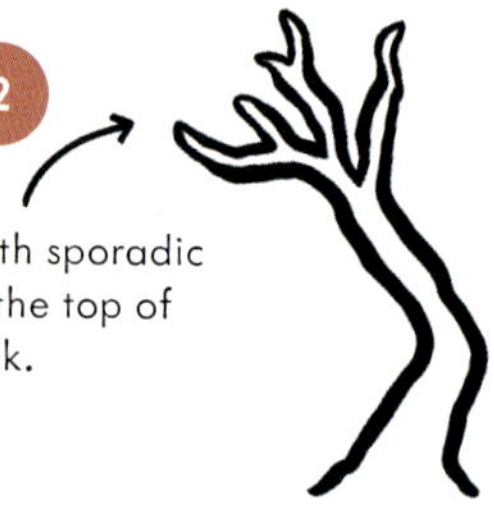

3

Cap your branches at their tops and draw a spiky tree shape around them in any shape that feels right to you.

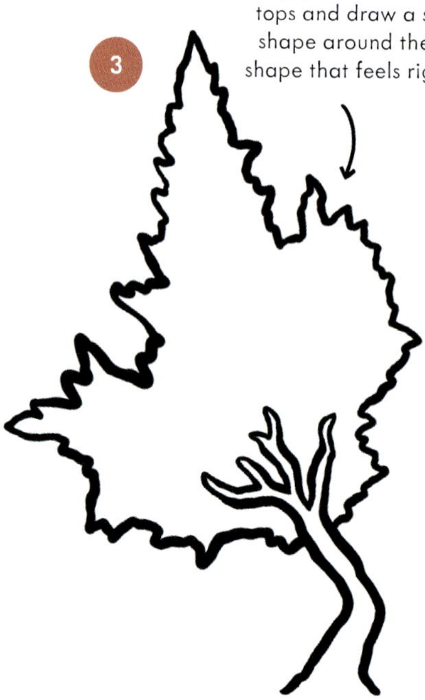

4

Shade in your foliage.

Add a few veiny lines to the trunk for a bark effect.

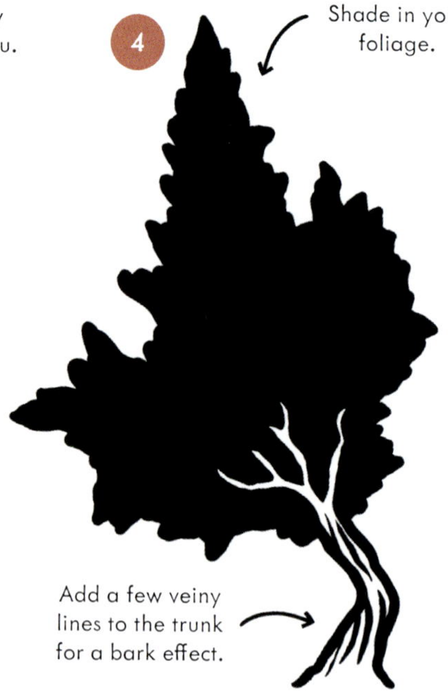

Spiny Succulent

These plants are great at storing moisture in the desert and ward off those looking for a drink with thick skins and scary spikes! Tough on the outside but beautiful, their unique forms can be recreated using a surprisingly simple technique of layering a series of pointed leaves.

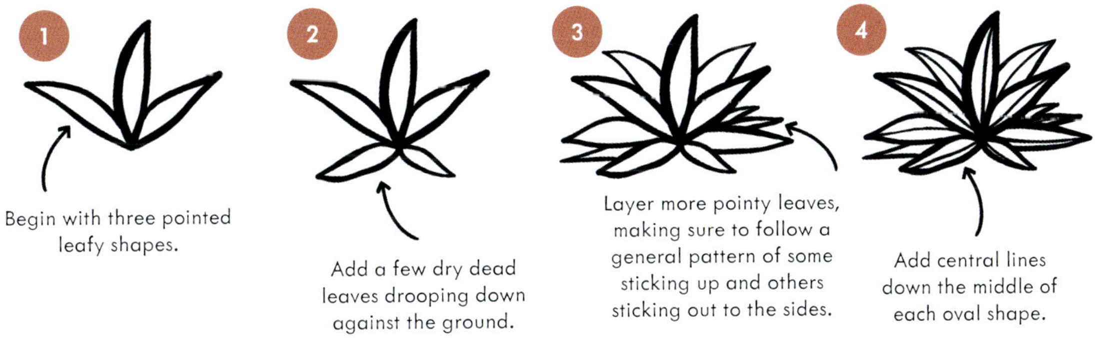

Bunch Grasses

Grass may seem like a tangled mess, but don't worry! These grasses are fun and easy to draw. With a few basic strokes, you can capture the essence of these landscape staples and they can be used in many ways in a variety of landscapes. Vertical dashes are the building blocks you need to create lush meadows and grassy hills in your drawings.

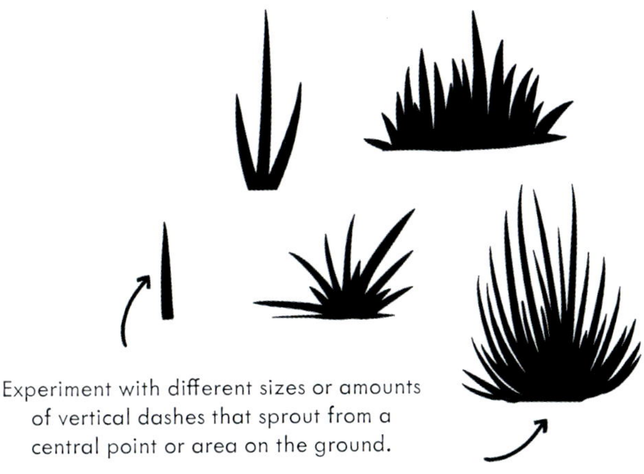

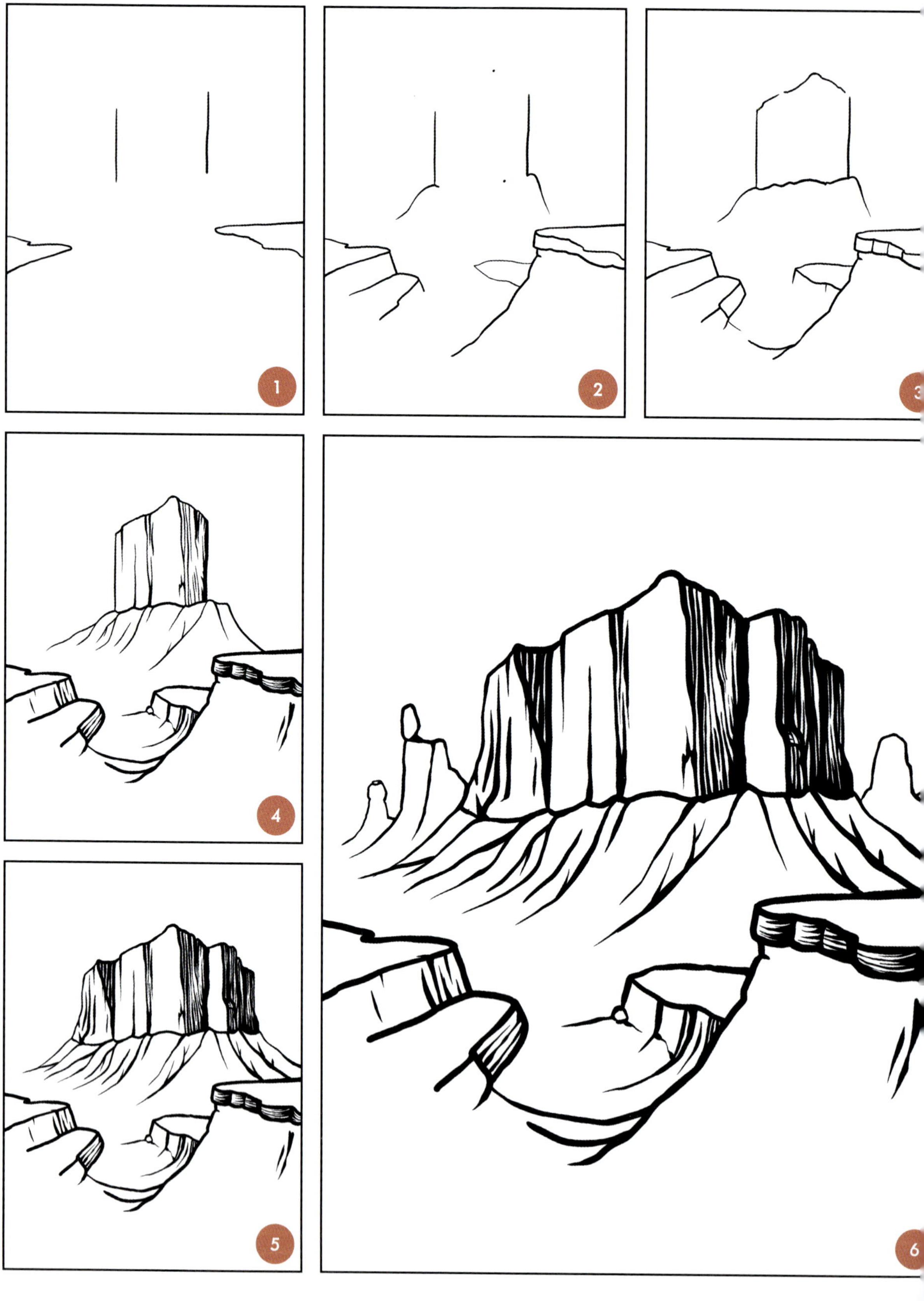
1
2
3
4
5
6

Now, Let's Draw the Scene

(See full image on page 12)

1. Start with some sideways V shapes on each side of the frame that are slightly level to each other. Draw two parallel vertical lines spaced apart in the center above those Vs, leaving a good amount of space between them.

2. Turn the V shapes into flat tops by adding some jagged cliff lines down from their points and another layer of flat tops below. Draw small curved slopes on the bottom of each parallel line. Add two reference dots in between the parallel lines at the top and bottom.

3. Using the dots, add wiggles that connect the slopes at the bottom and the top of the parallel lines, creating a pointed peak. Connect your mesas at the bottom with a curve in the center and add a few dashes down the flat tops.

4. Begin adding rocky texture with a variety of vertical lines up and down the central mesa, concentrating them on the right side. Add cliff faces by drawing lines on the bottom of the mesa that trail outward. Draw horizontal and vertical dashes to create shading under the flat tops.

5. Build more grandeur into your giant mesa by creating similar shapes on each side and lines trailing down the sides. Draw more of those vein-like lines on the bottom of your mesa.

6. Add distant mesas and get creative with their shapes; you can even add precariously balanced rocks on top.

(continued)

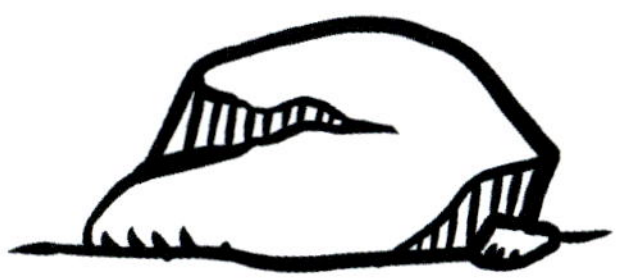

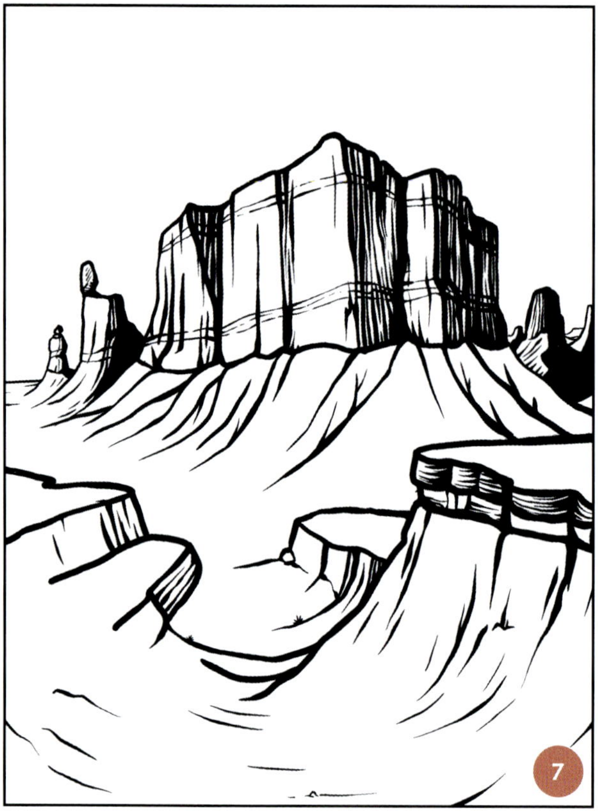
7

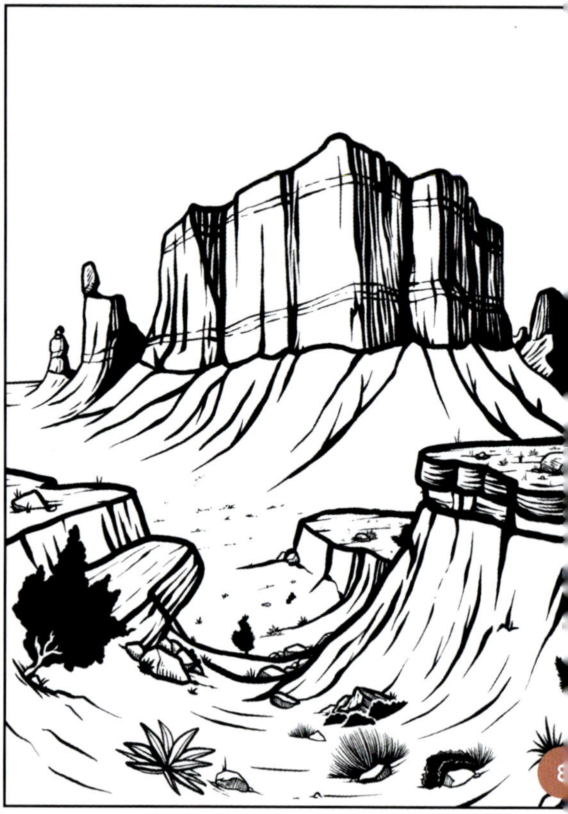

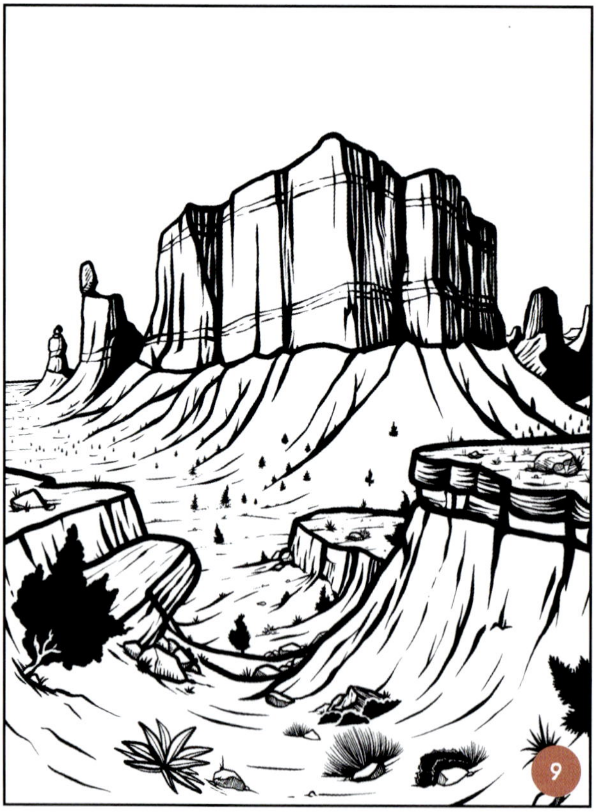
9

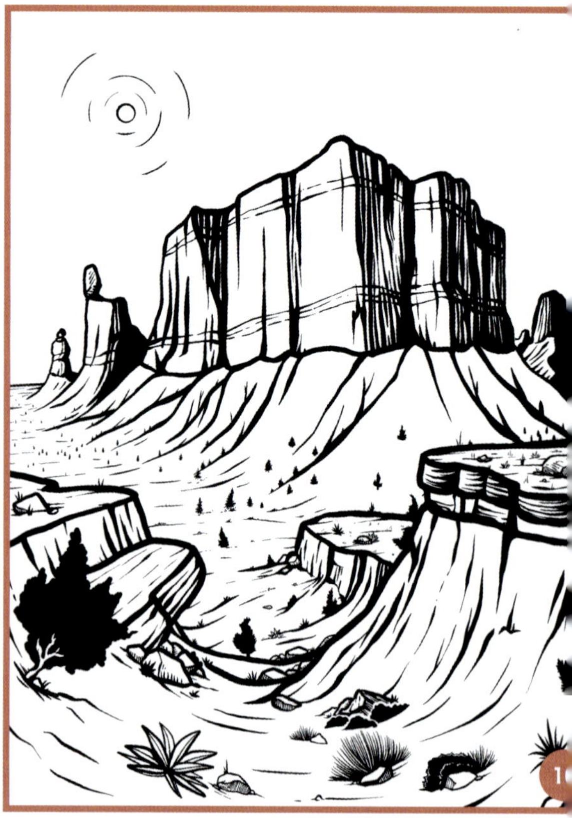

Now, Let's Draw the Scene (Final Steps)

7. Shade the right sides of these distant rocky shapes and add some details. Then draw horizontal striations along the top and bottom of your mesa, following the shape of the cliff face. Add some curving dashes to the foreground to indicate where the mesas connect to the desert ground.

8. Draw in desert shrubs in the foreground and on the mesa tops. Try a variety of Desert Chaparral (page 13), Spiny Succulents (page 15) and Bunch Grasses (page 15) in different sizes and shapes. Add a few Juniper Trees (page 14) and Rocks (page 13) in the fore and middle ground.

9. Add even more juniper trees in the middle ground with varying sizes of scribbly triangles and dashes that get tinier on the sides of the frame. Draw small lines throughout the ground that follow the natural curves of the landscape. As always, keep them smaller in the distance to create more depth.

10. Add a small sun in the sky and surround it with parentheses that radiate out around it to create a scorching effect.

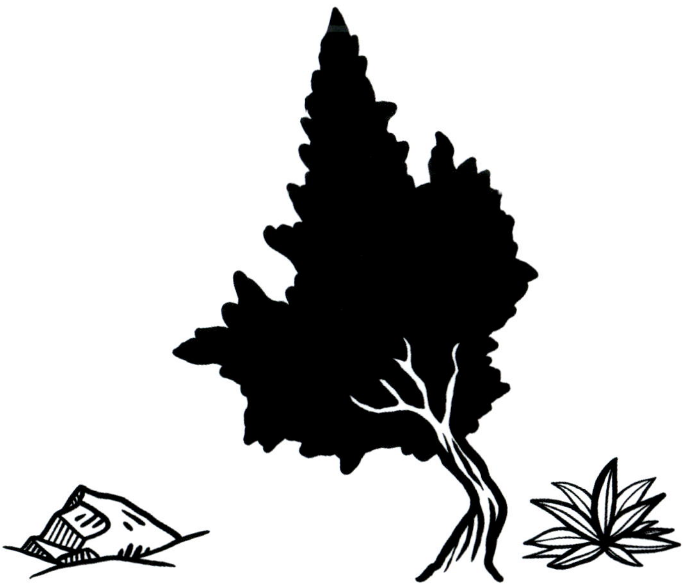

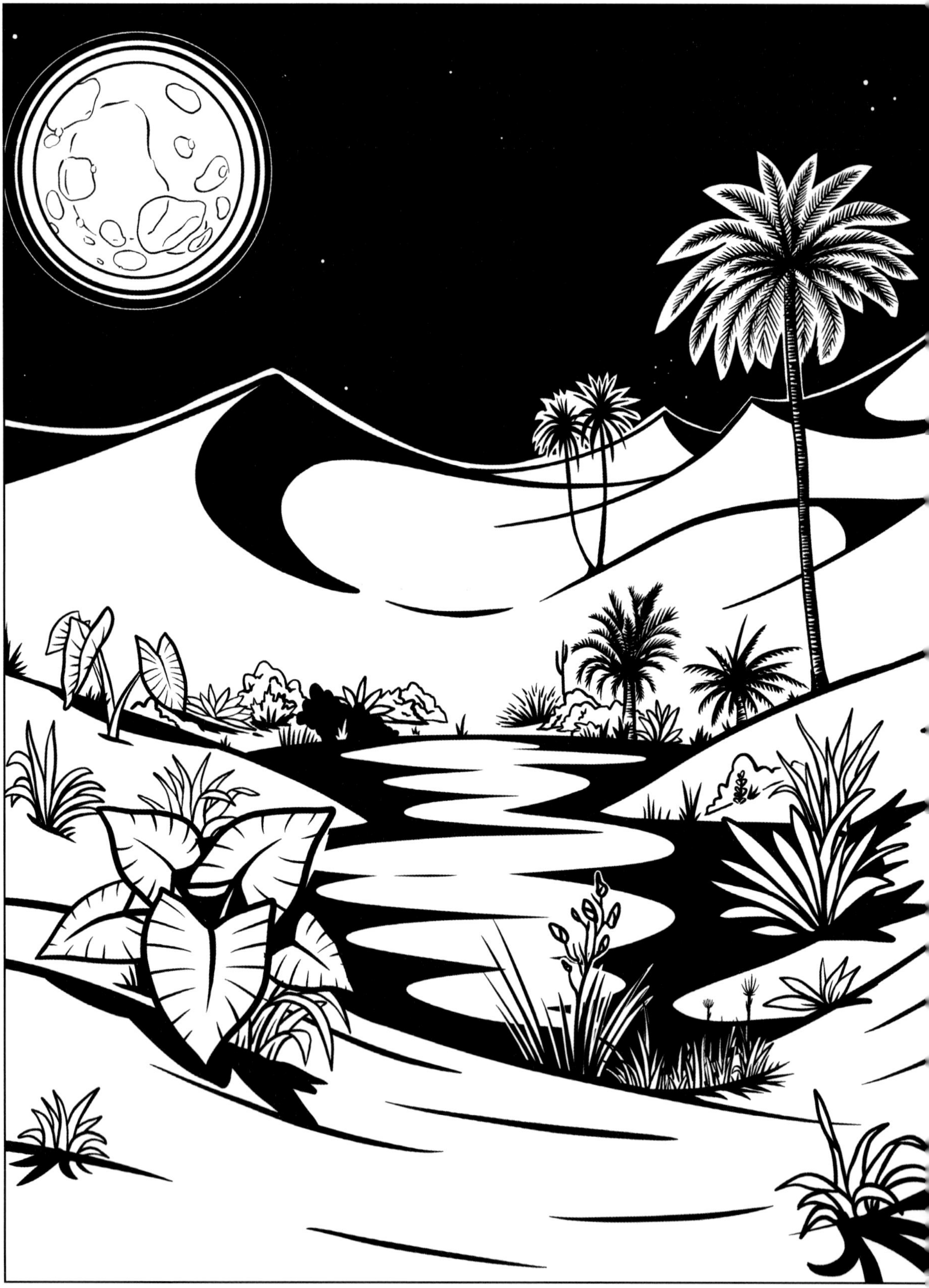

3. Oasis Tranquility

Imagine stumbling upon a hidden oasis after a long trek through the unforgiving desert heat. Lush palm trees sway gently in the cool evening breeze, their fronds silhouetted against the glow of the moon. The gentle murmur of water replaces the day's harsh winds, creating a symphony of tranquility. Here, amidst the stark desert landscape, lies a haven of life where we will delve into a new skill: depicting detail with lush vegetation. We'll learn how to translate the intricate shapes and textures of palm trees and leaves transforming them from simple lines into lifelike elements within your drawing. This night scene will be our first foray into the magic of shadowy landscapes to create atmosphere. We'll explore how to depict the soft glow of moonlight, casting long shadows. Grab your pens and add a touch of mystery and intrigue to your artwork.

Taro Plant

A jewel amidst the desert! The taro plant, with its magnificent, large leaves, adds a vibrant touch to any oasis scene. Using simple heart shapes as a foundation, we'll explore layering techniques to build lush, textured leaves.

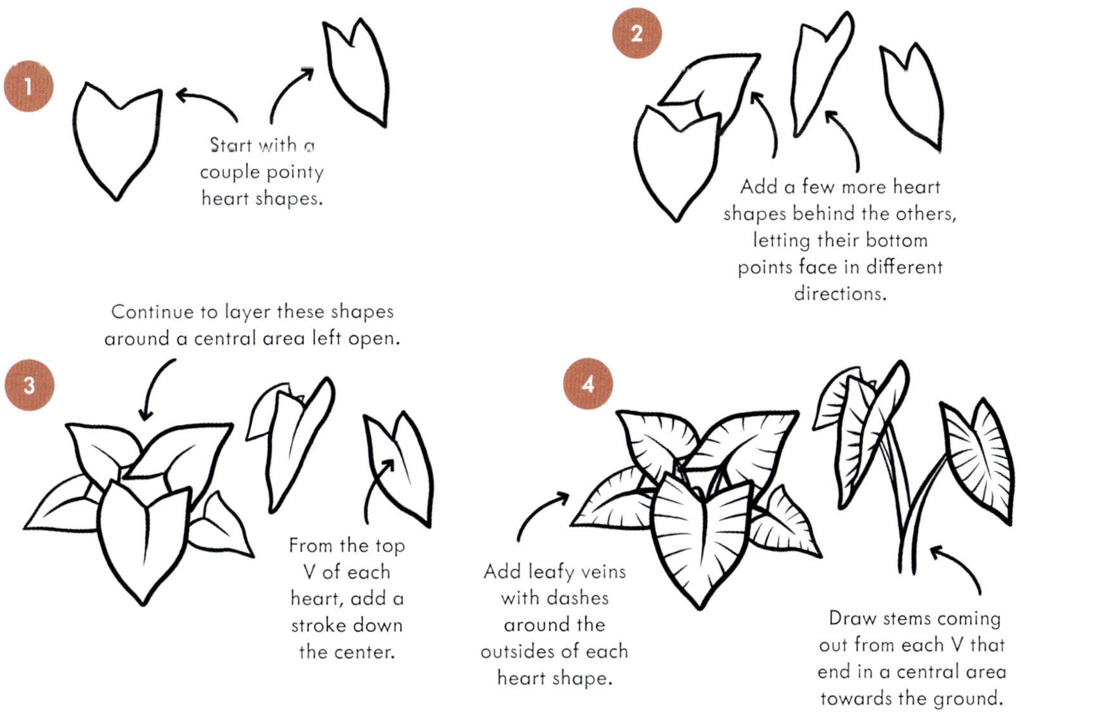

Date Palm

Desert fireworks in bloom! Date palms, with their unique crown of fronds, add a dramatic touch to your oasis scene. Learn to capture their form using a "firework" technique. We'll build on simple lines to create the structure and then explode with details, transforming them into stunning silhouettes against the moonlit sky.

1

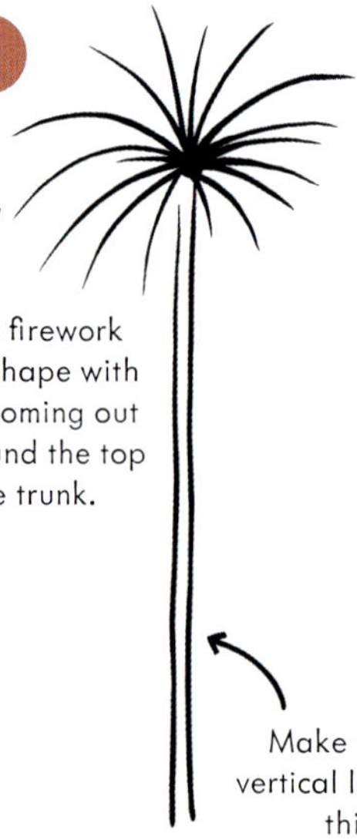

Draw a firework kind of shape with dashes coming out and around the top of the trunk.

Make two parallel vertical lines to make a thin trunk.

2

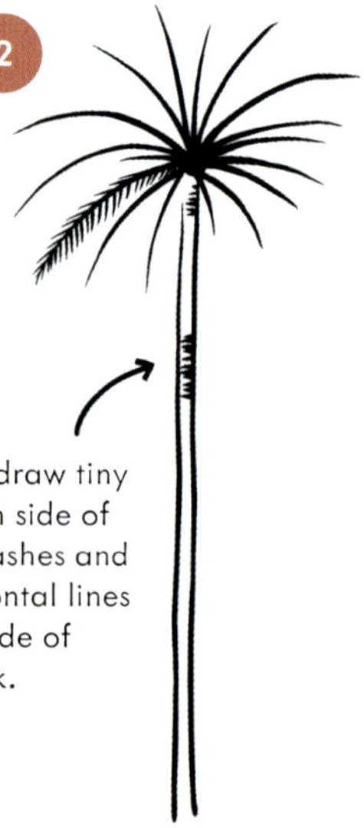

To add details, draw tiny strokes on each side of the firework's dashes and add small horizontal lines along one side of the trunk.

3

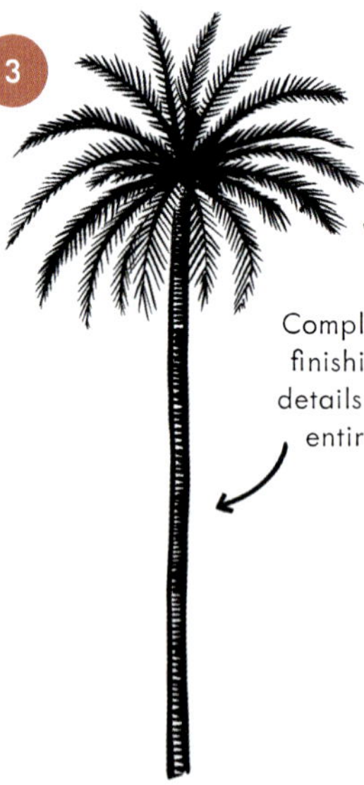

Complete it by finishing with details over the entire tree.

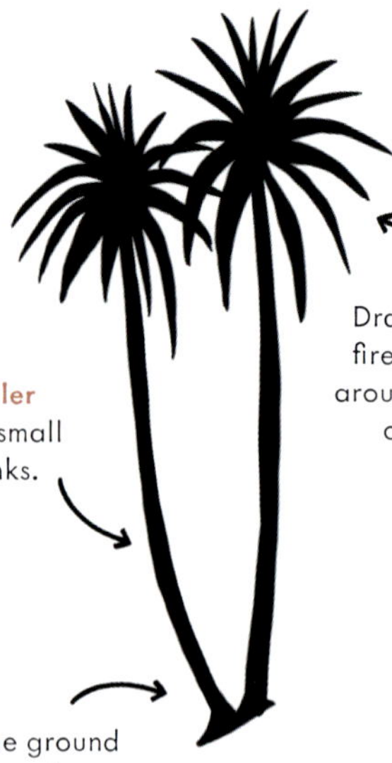

Draw the same firework shape around the top of one trunk.

To make smaller palms, make a small V for two trunks.

Add a line for the ground underneath the palms.

Leafy Grasses

Bring your oasis to life with leafy details! Leafy plants add a touch of lushness and variety to any nature scene, especially around a tranquil desert oasis. We'll explore layering techniques to build dimension and folds, transforming them into lifelike additions to your moonlit landscape. Leafy plants can add lots of interest and detail to a nature drawing. Try observing examples in real landscapes in order to get ideas!

Start with two pairs of eyebrow shapes close to each other. Add a pointy leaf arching up towards the sky between them.

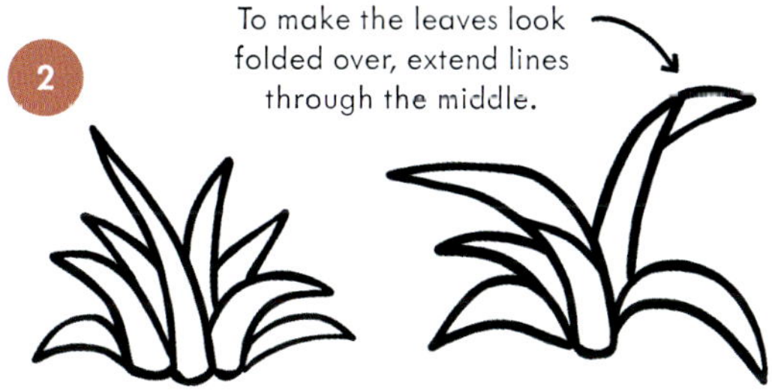

Draw more leaves sticking out from between the eyebrows around the central leaf.

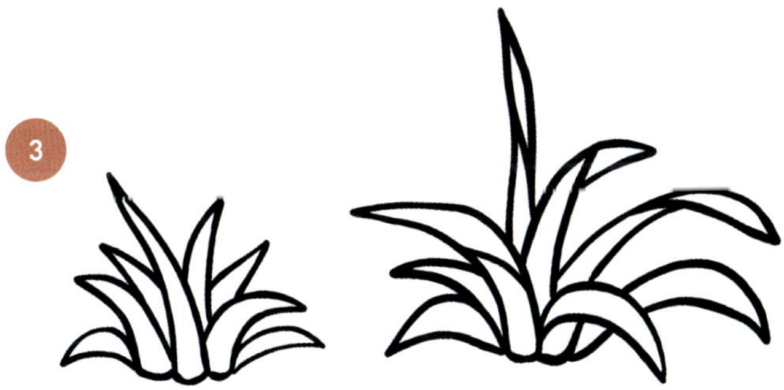

Continue to layer your leaves and fold some over themselves with lines that cross through. Add more leaves along the sides of your plant, making sure they all start from a central area to stay bunched.

Reeds

The gentle whisper of the oasis! With their swaying stalks and wispy plumes, reeds add a touch of movement and life to any tranquil waterside scene through simple shapes and layering techniques.

1

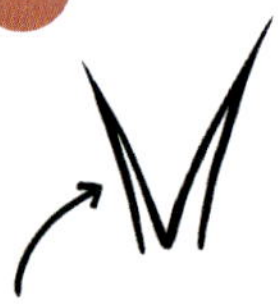

Start with a small arching V, then create leaves by adding two lines around it.

2

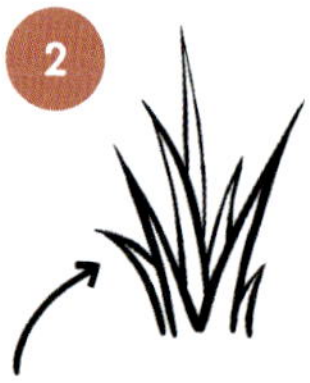

Layer more pointy leaves behind your central V shape, letting some stick out behind others.

3

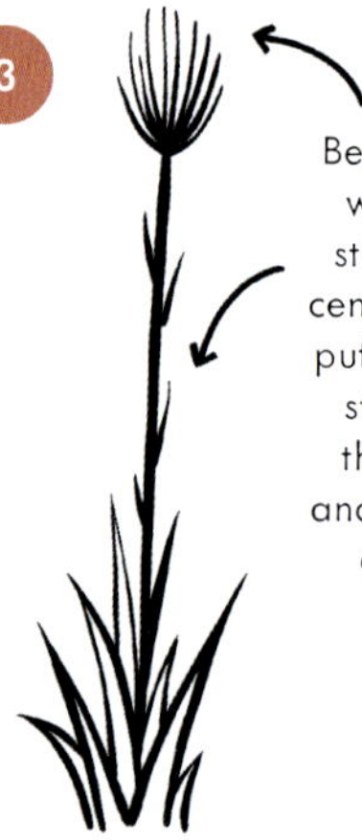

Begin your reed stalk with a vertical line sticking up from the central leaves. Make a puff of vertical dashes sticking up around the top of the stalk and add tiny diagonal dashes down the stalk as well.

4

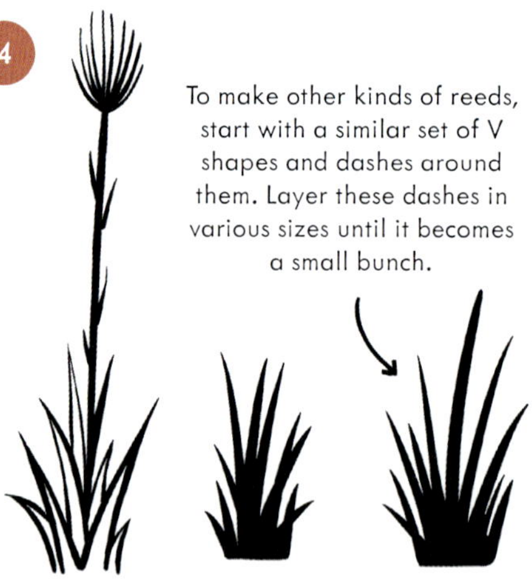

To make other kinds of reeds, start with a similar set of V shapes and dashes around them. Layer these dashes in various sizes until it becomes a small bunch.

5

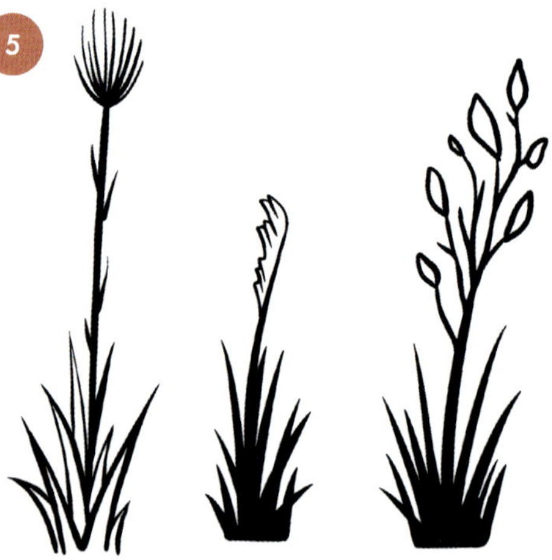

Try out different reed styles! Draw some stalks and add leafy shapes and branches around one, and a feathery shape on the side of the other.

Moon

The moon, with its cratered surface and soft glow, adds a touch of mystery and wonder to your tranquil oasis scene. We'll build texture with these easy wobbly shapes, capturing the subtle light and shadows that bathe the moon in its ethereal glow.

1

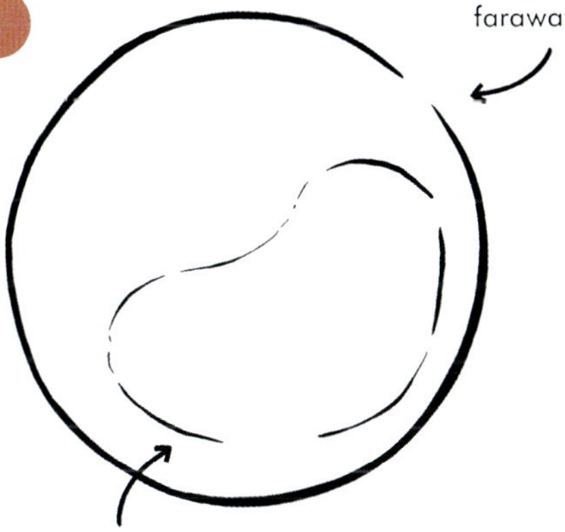

Leave tiny gaps in a circle to give it a vague faraway look.

Draw a large bean shape to the bottom area of the circle including those same gaps throughout.

2

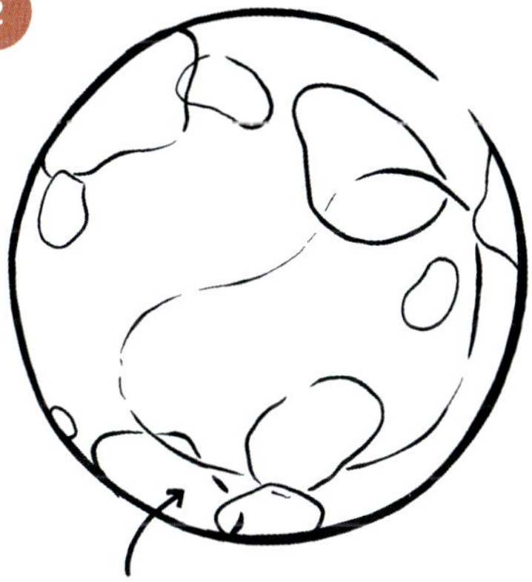

Add more organic circular shapes around the sides of the moon, letting some slightly overlap the bean shape and leaving little gaps in the lines here and there.

3

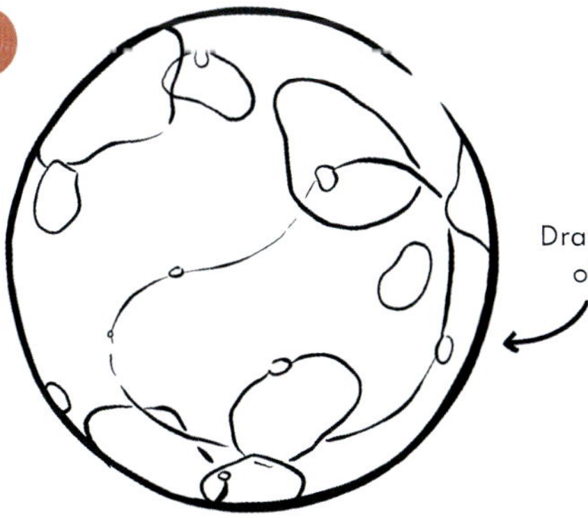

Draw tiny circles in between some of the gaps to complete your crater-covered moon.

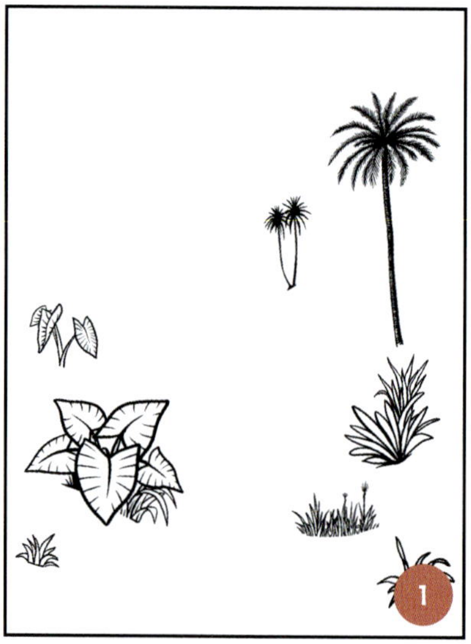
1
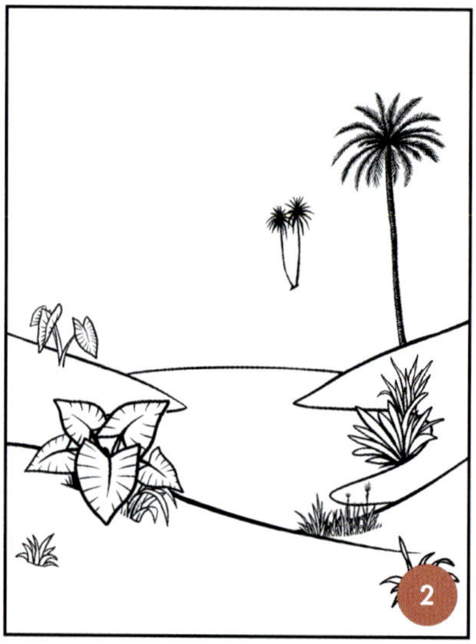
2
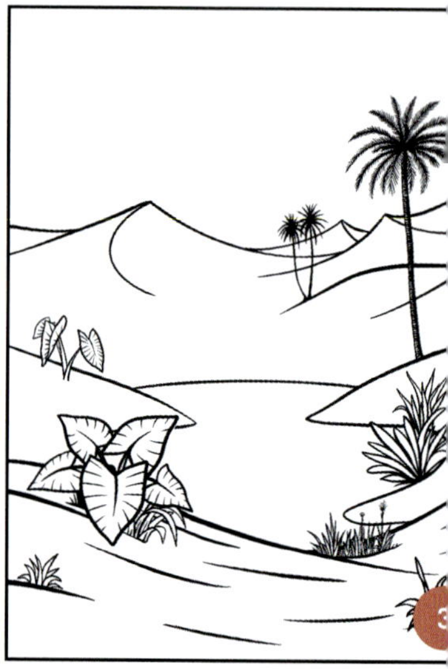
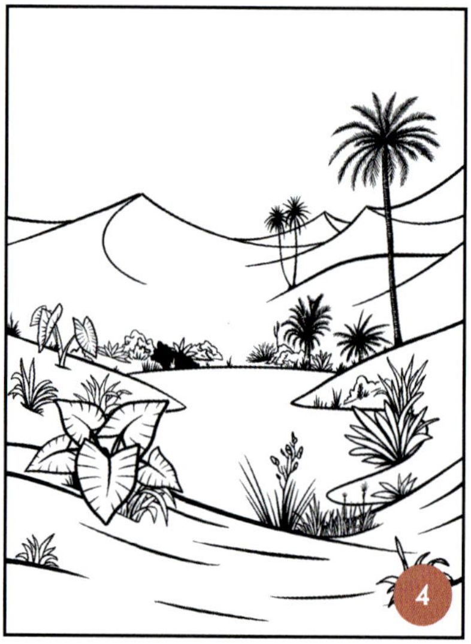
4
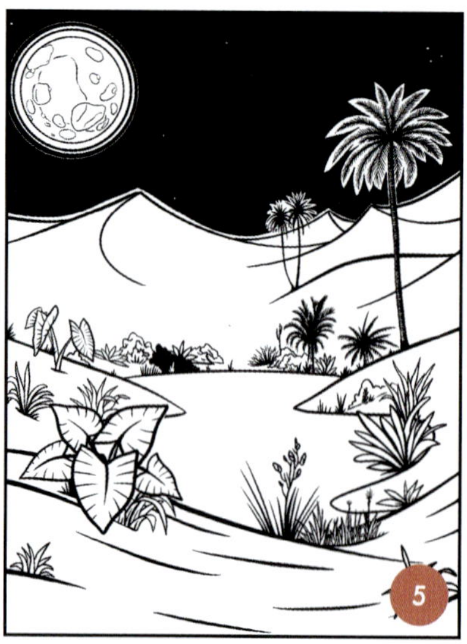
5
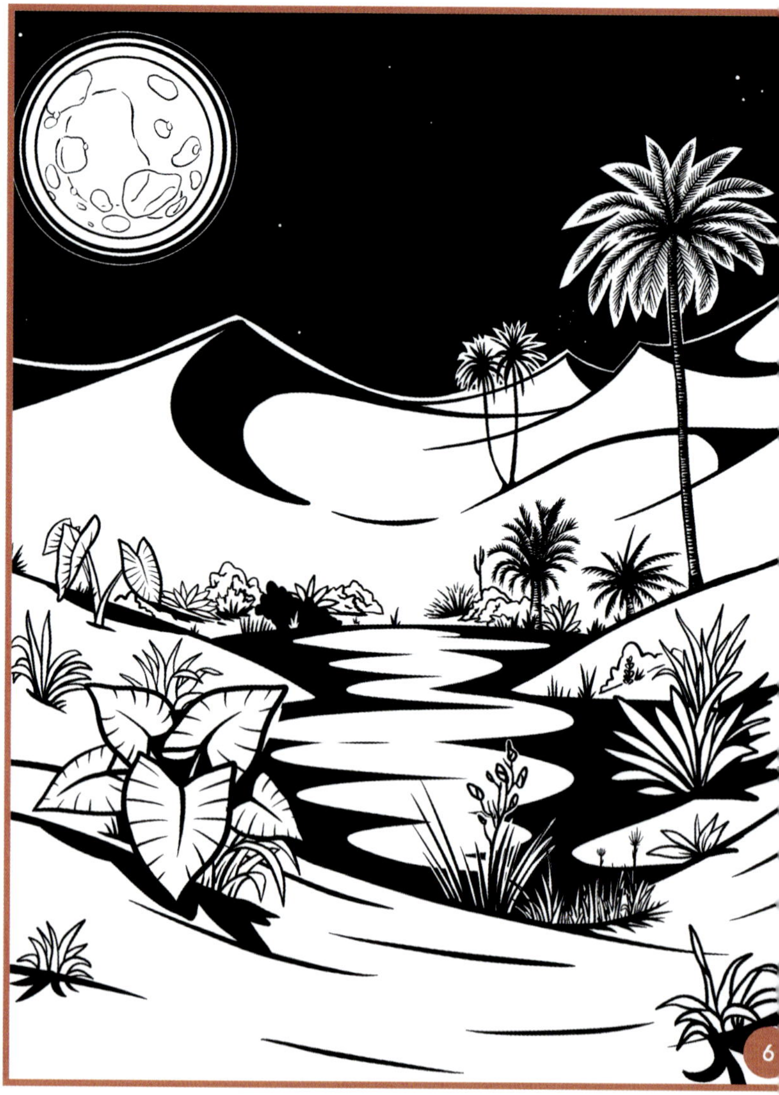

Now, Let's Draw the Scene

(See full image on page 20)

1. Start with a Taro Plant (page 21) in the foreground. Add some small Reeds (page 24) elsewhere. Draw Leafy Grasses (page 23) randomly around the bottom third of your frame. On the right side, add one large Date Palm (page 22) and some smaller ones in the middle ground.

2. Begin drawing your oasis! Start with a curvy slope behind your Taro plant and meet it with another slope behind the reeds. Draw a curve behind the leafy grasses and two hilly humps on the left and right sides. Then add a curving horizontal line in the middle to connect them all to create the base of your tranquil pool.

3. Draw some dunes in the background using what you learned from the Ever Shifting Sand Dunes tutorial (page 11). Add some small lines that follow the slopes in the foreground and underneath the leafy grasses.

4. Lay in more plant life around the oasis! Try drawing more leafy grasses, small bushes, and a few more date palms. Continue drawing a variety around the center until your oasis is bursting with life.

5. Make this a nighttime scene and add a full Moon (page 25) to a dark sky. To let your features stand out, leave a small outline of light around the dunes and palm trees in the background, and leave a few light circles around the moon for glowing moonbeams.

6. The best way to draw reflective water is to start with a variety of horizontal arches on the left and right of the pool whose points face the center but leave a space between. Then shade in the left and right sides of these arches to leave highlights in the middle of the water.

Add more shadows under your plants and trees and along the curves of the dunes on their right sides.

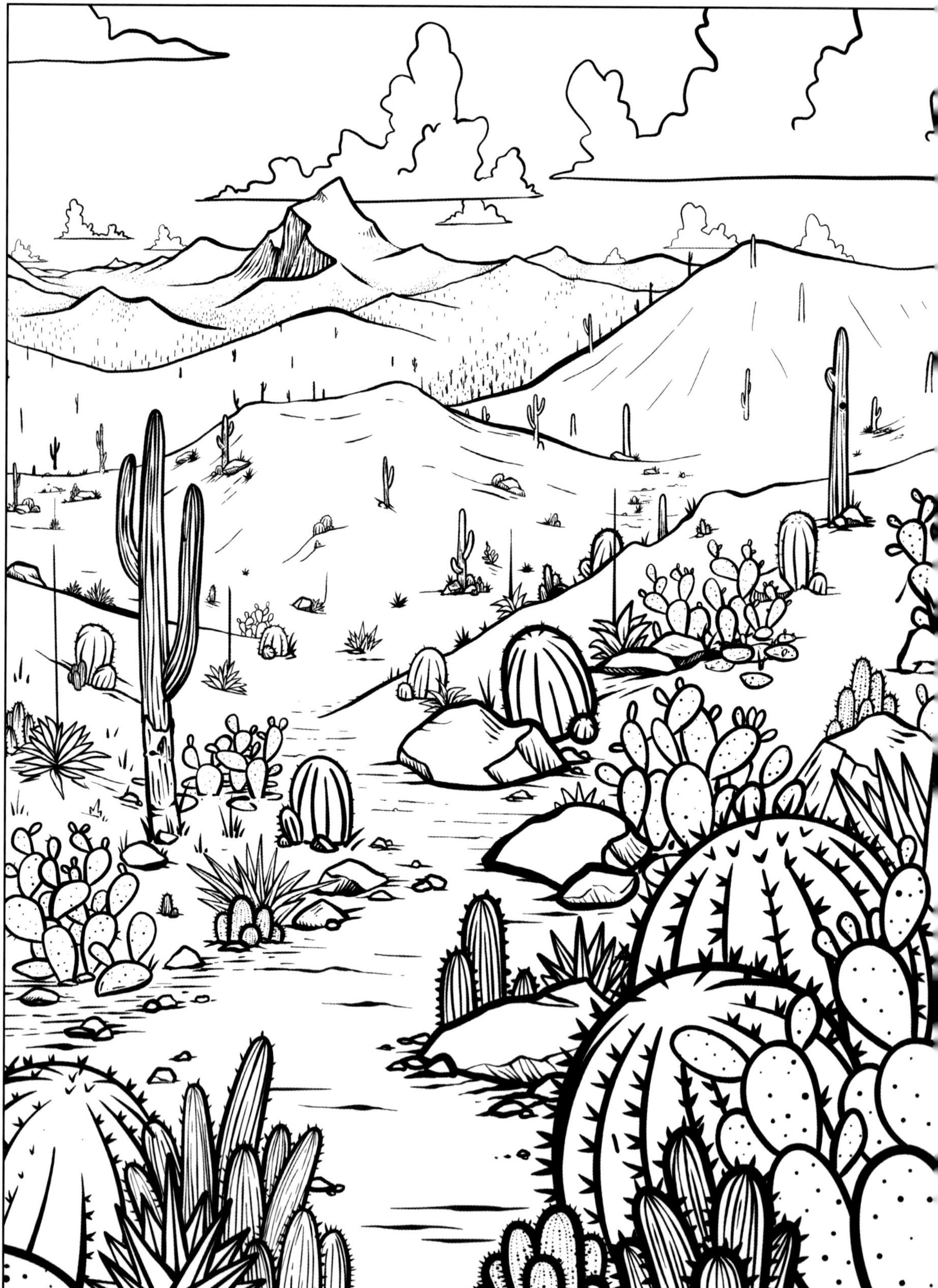

4. Cactus Shrublands

In the parched heart of the Southwest, amidst a sea of sun-scorched earth, cactus shrublands emerge as thorny forests, a testament to life's resilience. These remarkable plants stand strong against harsh conditions, each uniquely adapted to survive. As we illustrate the beauty of these shrublands, we will unlock a fundamental artistic technique: building depth and composition through layering. By strategically stacking and positioning plants and other elements, you'll learn to create a sense of depth and dimension in your drawings. This technique shines in cactus shrublands, where the unique shapes and sizes of cacti offer endless opportunities for creative composition. Grab your pens and prepare to be amazed by the possibilities of layering. We'll delve into the fascinating world of cacti, exploring their diverse shapes, textures and spines. With each mindful line, you'll not only master the art of depicting these desert dwellers but also discover how to use them to create compositions that tell the stories of the cactus shrublands.

Here arid landscapes, sculpted by relentless winds and unforgiving sun, teem with an array of prickly inhabitants, each adapted to survive in this harsh environment.

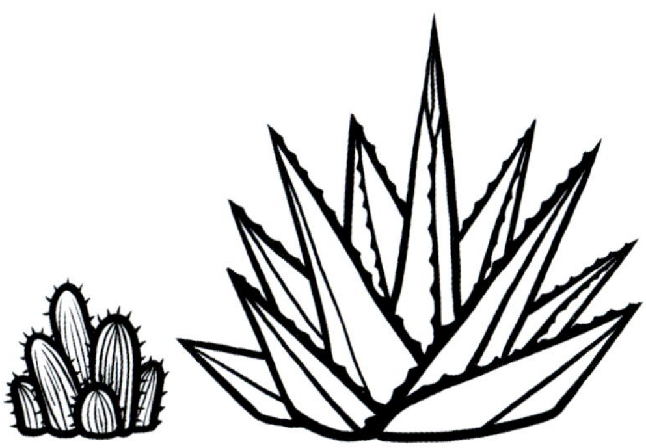

Yucca

Yucca plants, with their tall, majestic forms and spiky leaves, add a touch of height and drama to any cactus shrubland scene. We'll build your yucca step by step, strategically layering spiky leaves and wispy flowers to create a desert dweller that stands out in your landscape composition.

1

Start with three thin, pointy leaves coming out around a single point in the ground.

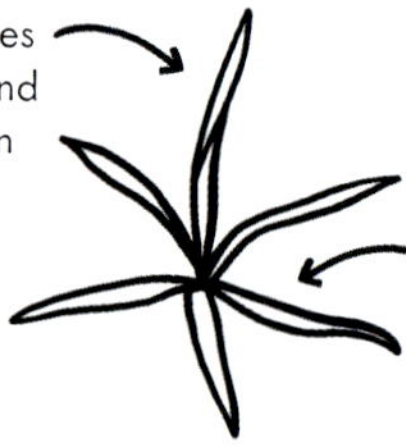

Mirror those leaves in the opposite direction for three leaves growing along the ground.

2

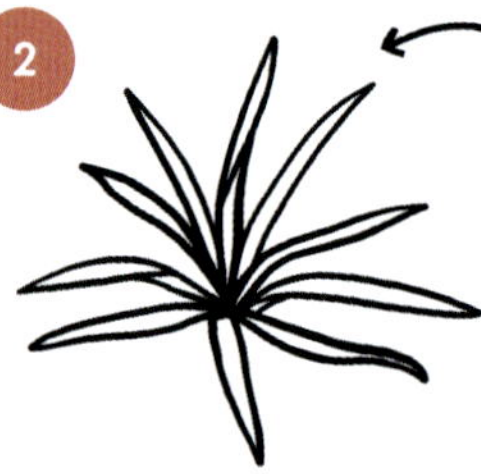

Draw more leaves sticking out sideways between the others.

3

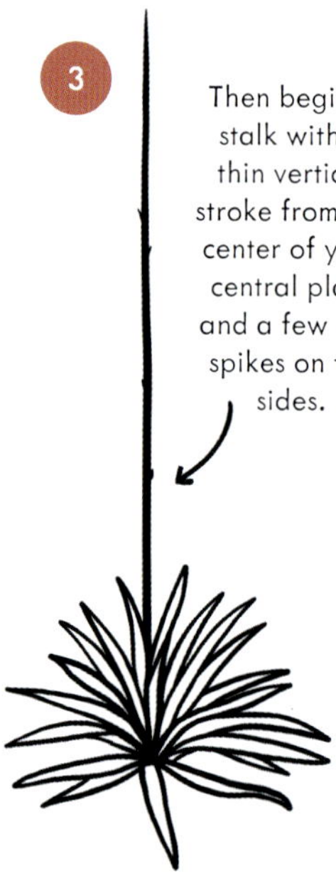

Then begin a stalk with a thin vertical stroke from the center of your central plant and a few tiny spikes on the sides.

Continue to layer these thin pointy leaves all around your central plant, letting them overlap naturally.

4

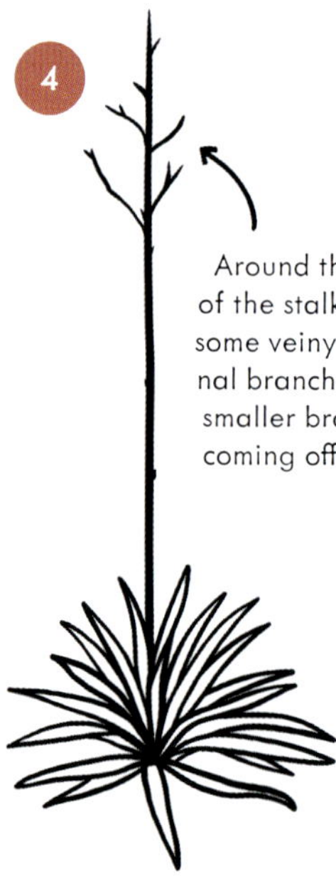

Around the top of the stalk, draw some veiny diagonal branches with smaller branches coming off them.

5

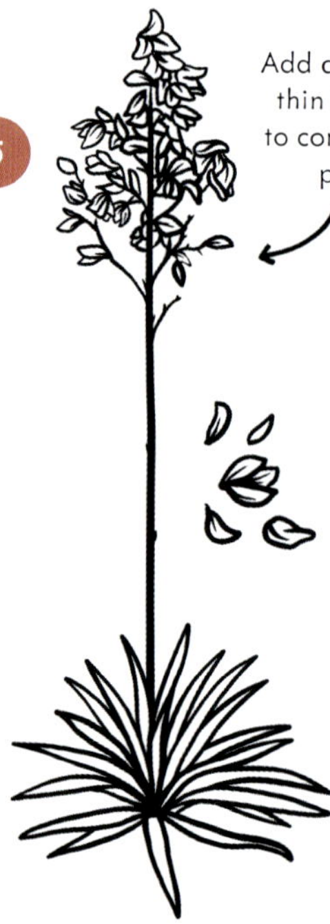

Add a few more thin branches to connect your petals.

Add loose petal shapes around these branches, letting some blow away with the wind; don't be afraid of making these too specific, because the more random they are the more natural it looks! For a further breakdown of these petals, start with an oval-like shape, draw a center line and layer curvy wavy petals around them.

Bunch Cactus

Bunch cacti, with their clustered forms and spiky textures, add a touch of character and variety to any cactus shrubland scene. We'll build them up layer by layer, starting with foundational shapes and adding spikes to bring these prickly veterans to life in your landscape composition.

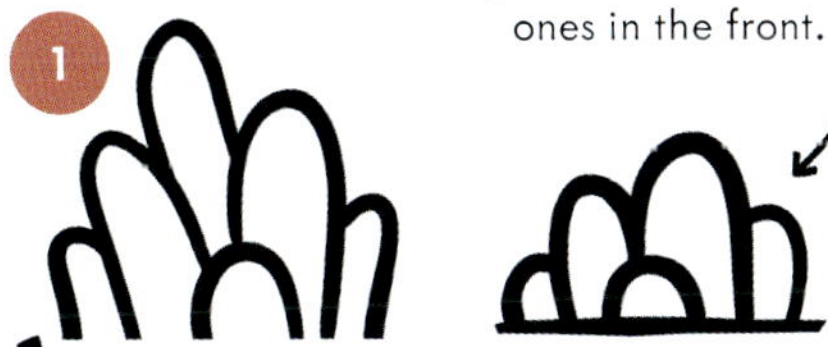

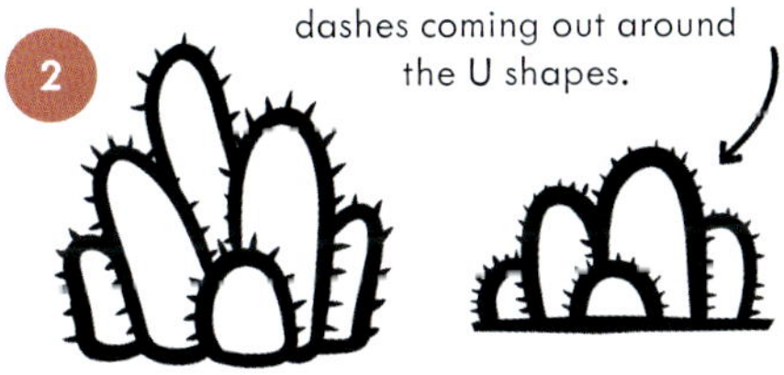

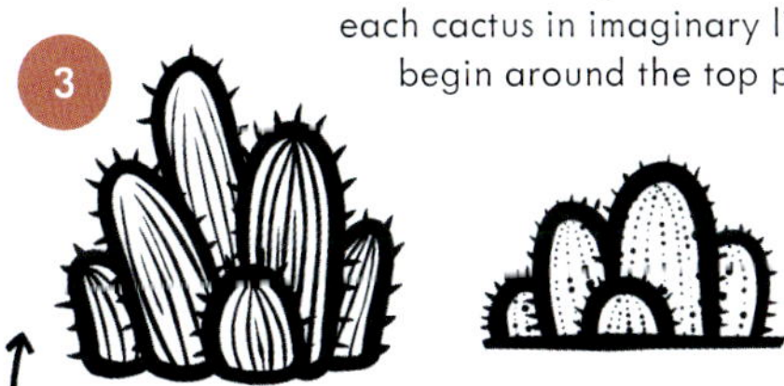

Agave Plant

Agave plants, with their sharp, symmetrical forms, add a touch of diversity to any cactus shrubland scene. Building this agave step by step will strengthen your skills in layering for creating depth and texture.

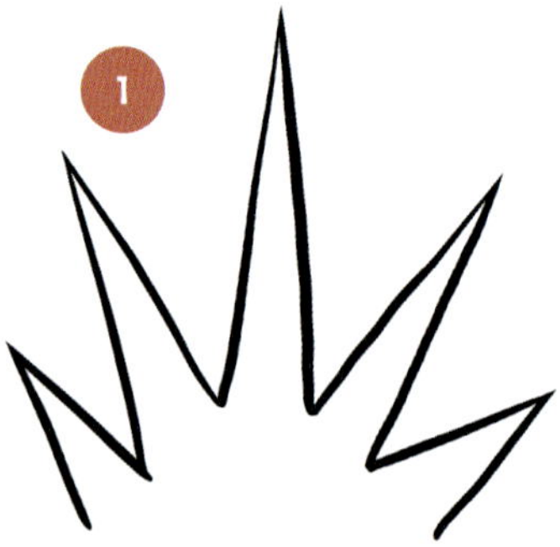

Start with an extra spiky shape that arches out around the ground with a central spike taller than the others.

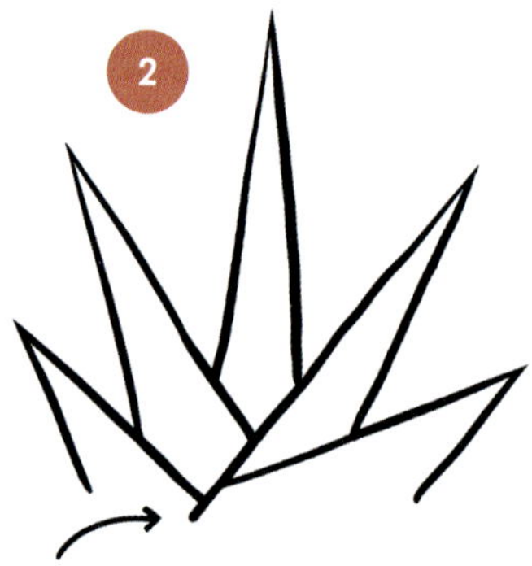

Create an overlap in the middle with a Y shape. Connect the front spikes to the Y shape by continuing their diagonal lines to the center.

Layer more spiky shapes in between the others.

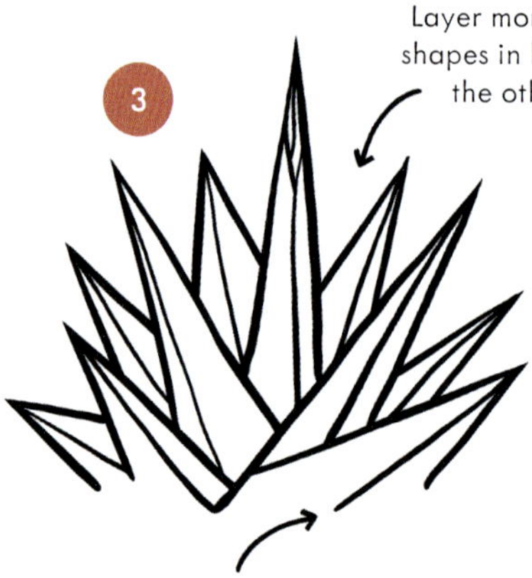

Add central lines down each of the spikes.

For the spines, draw small bumpy ripples along one line of each spike. This can be in the middle or along their sides.

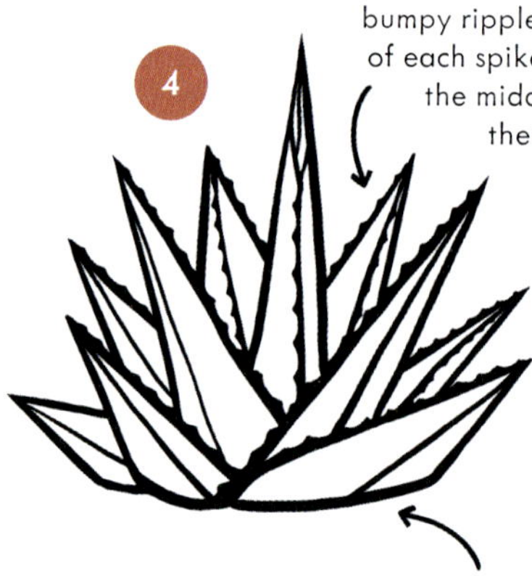

Cap off the bottom shape with some rounded lines.

Saguaro

Desert giants reaching for the sky! Saguaro cacti, with their towering silhouettes and iconic branching arms, are the undisputed kings of the cactus shrubland and they will help you bring your layering skills to the next level! Learn how to create a sense of depth in your composition by incorporating background cacti and foreground elements, transforming these majestic giants into the focal point of your desert landscape.

1

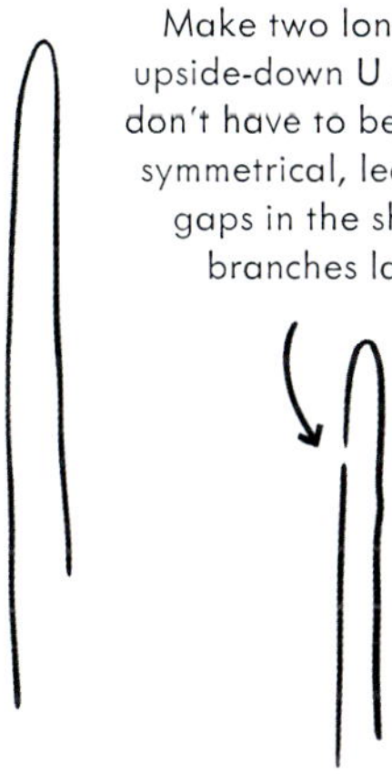

Make two long, narrow upside-down U shapes that don't have to be completely symmetrical, leaving some gaps in the shapes for branches later on.

2

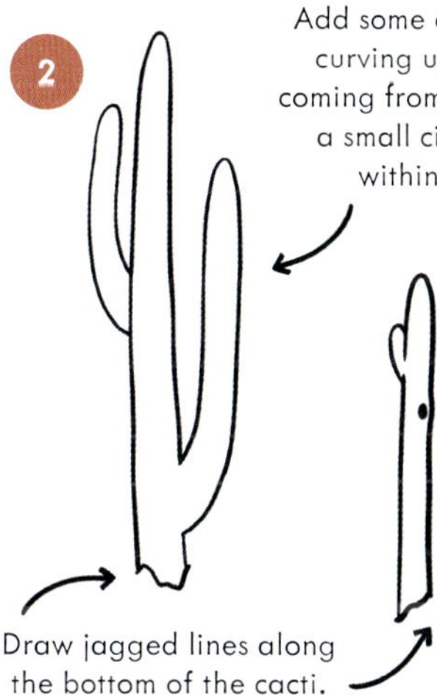

Add some cactus arms with curving upside-down Us coming from the gaps or add a small circle for a hole within the cactus.

Draw jagged lines along the bottom of the cacti.

3

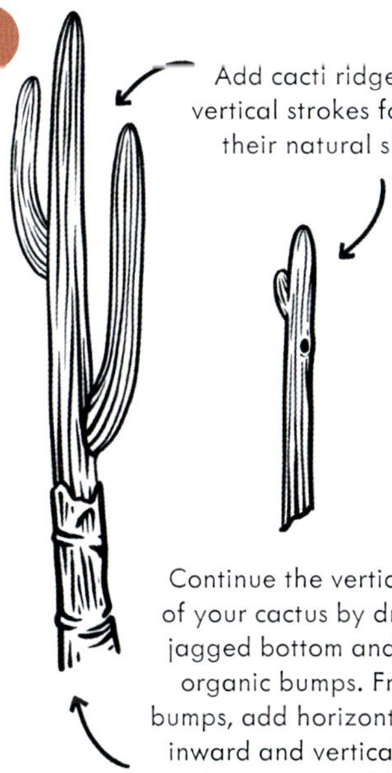

Add cacti ridges with vertical strokes following their natural shape.

Continue the vertical trunk of your cactus by drawing a jagged bottom and adding organic bumps. From the bumps, add horizontal dashes inward and vertical dashes underneath to add texture.

4

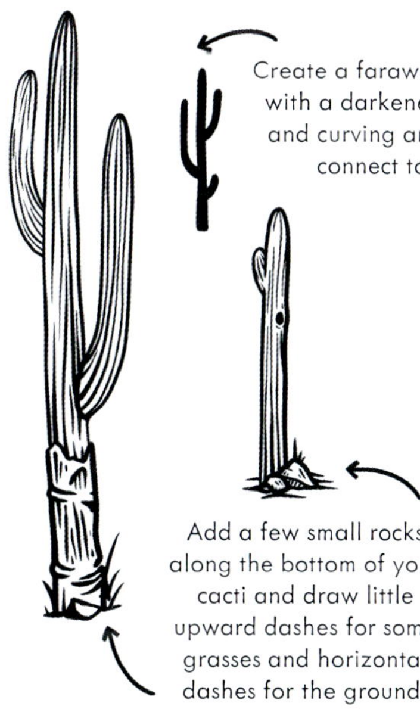

Create a faraway cactus with a darkened trunk and curving arms that connect to it.

Add a few small rocks along the bottom of your cacti and draw little upward dashes for some grasses and horizontal dashes for the ground.

Prickly Pear

The prickly pear cactus! A true desert icon, it stands out amongst its spiny brethren with its unique flattened pads. The prickly pear boasts a fascinating structure of segmented "paddles" covered in a striking array of tiny spines. Let's unlock the secrets of the prickly pear and bring its desert beauty to life!

2

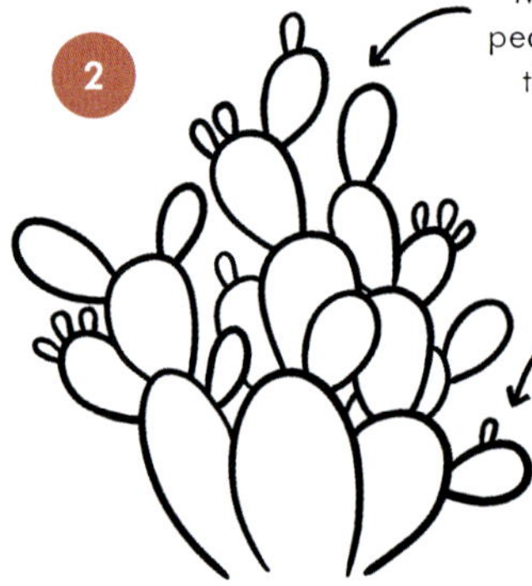

Make the upper prickly pear layers slightly smaller than the initial ones to indicate they are new growth.

Make cactus buds with tiny U shapes along a few of your prickly pear edges.

1

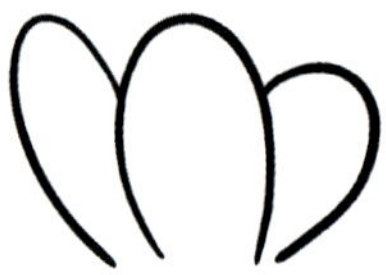

Start with three round, upside-down U shapes bunched together.

Layer more U shapes on the tops and sides of your initial bunch and build these upwards and slightly outwards in various shapes and sizes.

3

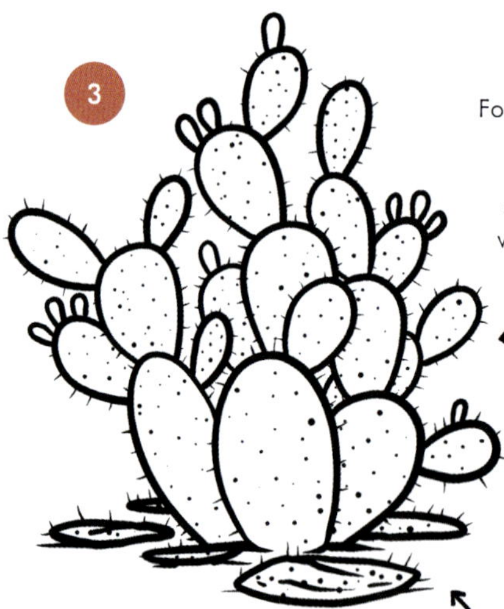

For spines, simply add dots randomly throughout your prickly pears, making some slightly bigger or smaller. Draw spikes sticking out with some thin dashes around the outline of your cactus.

Add a few flat prickly pear "paddles" that have fallen off around the bottom of your cactus.

Barrel Cactus

In the unforgiving desert landscape, the barrel cactus stands out. Forget the spindly silhouettes—this robust beauty boasts a unique, rounded body, perfectly adapted to the scorching sun. Wrapped in a crown of sharp spines, a testament to its desert toughness, the barrel cactus thrives with surprising efficiency.

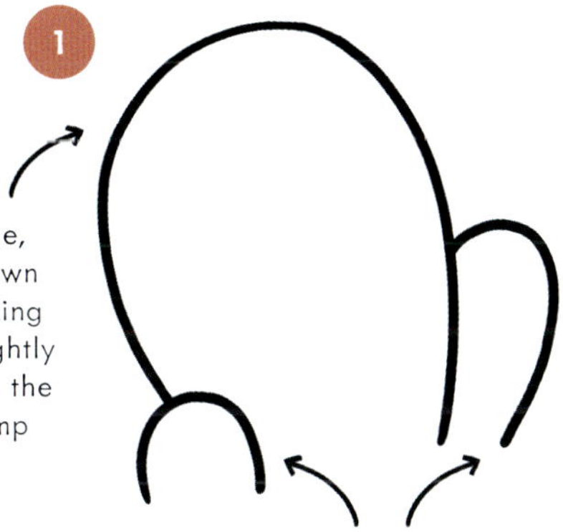

Make a large, fat upside-down U shape, making the bottom slightly narrower than the rounded bump on top.

Add half of an upside-down U to the side and a small squat one in the front.

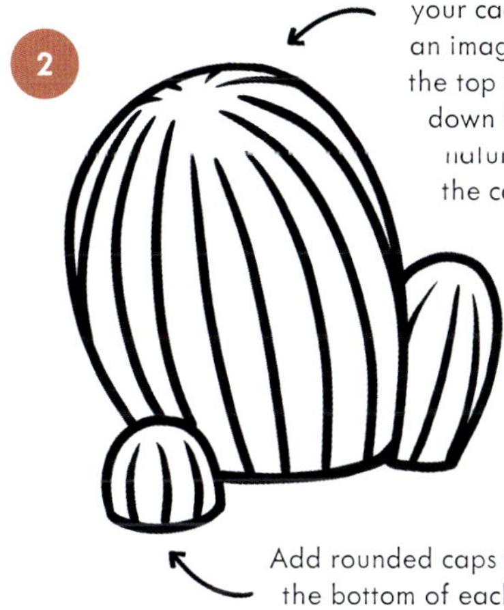

To add the ridges of your cactus, start from an imaginary point on the top and draw lines down following the natural curves of the cactus shape.

Add rounded caps to the bottom of each shape.

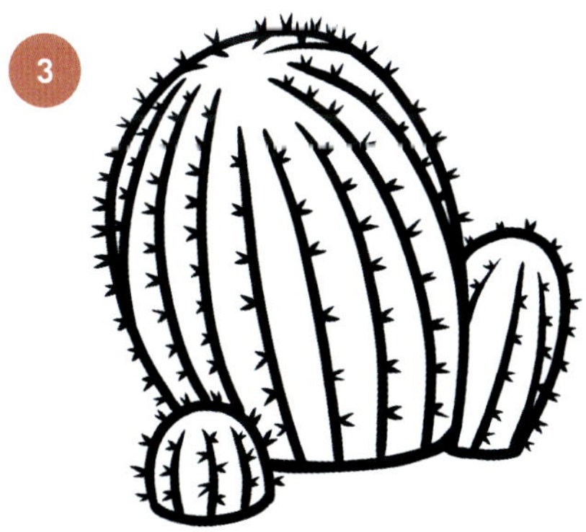

Add spines along these ridges by drawing tiny Vs evenly spaced apart on the lines. Have them face towards the left side of the cactus on the left side, and towards the right on the right side.

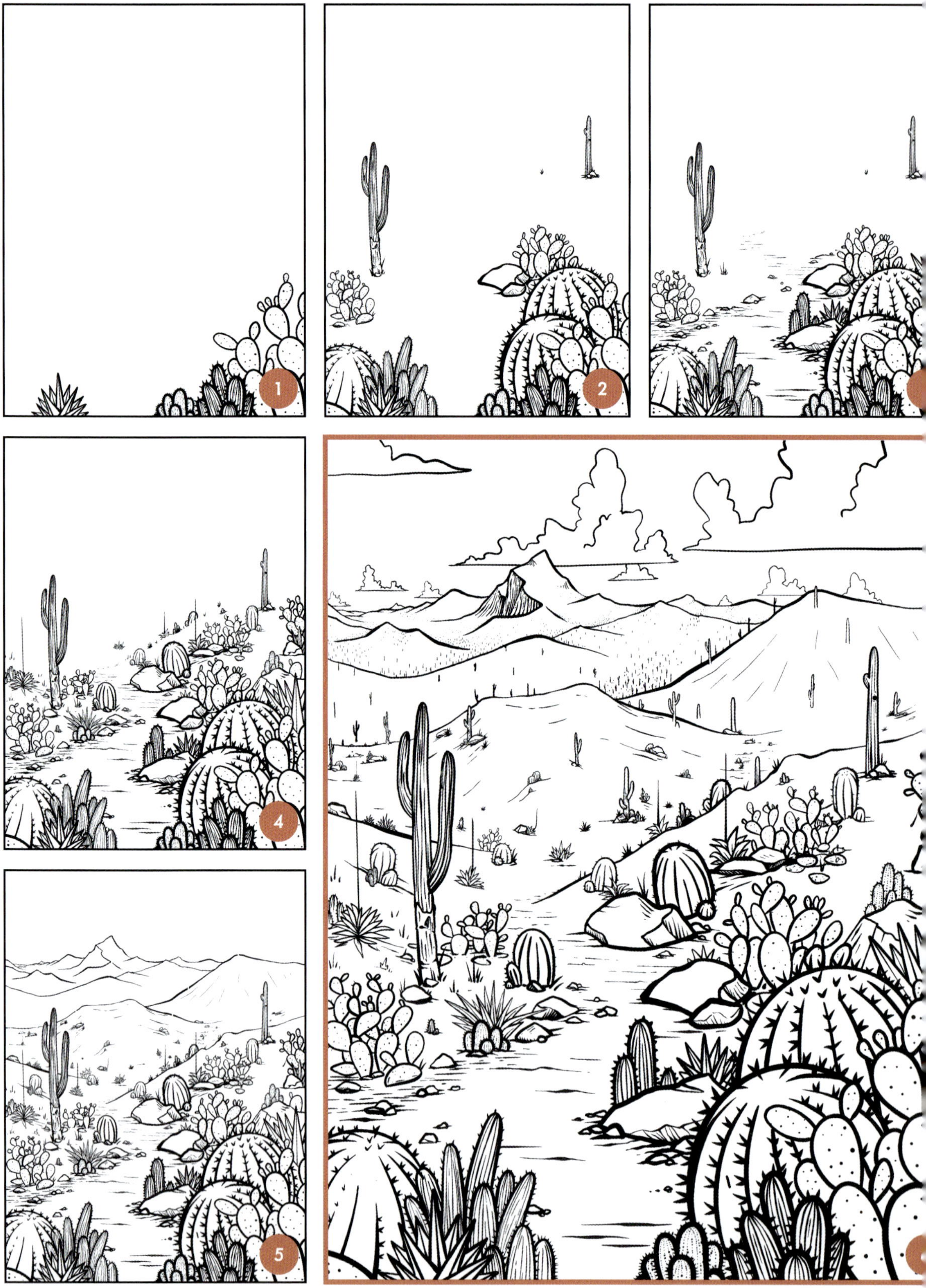
1
2
4
5

Now, Let's Draw the Scene

(Sell full image on page 28)

1. Begin the foreground with an Agave Plant (page 32) and a Bunch Cactus (page 31). Layer the bottom right corner with another cactus and a Prickly Pear (page 34).

2. Continue to layer behind your plants with more cacti, prickly pears and some big Barrel Cacti (page 35). Add some Saguaro (page 33) slightly farther in the distance and be sure to leave some space around the center of the frame. Add a few rock shapes throughout.

3. Start to develop a sandy trail through the shrubland with small horizontal dashes following an imaginary curving line that gets smaller heading towards the horizon. Add more succulents and some small Rocks (page 13) along the trail as well.

4. As you continue building your shrubland around your trail with more of the same plants, add a hill shape on the right side of the frame.

5. Draw distant mountains with some wobbly horizontal lines across the background. Feel free to experiment with different sizes of peaks and valleys! Add details to your closest desert hills by drawing sloping lines with shrubs or rocks on top. Making the slopes follow the outline of the hill will help to add realistic texture, and some thin diagonal lines on other mountains will help to create steep cliff sides.

6. Follow up with an extensive cactus field by drawing saguaros on the mountains in the foreground, making them smaller and less detailed until they are tiny vague shapes dotted throughout the mountains in the background. Add depth to your tallest peak by shading the left mountain face with vertical lines.

Draw magnificent clouds by starting with a straight horizontal bottom then adding a puffy, wiggly shape above. Adding a few more puffy squiggles to the middle of the cloud gives it more shape. Create a truly endless desert sky by drawing much smaller clouds closer to the mountainous horizon!

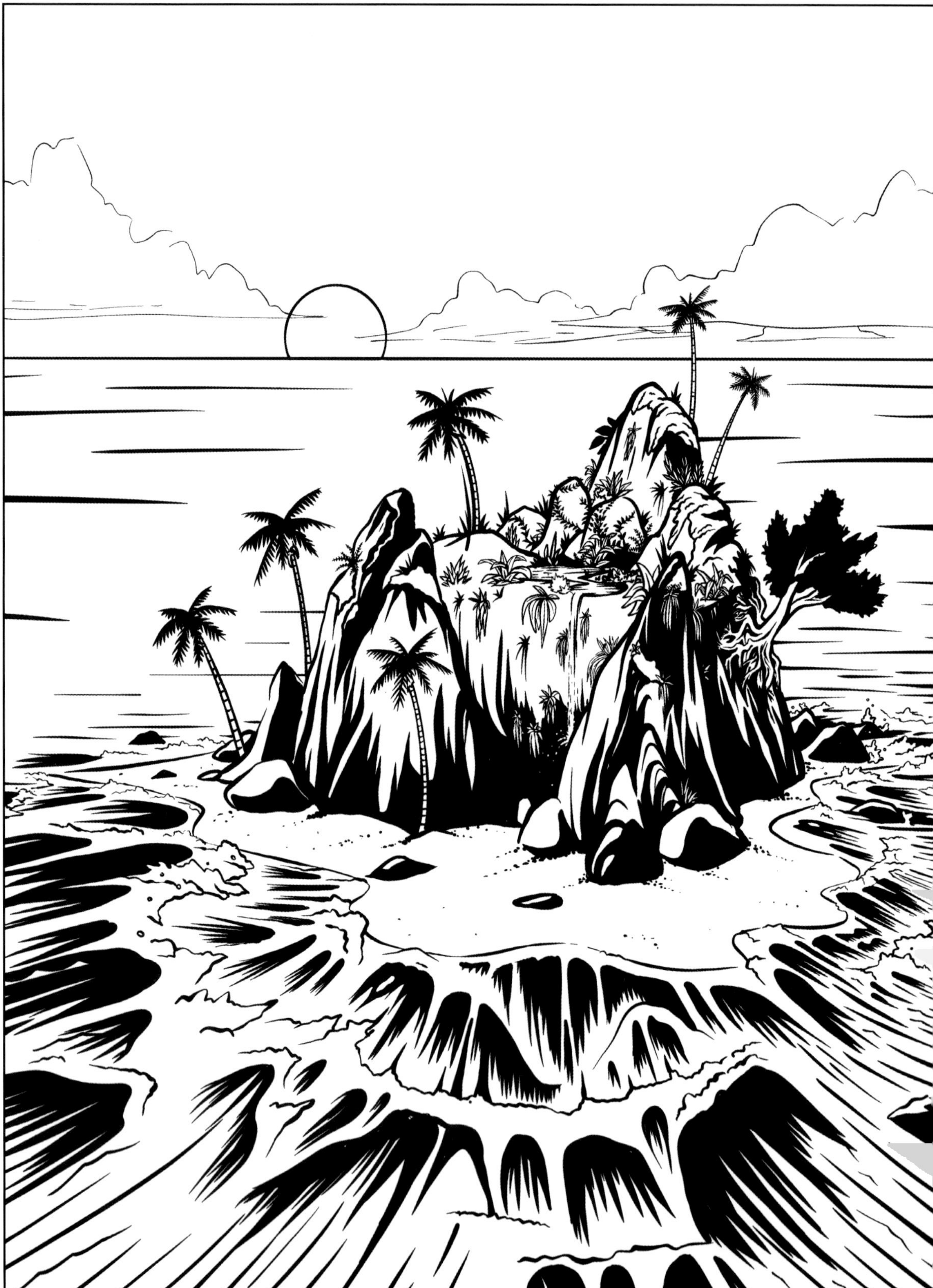

5. Desert Island

Emerging from the vast expanse of the ocean, desert islands stand as solitary beacons of life, their rugged beauty a testament to nature's resilience. These secluded sanctuaries, battered by relentless waves and scorching sun, harbor unique ecosystems of flora and fauna, adapted to thrive in isolation.

Air Plants

Air plants, with their wispy forms and surprising resilience, add a touch of life to even the harshest desert island. Showcase their intricate details using simple shapes as a foundation. We'll explore layering techniques to build realism through symbolism, transforming them from basic forms into impressive elements clinging to your dramatic desert island scene.

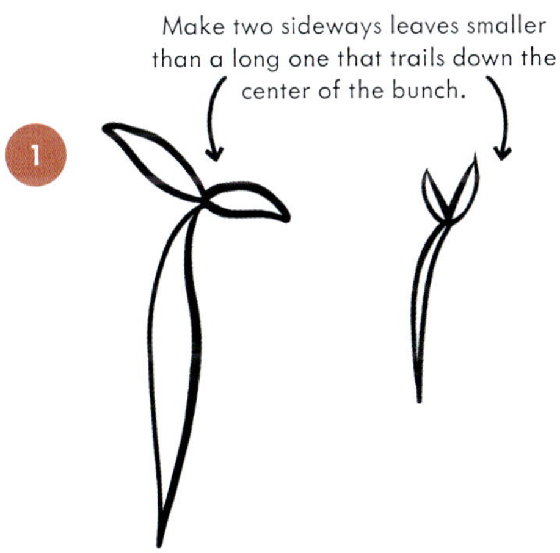

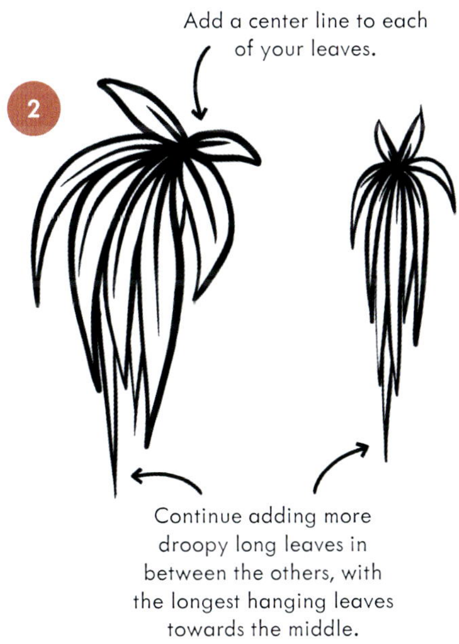

Vines

Vines, with their twisting forms and trailing leaves, add a touch of movement and life to your desert island scene. This tutorial will show you how to create a variety of vine styles using simple lines and shapes. We'll explore different leaf designs and layering techniques, allowing you to recreate the intricate details of these plants and add a sense of flow and texture to your dramatic island landscape.

1

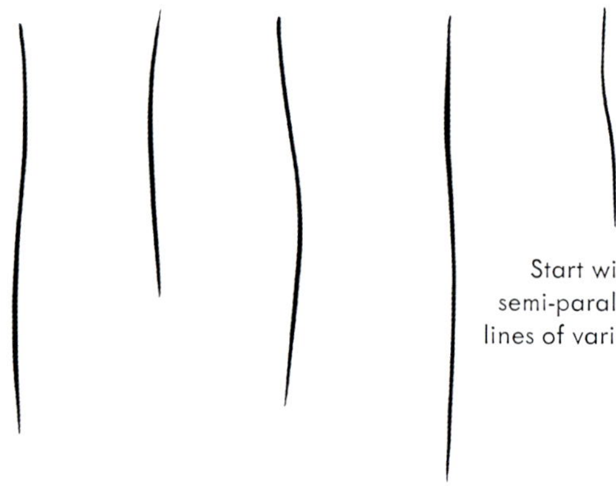

Start with some semi-parallel vertical lines of various lengths.

2

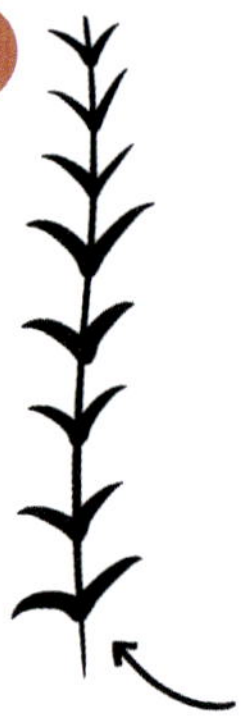

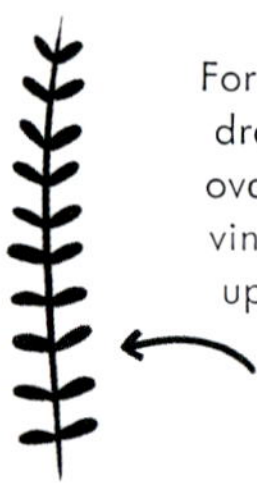

For a different style, try drawing small narrow ovals on each side of a vine that point slightly upwards for rounded leaves.

Create leaves by drawing thick V shapes around the center of a vertical line and filling them in.

3

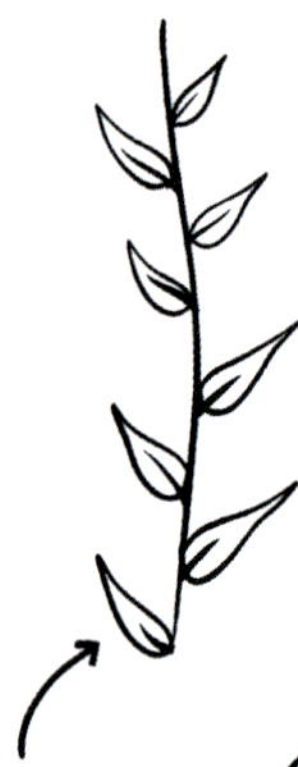

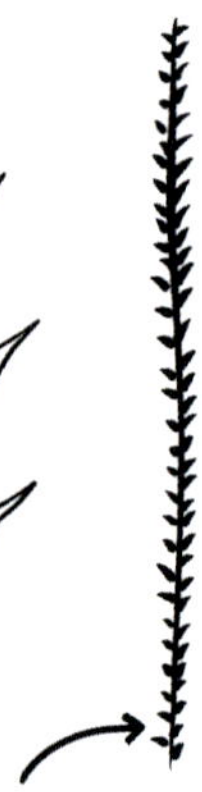

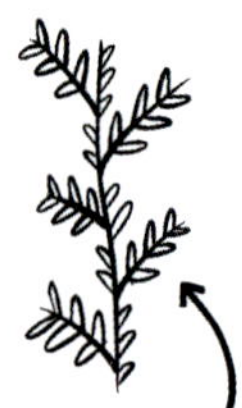

For another option, add small branches out of the center line and draw round leaves on each side.

Continue to experiment with different leaf designs! Try large, pointed leaf shapes or simple tiny ones growing closely together.

Ficus Tree

Ficus trees, with their sprawling branches and dense foliage, can add a touch of life and protection to your desert island scene. Even on a windswept rock, these resilient trees can find a foothold. This tutorial will guide you through capturing the details of this island survivor, using simple lines and shapes as a foundation. We'll explore techniques to draw a textured trunk, branching canopy and root system, creating a beautiful tree that provides shade and visual interest in your dramatic island landscape.

Have the top ends of the lines slightly branch away from each other.

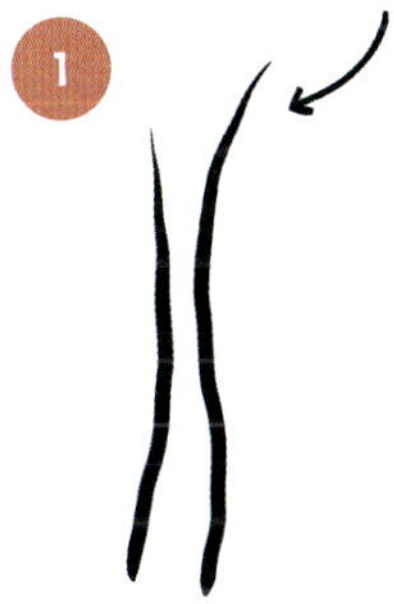

Start with some wobbly, semi-parallel vertical lines to make a trunk.

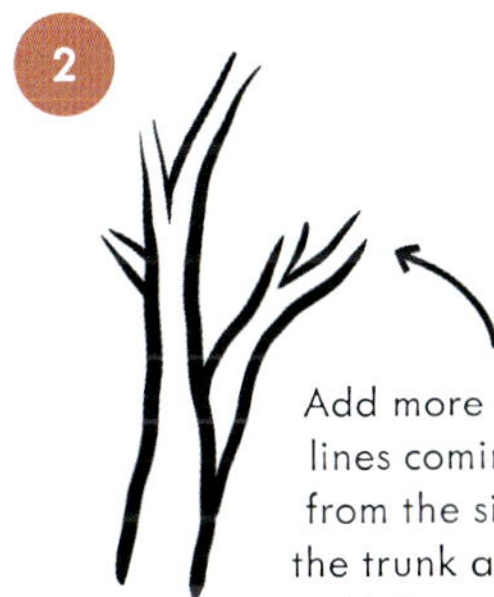

Add more sets of lines coming out from the sides of the trunk and add a V shape to the middle of those lines to begin your tree branches.

Make your tree canopy with a scribbly shape around the top of the trunk and branches.

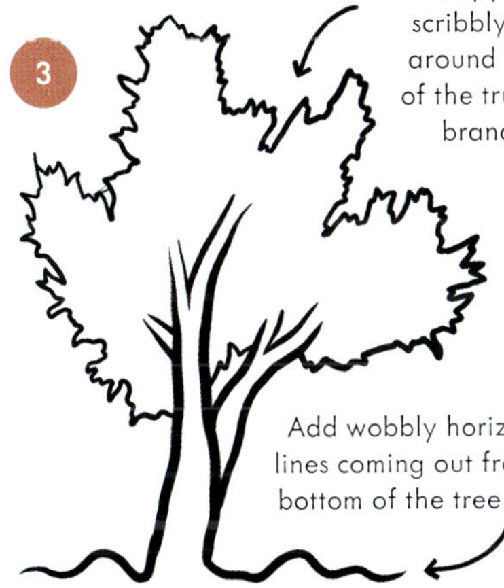

Add wobbly horizontal lines coming out from the bottom of the tree trunk.

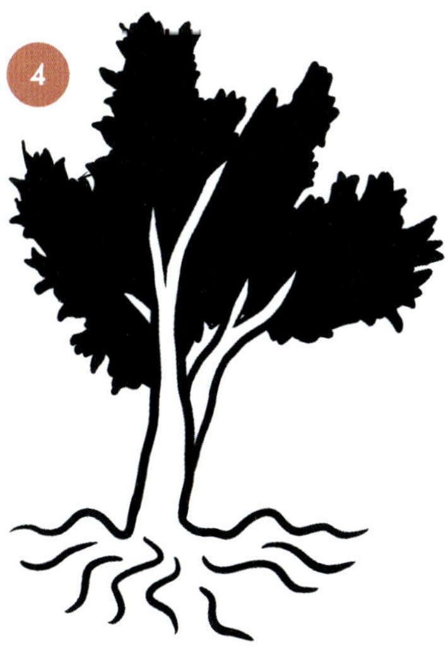

Draw more squiggly lines underneath the tree trunks to add roots and shade in your tree shape completely.

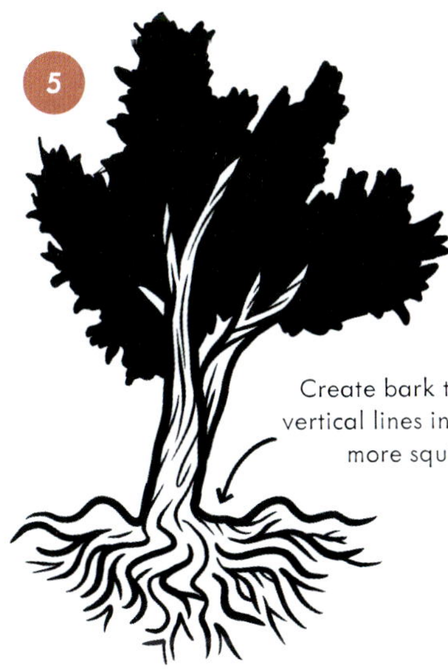

Create bark texture with curvy vertical lines in the trunk and add more squiggling roots.

Simple Coconut Palm

Coconut palms, with their tall, slender trunks and cascading fronds, are the quintessential symbol of a desert island paradise. This tutorial will show you how to draw the intricate details of this iconic tree, step by step. We'll build on basic shapes to create a realistic structure, then layer on delicate textures to bring this life-giving island resident to life in your dramatic landscape.

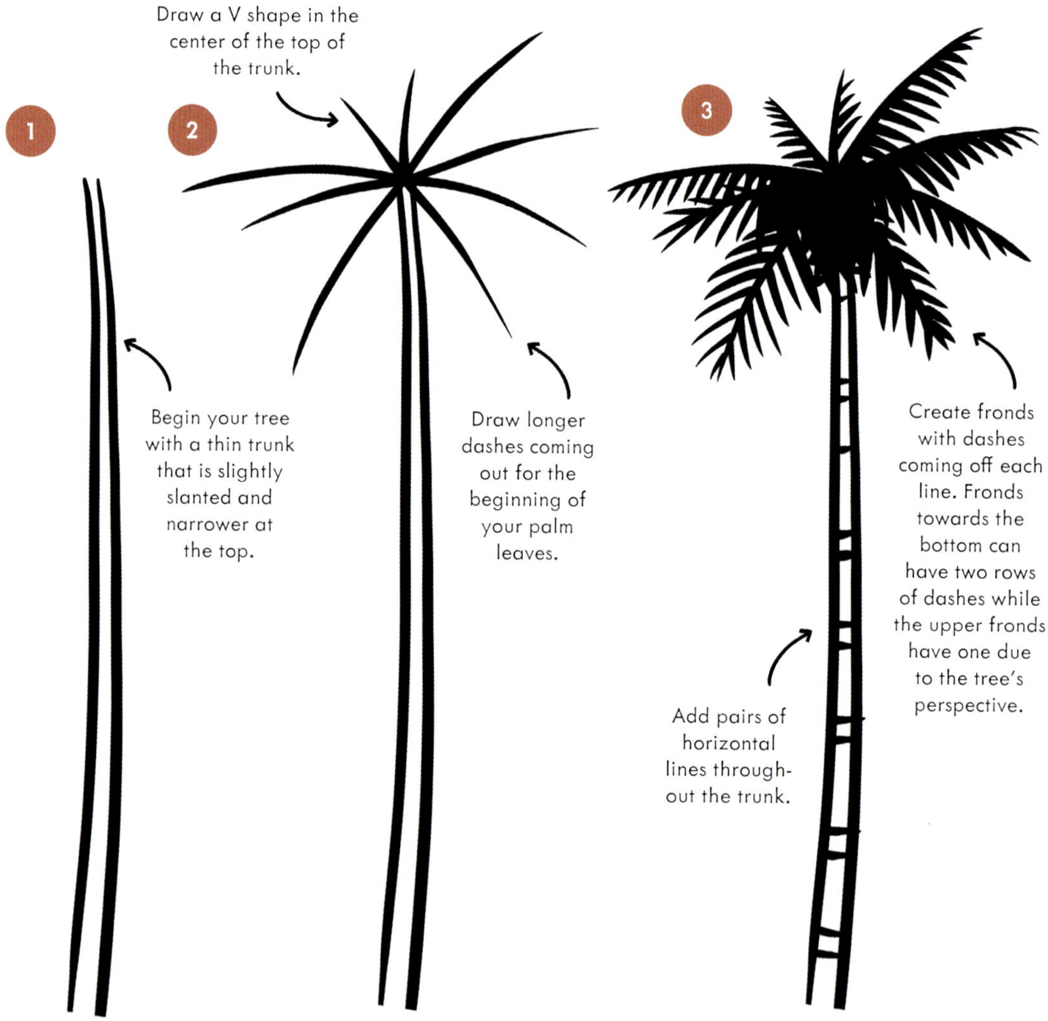

Waves

Waves, with their crashing power and ever-changing form, are a vital element of any desert island scene. This tutorial will guide you through capturing the movement and texture of waves, using basic shapes and layering techniques. We'll explore how to create the foamy crest, the rolling curves of the water, and the interplay of light and shadow, transforming them into a dynamic element that adds drama and energy to your desert island landscape.

1

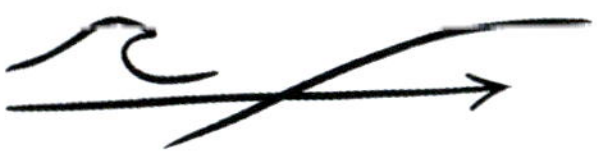

To start a wave, first figure out which direction the wave is going. For most of these drawings, the waves will be going towards land.

2

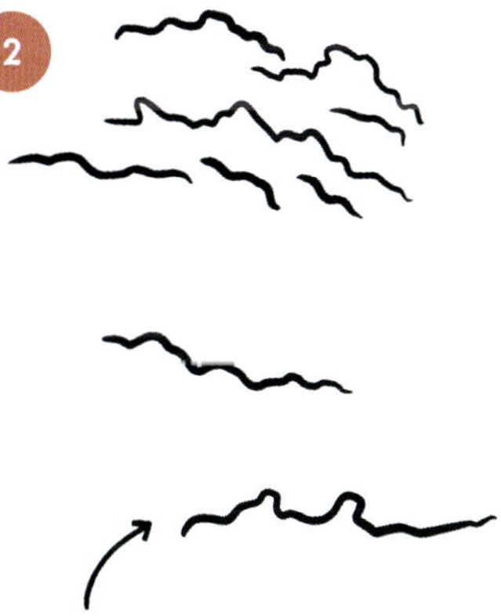

Since this wave is going towards the right of the frame, create the foaming crest with some wiggly lines on the right side that can be slightly layered on top of each other.

3

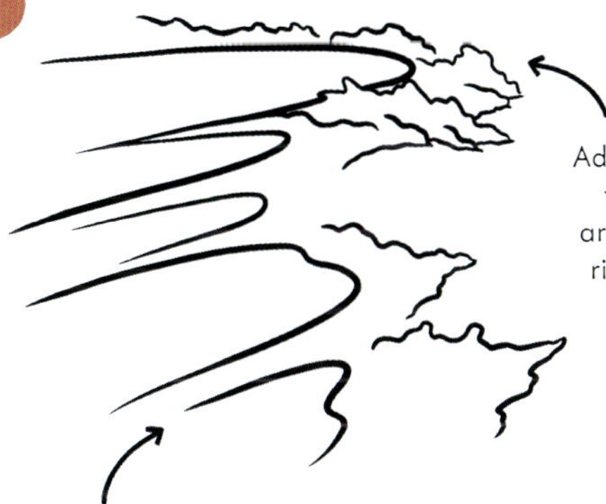

Add a few more foam crests around the top right of these arches.

Add swooping sideways arches going towards the squiggles.

Draw some tiny circles around the foam for extra bubbly texture.

4

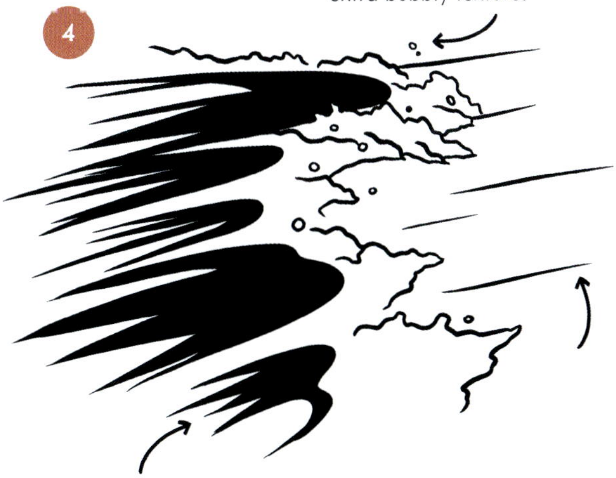

Fill in the waves with dark thick dash lines and shade in the arch shape completely. Create the presence of a shoreline or more water with some horizontal dashes on the right side of the foaming crest.

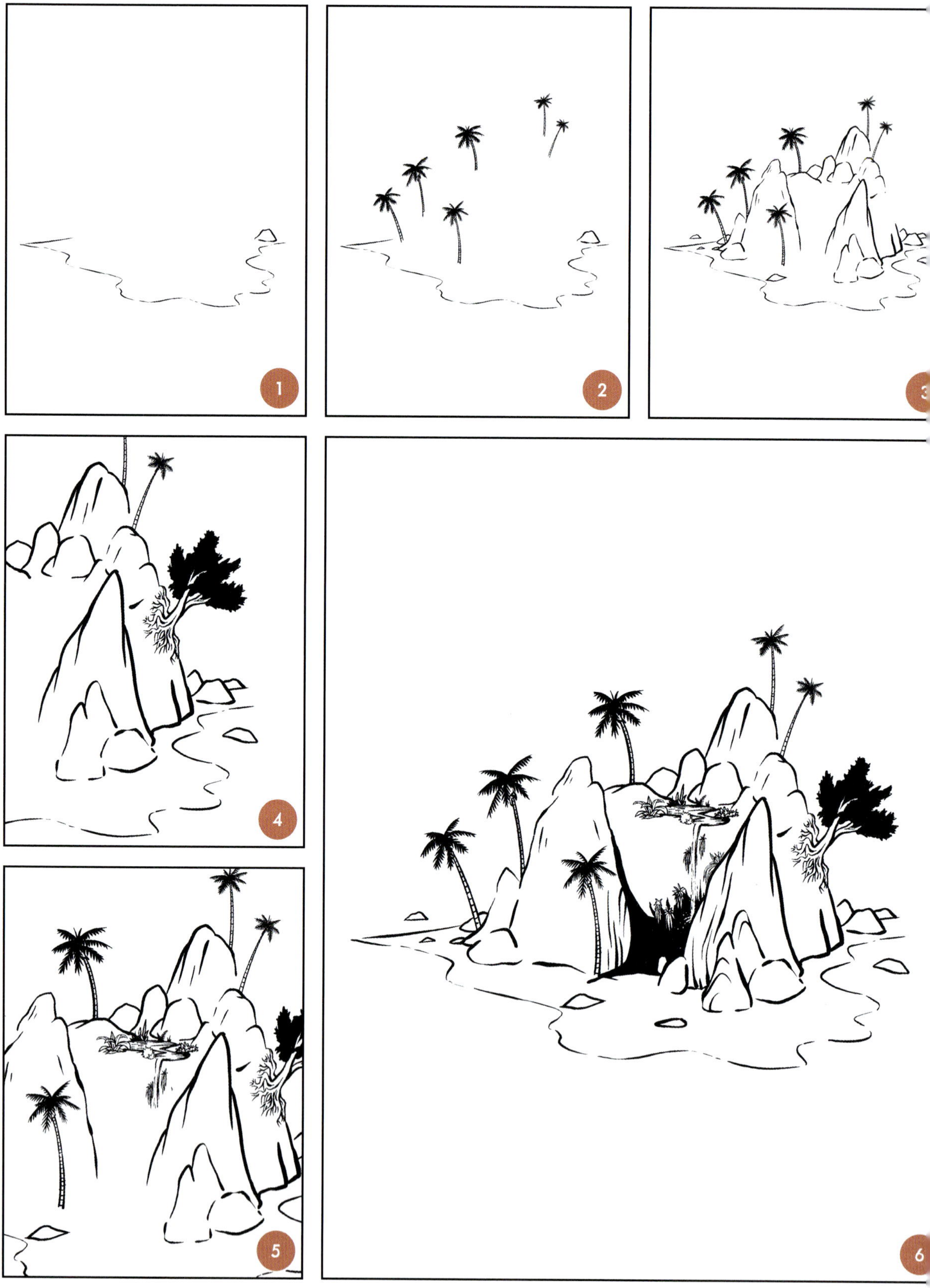
1
2
3
4
5
6

Now, Let's Draw the Scene

(See full image on page 38)

1. Start with a gently wiggling line across the center of the frame to indicate the island's beachy edges. Create some island corners by adding a sloping line on one side and a rock on the other.

2. To decide on your island's size and shape, draw in some Simple Coconut Palms (page 42) throughout the space above the island edge you just created, adding as many trees as you like wherever you see fit.

3. From those trees, draw steep and narrow rocky cliffsides with some bumpy upside-down V shapes. Add a few smaller boulders to the bottom of the cliffsides and around the beach as well.

4. Add a perilously perched Ficus Tree (page 41) to the side of one cliff by drawing some wiggles that branch out from a trunk sticking up diagonally. Draw in the tree's foliage by making a scribbly outline around the trunk and filling it in.

5. Create a small pond and waterfall for the top of your island! Start by drawing a few small Air Plants (page 39) and bushes, then create a pond with lines around an imaginary narrow oval, letting the ends trail down the side of the cliff to make the waterfall. You can even draw some air plants clinging to the sides of the cliff along the waterfall for extra detail.

6. Add in more trailing plants down the side of the cliff and add more texture to the island rocks with lines inside them that mimic their outer shape. Drop in some dark shadows to the very lowest portion of the cliffside that is surrounded by rocks on both sides.

(continued)

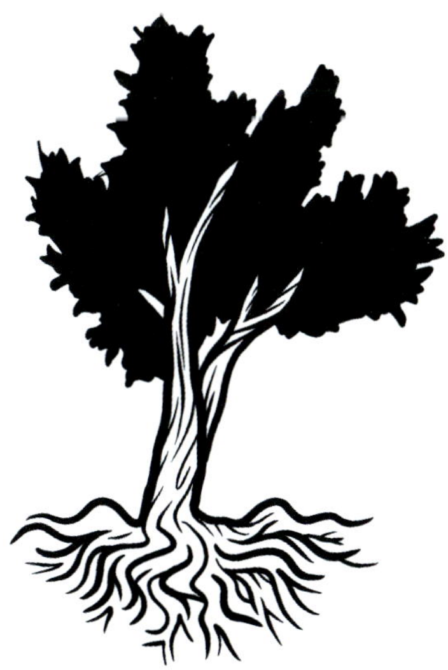

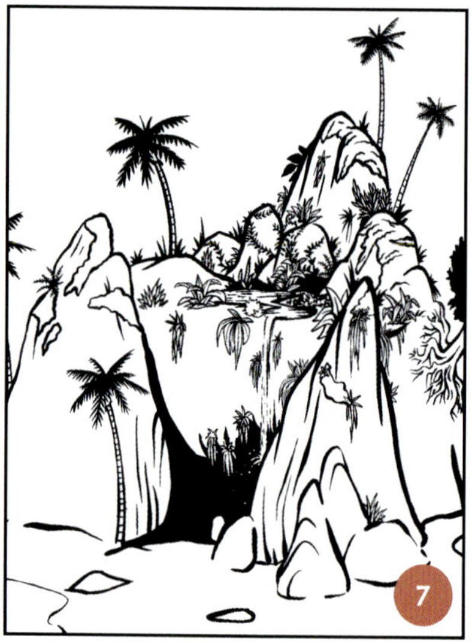
7

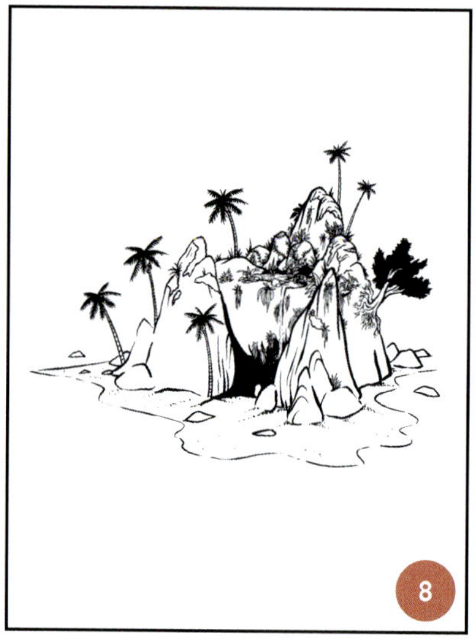
8

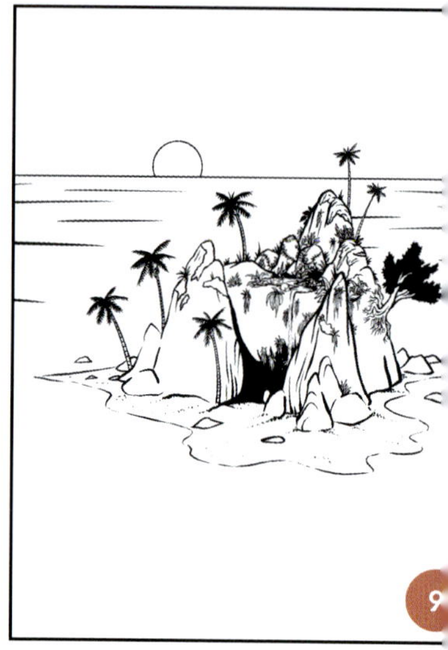
9

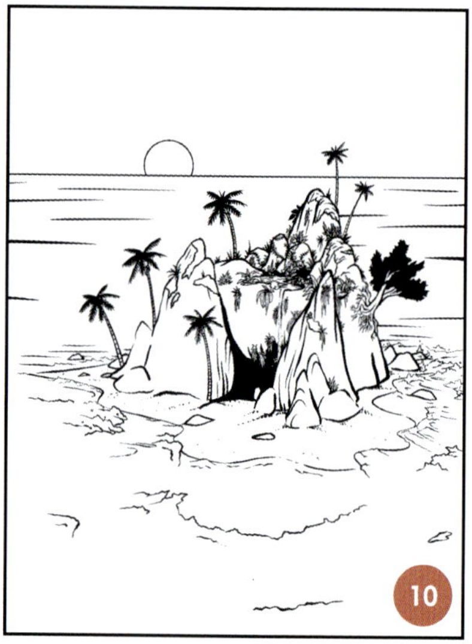
10

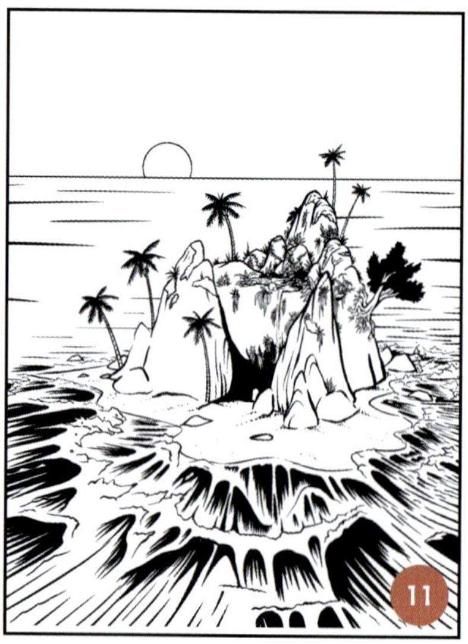
11

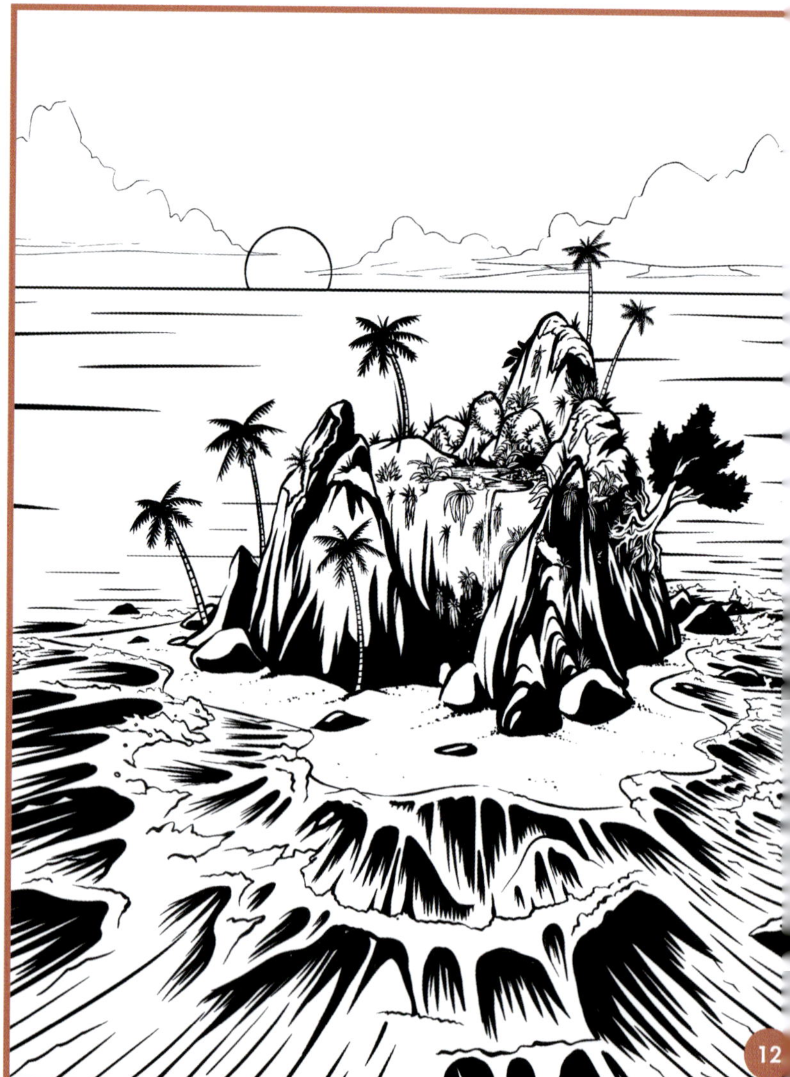
12

Now, Let's Draw the Scene (Final Steps)

7. Get creative while adding vegetation to your island! Draw some sprouting Bunch Grasses (page 15) and Vines (page 40) and add moss with wiggly shapes on the tops of the rocks. Be sure to concentrate the most plant life around the water.

8. Add sandy texture to your beach by sprinkling dots in trailing lines coming off the rocks and add more sparse dots around the shore.

9. Draw your horizon line behind the top of the island and put a circle peeking out from the top for a setting sun. Begin to draw your ocean by starting with horizontal strokes coming from the sides of the frames.

10. To draw the Waves (page 43) begin with their foamy peaks that are washing up towards the shore. Add some overlapping wiggly lines on the back of the island and some longer arching ones in the foreground to indicate a larger wave approaching.

11. Slightly behind the lines you just drew, add lots of arching U shapes of varying sizes surrounding the island. Shade in these areas with long downward strokes following the Us, then shade in the areas closest to the foaming fronts of the waves.

12. To draw shadows on the island, darken the areas where the setting sun would not reach, such as the lowest areas of the cliff sides and the rocks on shore. To make it more realistic, do not make the shadows fully solid shapes and instead let zigzagging streaks of light show through.

Finally, draw some puffy wisps of clouds slightly above the horizon line with lighter lines, letting parts of them overlap the sun.

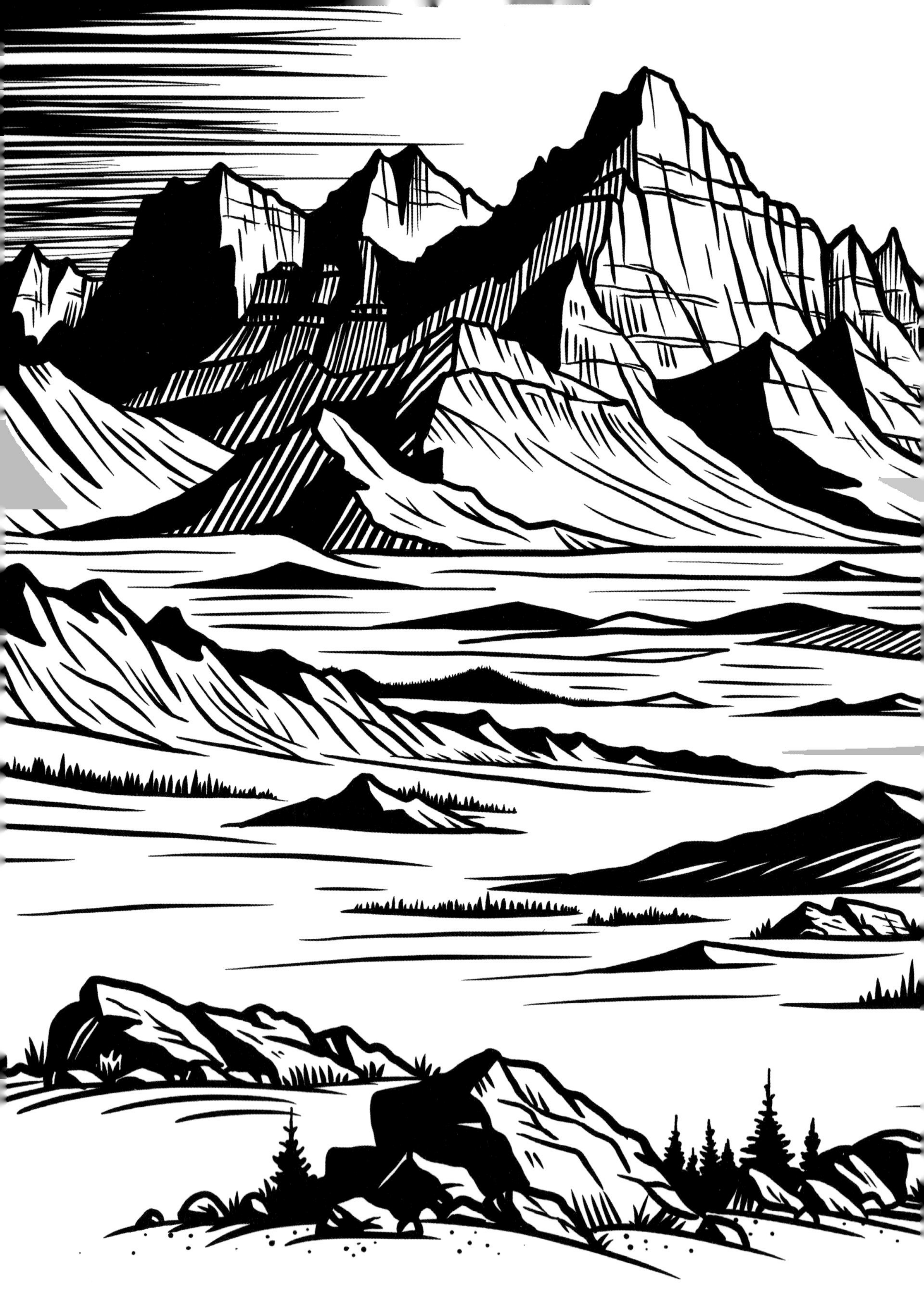

THE MOUNTAINS ARE CALLING

Ah, mountains, the embodiment of nature's grandeur. Each mountain is unique and silent; their peaks pierce the sky. These impressive places beckon adventurers seeking solace and rejuvenation in the embrace of the wild, from the crisp lines of Snow-Capped Peaks (page 65) to dramatic waterfalls in the Cliffs and Rocky Ranges (page 71).

Mountain ranges, sculpted by eons of relentless forces, stand as testaments to the awe-inspiring power of nature. Whether snow-capped peaks of the Himalayas (page 65) or active Majestic Volcanos (page 51), mountains come in all shapes and sizes, each with its own unique character and allure. From the tranquility of Alpine Lakes and Water (page 55) to the adrenaline-pumping rush of thousand-foot cliffs, mountains offer a tapestry of experiences, a sanctuary for the soul and a source of endless inspiration. Learn to draw in greater detail, develop your shading skills, and practice your rock textures.

Mountains are not merely static landforms; they are dynamic entities, constantly evolving under the relentless forces of nature. Wind, water and ice sculpt their slopes, creating breathtaking valleys, canyons and cliffs. Volcanoes, the earth's fire breathers, erupt with molten lava, reshaping the landscape and reminding us of the planet's immense power. A mountain's very presence commands awe and respect.

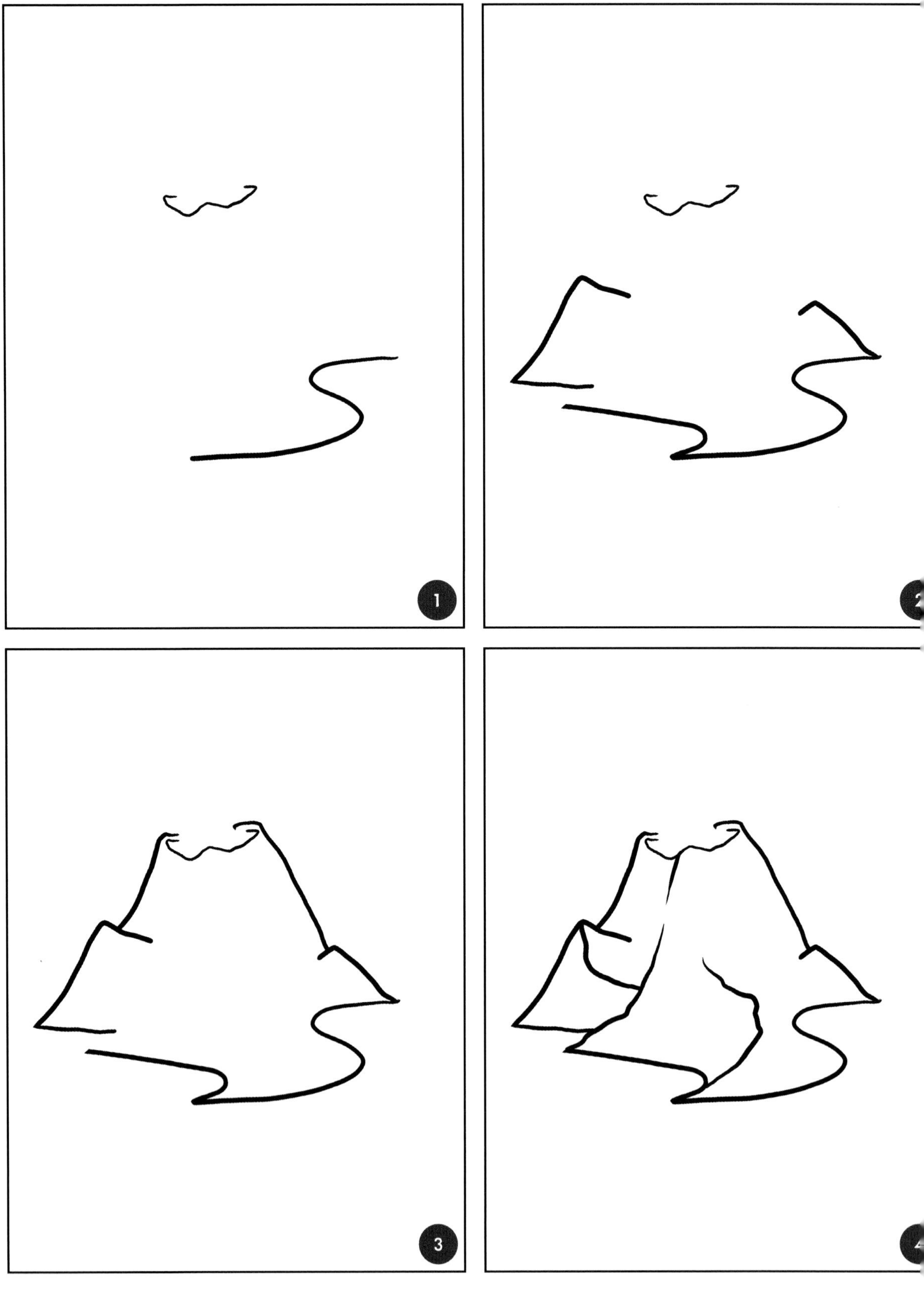
1
3

1. Majestic Volcanos

Volcanoes, with their awe-inspiring power and dramatic landscapes, have captivated artists for centuries. These fiery mountains, from the snow-capped peak of Mount Fuji to the active caldera of Kīlauea, offer a unique challenge and a wealth of inspiration.

In this tutorial, we'll embark on a journey to translate the raw power and beauty of a volcano onto the page. We'll start with basic shapes to construct the volcanic form, then layer textures to create the illusion of smoke, ash and molten lava. By the end, you'll have a powerful volcano illustration that evokes the essence of this incredible natural phenomenon.

Get ready to unleash your creativity and explore the artistic possibilities of these awe-inspiring mountains! This step-by-step guide will take you from basic shapes to a dramatic volcanic landscape, equipping you with the skills to create your own fiery masterpiece.

---

1. Start with an S shape that's lying on its side. To start the mouth of the volcano, draw a wide, wobbly W a few inches above the S shape.

2. Add a small horizontal line and a sideways J on the left that connects to the bottom end of the S. Then, draw the beginnings of the volcano with some points coming off the line on the right and the top of the S.

3. Draw the sides of the volcano with two lines coming up from those points and have them curve around the sides of the volcano mouth.

4. Draw a few ridgelines down the sides of the volcano.

(continued)

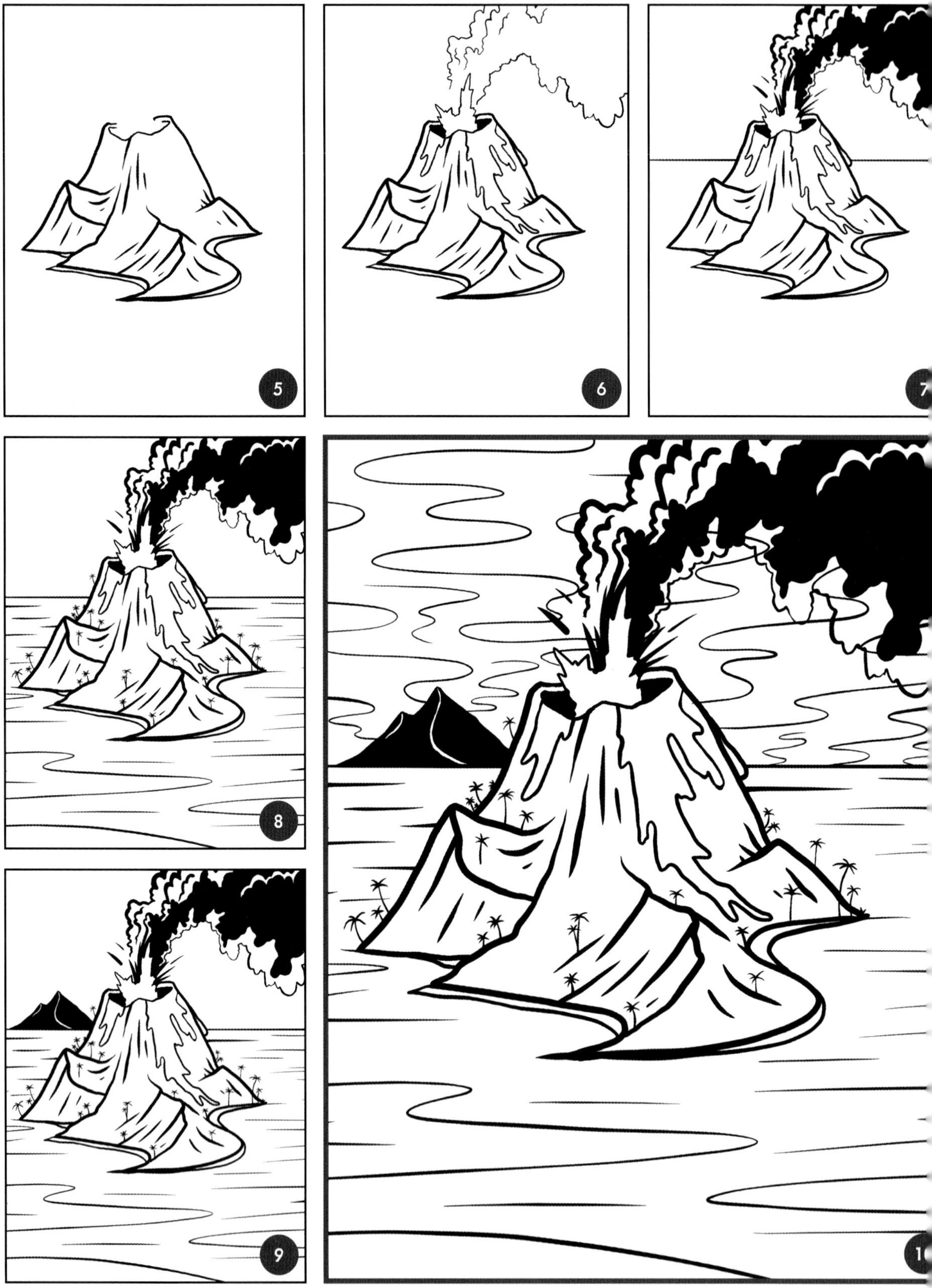
5
6
7
8
9

Majestic Volcanos (Final Steps)

5. Create more texture on your ridgelines with a few dashes coming off their sides. Add a coastline with a second line that traces around the bottom of the island.

6. Draw the lava with an upward explosion of wiggly lines from the mouth and some trailing down the sides of the volcano, then fill in the mouth completely. Add smoke by drawing puffy cloud lines coming out from the top of the volcano.

7. Make the smoke ashier by shading the central area of the smoke cloud darker. Add some upward dashes around the top of the volcano to indicate the powerful eruption. Draw your horizon line behind the top of your volcanic island.

8. Add tiny palm trees all over your island. Draw horizontal dashes underneath the horizon line to create the rippling ocean.

9. Make a distant island with a simple triangular mountain resting above the horizon line and shade it in.

10. Finally, create some ashy clouds with wiggling lines throughout the sky to complete your land-scape!

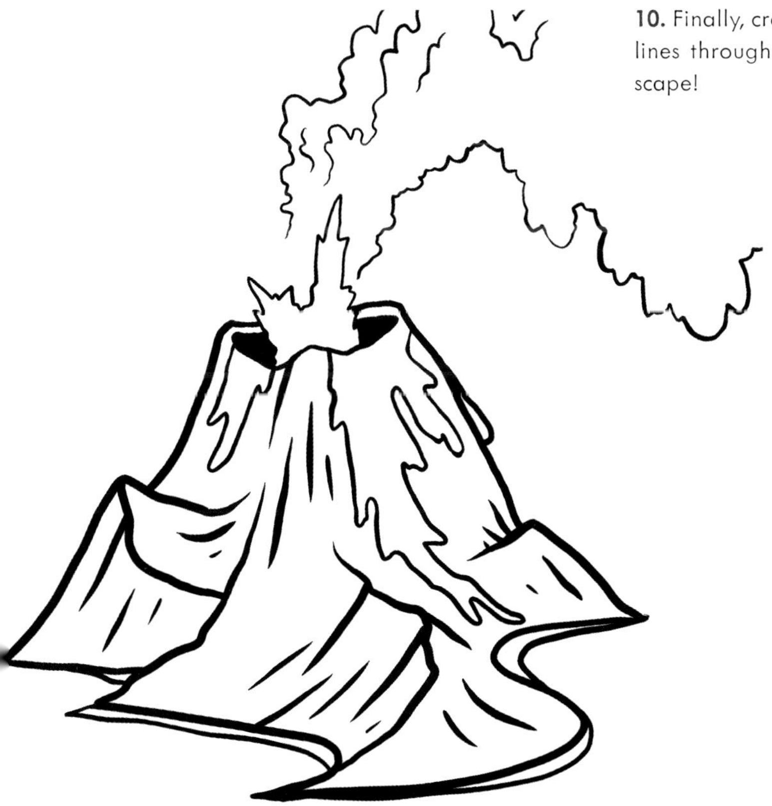

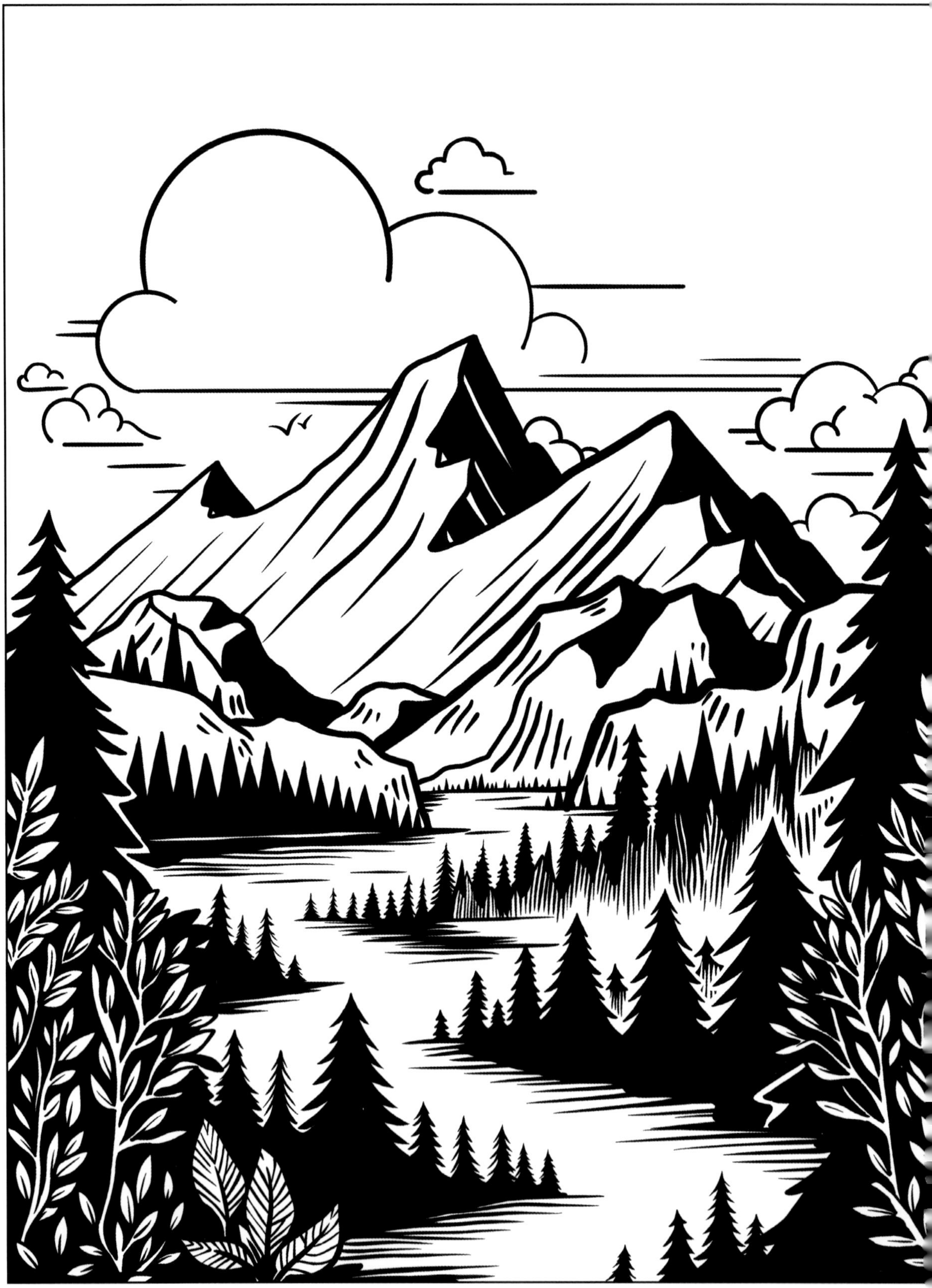

2. Alpine Lakes and Water

Nestled amidst towering peaks, alpine lakes offer a breathtaking scene. Their crystal-clear waters and majestic surroundings inspire artists of all levels. In this section, you'll learn how to depict the essence of these landscapes using drawing and line art techniques. We'll explore how to create the illusion of depth and realism in the water, depict the grandeur of the mountains through light and shadow and add details that catch the eye like vegetation and clouds. By the end, you'll be equipped with the skills to draw your own serene alpine lake scene. Get ready to unleash your creativity and explore the artistic possibilities of these mountain havens!

Small Leafy Hosta Plant

These shade-loving perennials add a touch of elegance to any doodle, and their simple form makes them a perfect subject for budding artists. In this tutorial, you'll capture the essence of a small leafy hosta using basic shapes and lines. Get ready to add a touch of botanical beauty to your drawings!

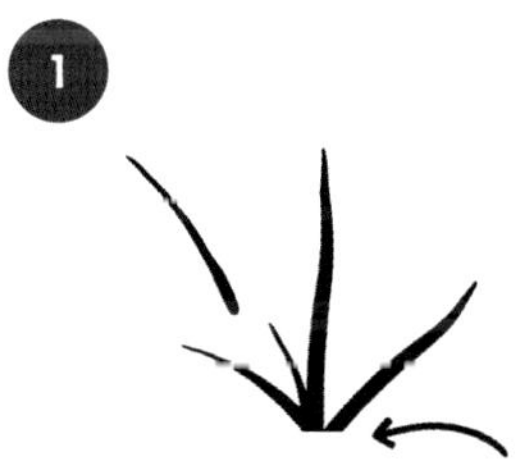

Begin with a few lines coming out around a central point at the bottom of the frame.

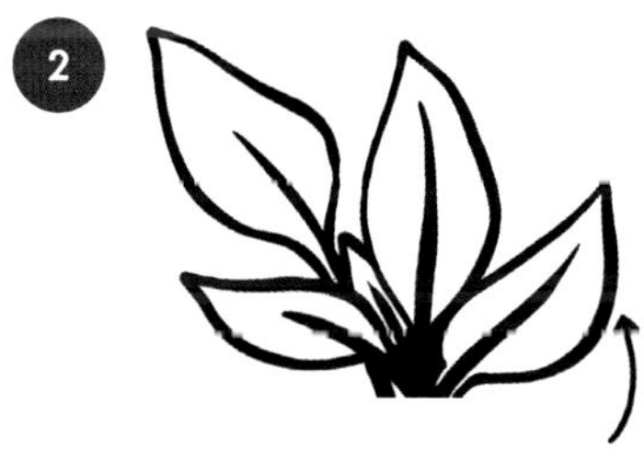

Draw round arcs ending in a point around each line.

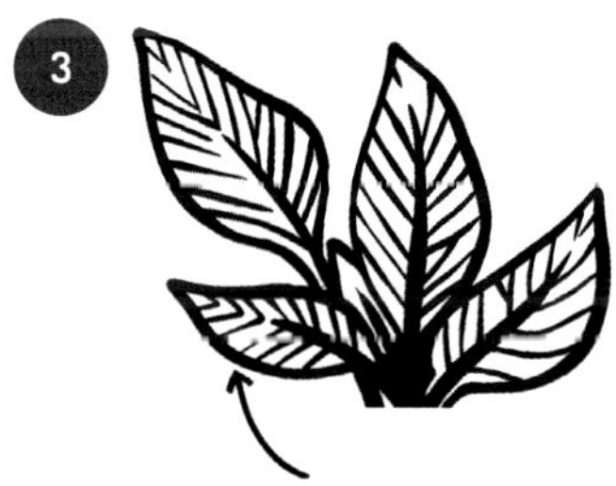

Draw dashes out from the center line of each leaf to signify the veins.

Cumulonimbus Clouds

Cumulonimbus clouds, with their towering forms and billowing tops, add a touch of drama to any landscape. Capturing their wispy textures and dramatic shapes can be a rewarding challenge for artists. In this tutorial, you'll create a realistic cumulonimbus cloud formation that perfectly complements your alpine lake scene.

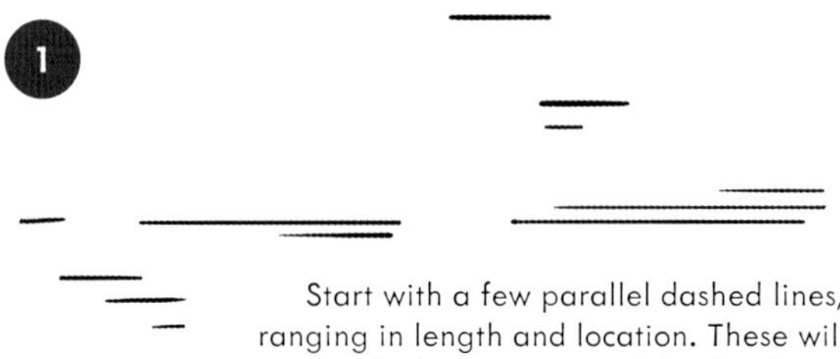

Start with a few parallel dashed lines, ranging in length and location. These will be the bottom areas of the cloud.

Roughly following the triangles, draw large arcing shapes to create the fluffy tops. Don't be afraid to experiment with their size and shape!

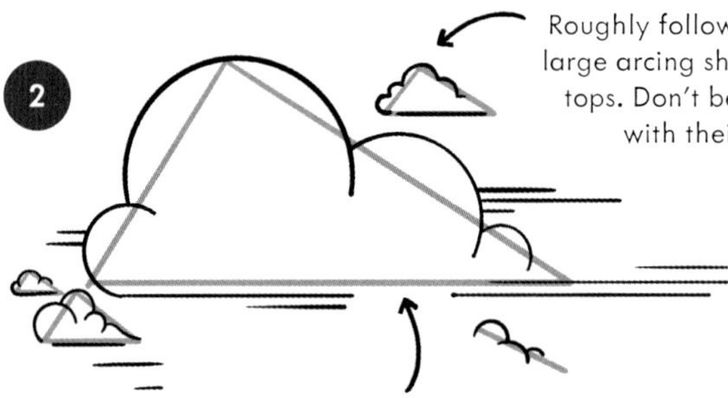

To lay out the overall cloud shape, envision a few uneven triangles on top of the parallel lines, with their ends narrower on one side. Using this shape will help create a windblown effect.

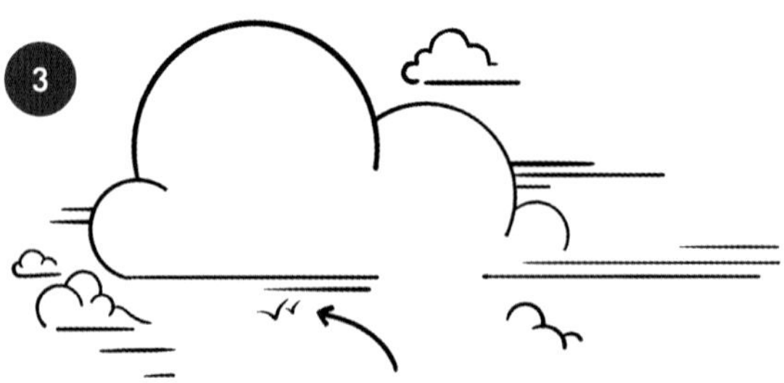

Add a few small flying birds by making Vs with rounded lines.

Sprouting Willow

Forget the towering giants of the forest—right now, we're focusing on the adorable side of willows! This tutorial will guide you through creating a detailed, yet approachable sprouting willow that brims with charm. Get ready to unleash your inner artist and bring this little bundle of leaves to life! We'll explore how to build the basic structure with simple shapes, then layer on delicate details to create a textured and whimsical willow.

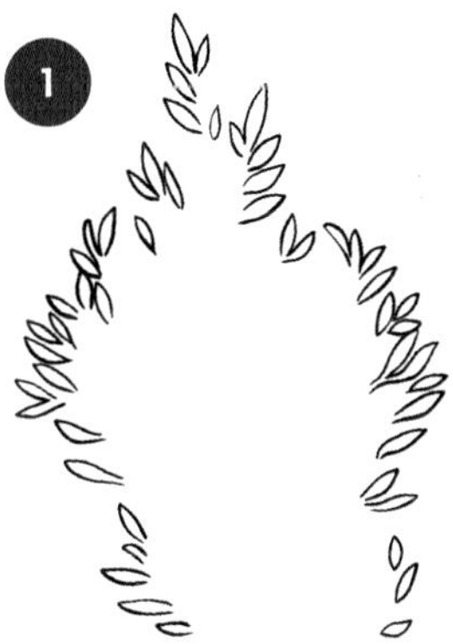

Create a frame of small leaves pointing out in an arc. Randomly place leaves of the same size around this arc. These will be the rough shape of the willow.

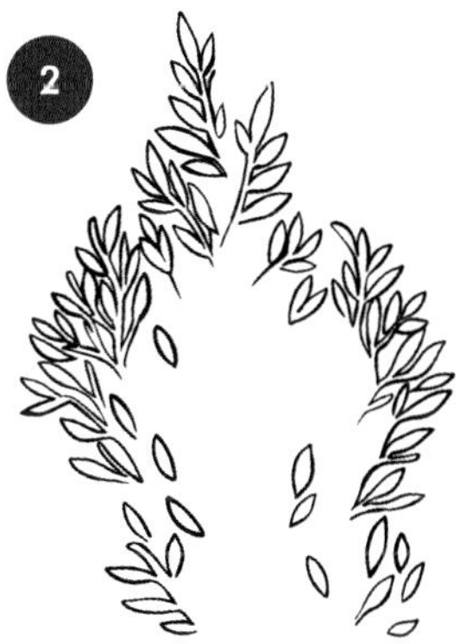

Start connecting a few of these outer leaf shapes with stems and draw in more loose leaves.

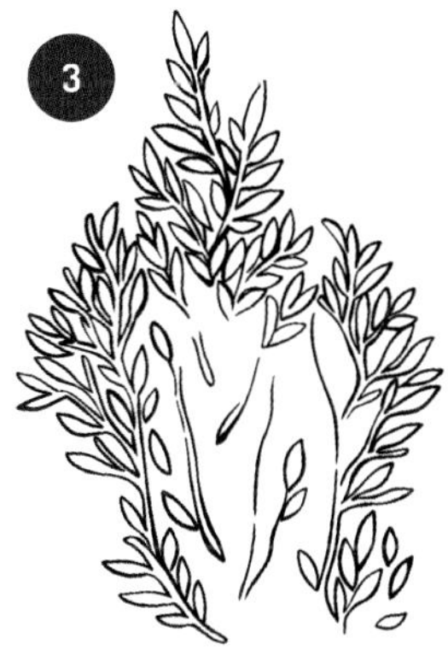

Draw some wobbly lines to the center to create more branches, while continuing to fill the outlining branches with more leaves.

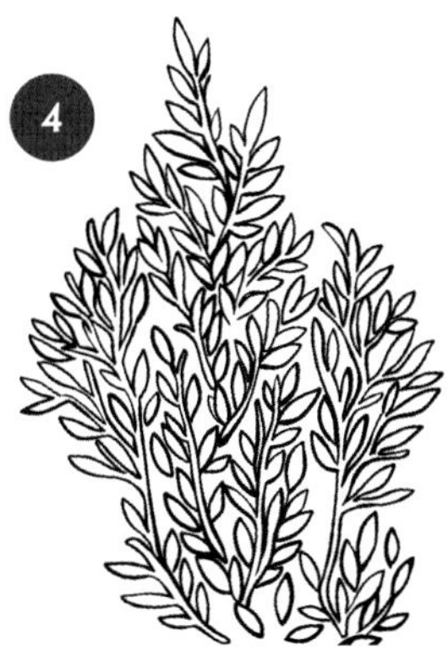

Fill the entire area with leaf shapes until the center is filled.

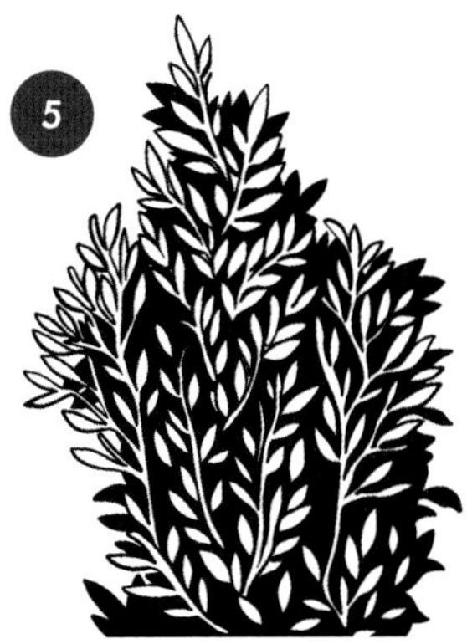

Shade behind each leaf and create an irregular leafy bush shape around the outside.

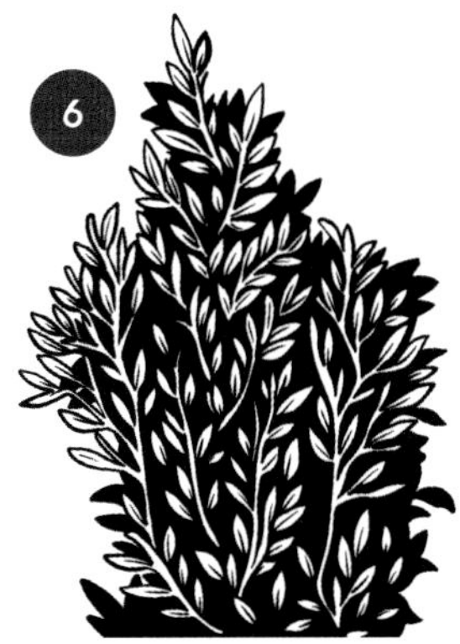

Add a line in the center of each leaf.

Simple Pine Tree

Alpine landscapes wouldn't be complete without their signature evergreens! In this step-by-step guide, create a simple pine tree that's perfect for adding a touch of whimsy to your alpine scene. Forget about meticulous detail—this pine tree is all about capturing the essence with fun and easy shapes. We'll start with a simple central line, then build upon it using playful zigzags to create a charmingly textured silhouette. Let's add a touch of cartoon magic to your alpine artwork!

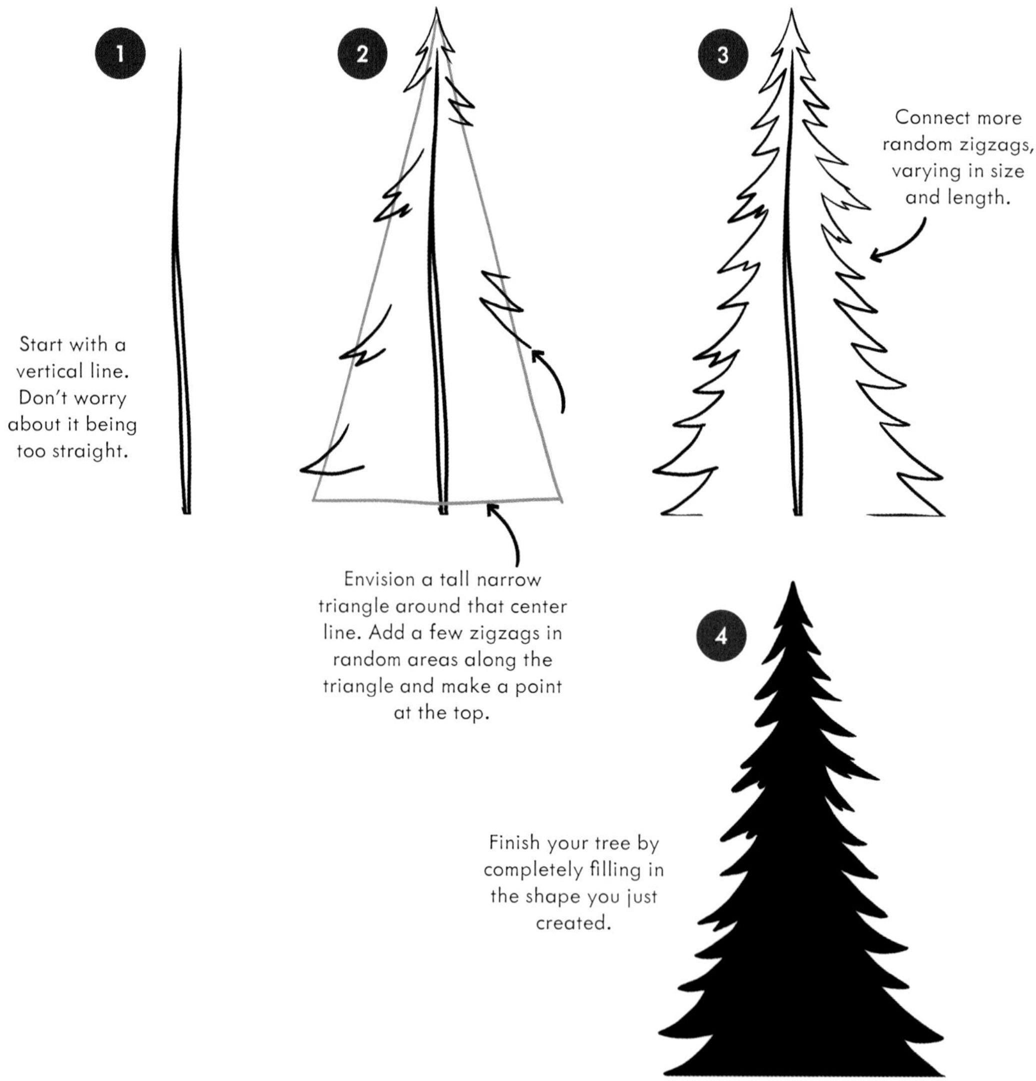

Jagged Mountain Range

Mountains are the giants of the natural world, and capturing their jagged peaks and dramatic slopes on paper can be both exciting and challenging. In this tutorial, we'll guide you through the process of drawing a majestic, jagged mountain range, perfect for adding a sense of awe and grandeur to your alpine scene. We'll explore the concept of erosion and how it shapes mountain landscapes. These particular mountains are created when blocks of earth are eroded and crumble away from a central ridgeline. You'll learn how to translate those forces into a rough, jagged line that forms the foundation of your mountain range. Step by step, we'll add details like angled slopes, textured ridges and strategic shading to bring your mountains to life.

Include a few taller points going in one direction.

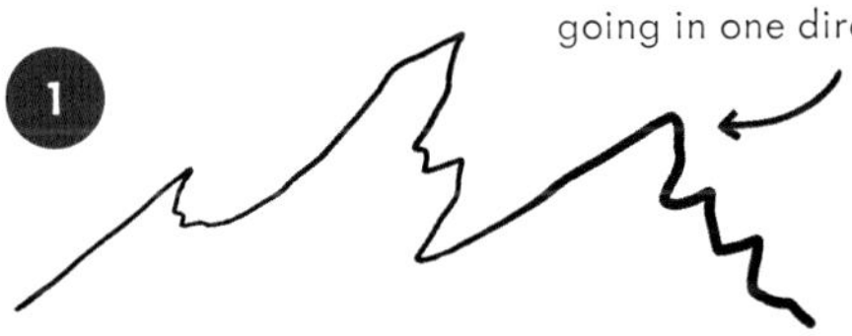

Begin with a rough jagged line.

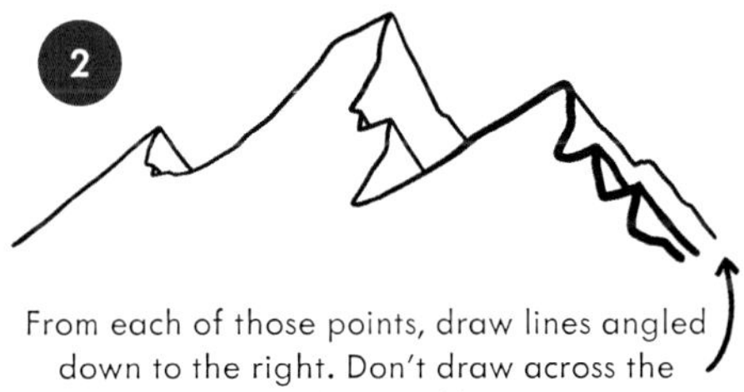

From each of those points, draw lines angled down to the right. Don't draw across the original jagged line.

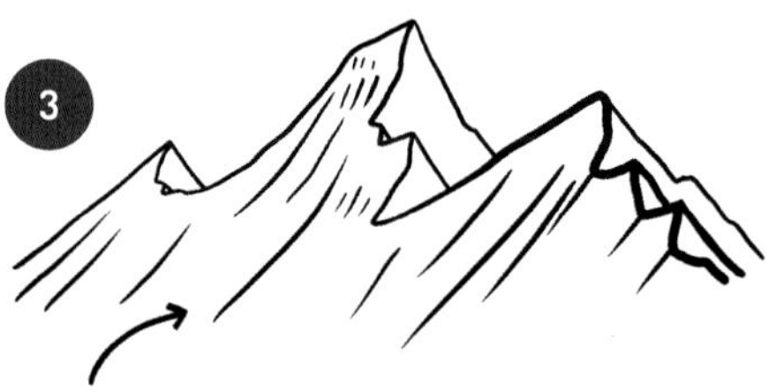

Add a few dashes that are random in length that run slightly parallel to the original line.

Shade in the right side of the mountain to create the shadow.

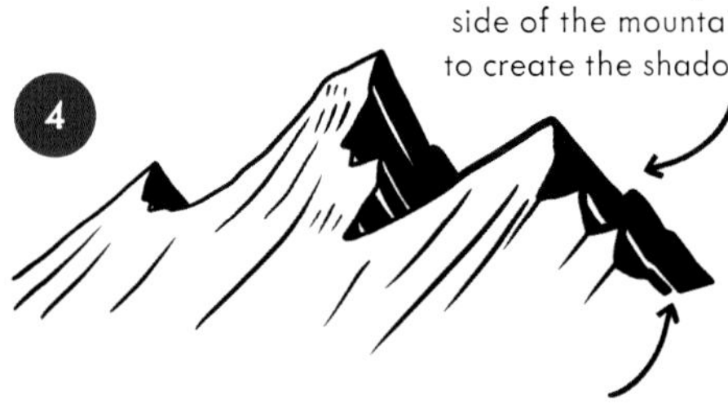

Leave areas of white peeking through the shadows to create even more depth.

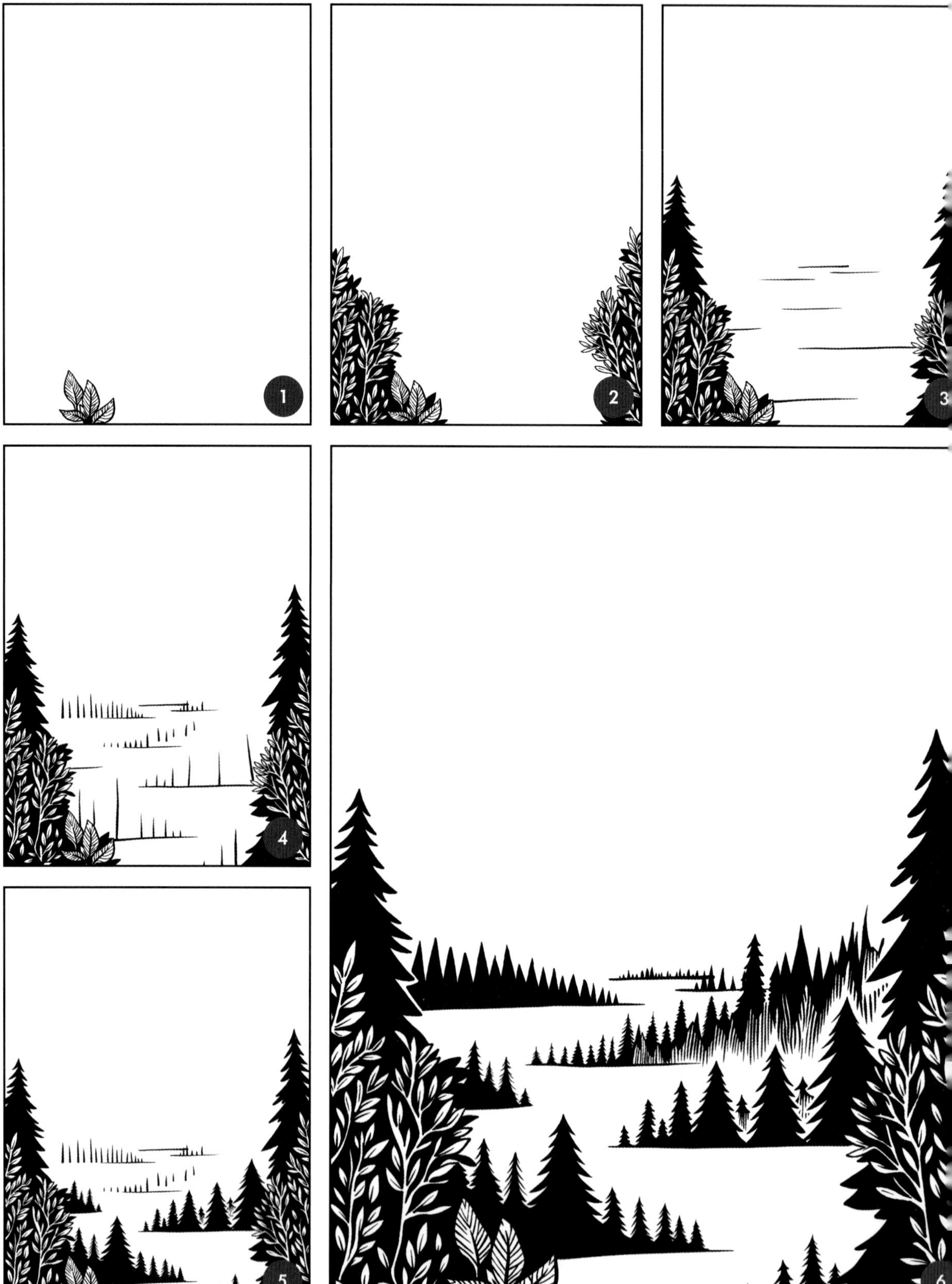
1
2
3
4
5
6

Now, Let's Draw the Scene

(See full image on page 54)

1. Start with a Small Leafy Hosta Plant (page 55) at the bottom of your frame.

2. Add in a few Sprouting Willows (page 57) to the left and right sides.

3. Add in some Simple Pine Trees (page 58) behind your bushes and draw a small horizontal line slightly lower than the center of the frame. Then, work your way down the frame adding a few more horizontal lines; those near the bottom of the page should connect to the side, while the lines closer to the center line remain floating.

4. From those lines, add some upward dashes, being sure to vary their length and spacing. These will serve as the beginning of some trees.

5. Begin adding in more pine tree shapes using the dashes as their center trunks. Feel free to add in more pine trees than you have lines for. Have fun with this step, as it's basically a bunch of scribbly jagged lines in the shape of triangles!

6. Create more depth by leaving a blank area above the tree line in the foreground and add more pointy treelike shapes on the dashes behind them. Add even more interest by including a middle area shaded by just adding in a bunch of small parallel vertical lines close together; this is known as vertical hatching. Make the trees smaller as you work your way into the background to show depth and distance.

(continued)

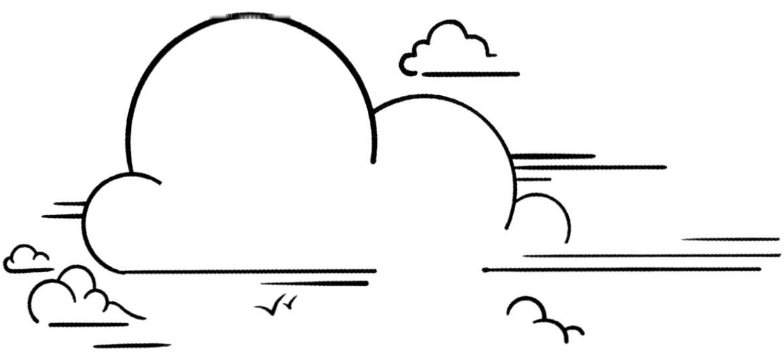

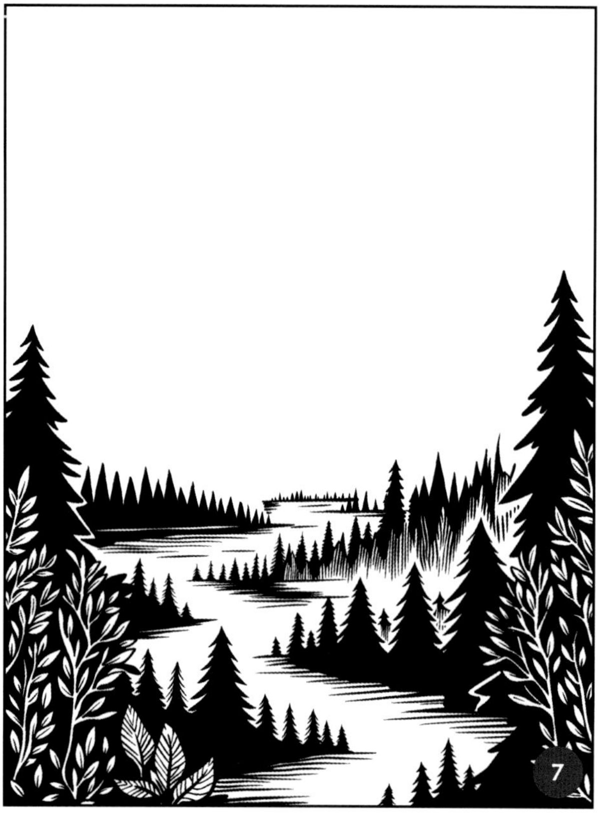
7
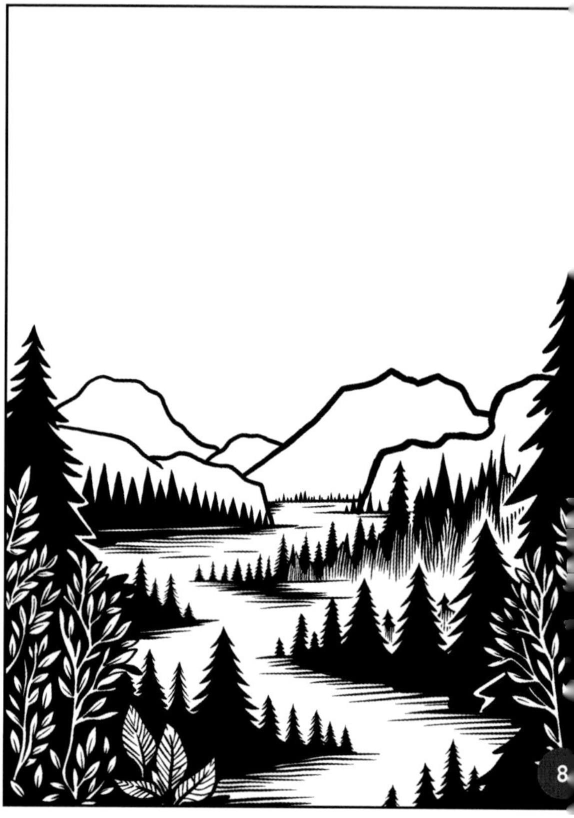
8
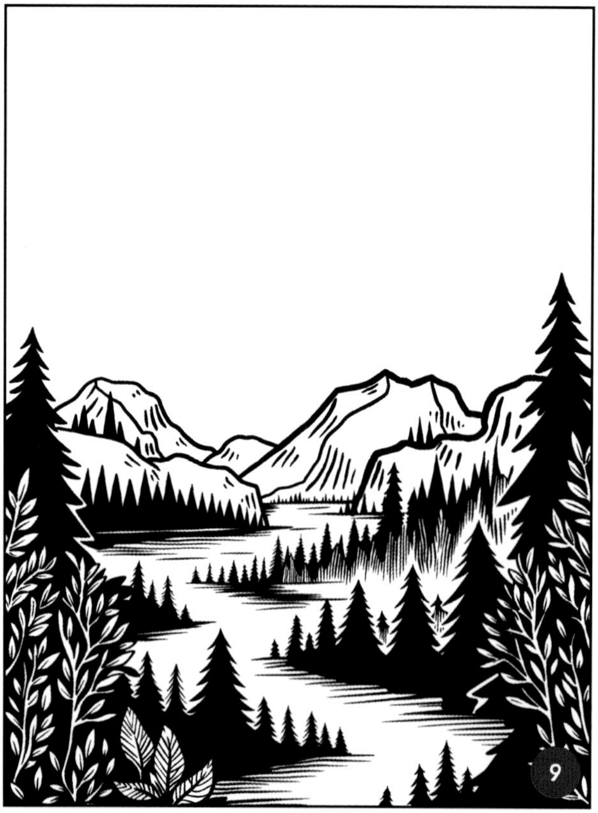
9
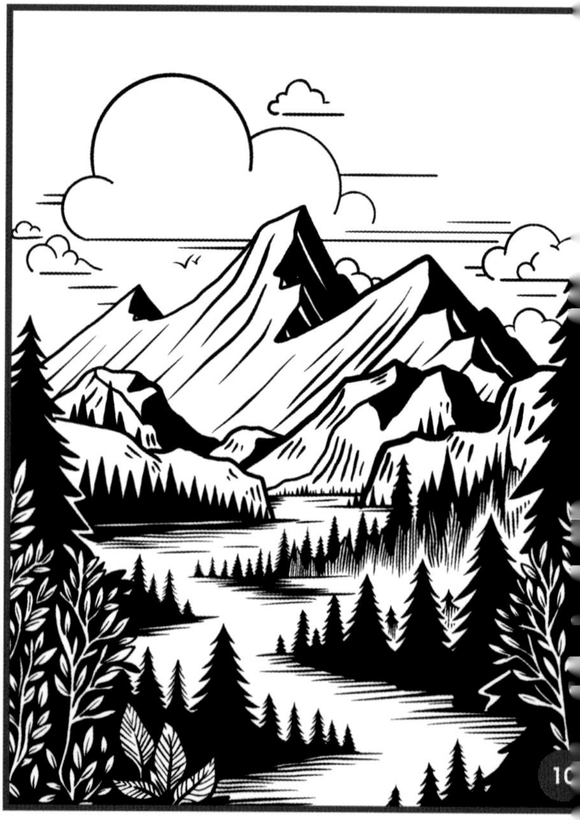
10

Now, Let's Draw the Scene (Final Steps)

7. This next part may look hard, but it's super easy! Draw horizontal lines as a reflection of the trees you just drew. Draw more lines on the sides by the trees, and fewer lines in the center.

8. To create the background, put in some random wobbly arcs behind the tree line farthest in the distance. Make them overlap however you like to create a hill range.

9. Make these mountains pop by adding some texture! Draw wobbly lines down to the left and right from any points on the arcs that you like. Then add a few diagonal dashes here and there to create more depth.

10. Make a majestic alpine peak in the background by adding in a Jagged Mountain Range (page 59). Give your mountains and hills some shadows by shading in the right sides of the ridgelines.

Finally, add in some puffy Cumulonimbus Clouds (page 56) and soaring birds behind the mountain.

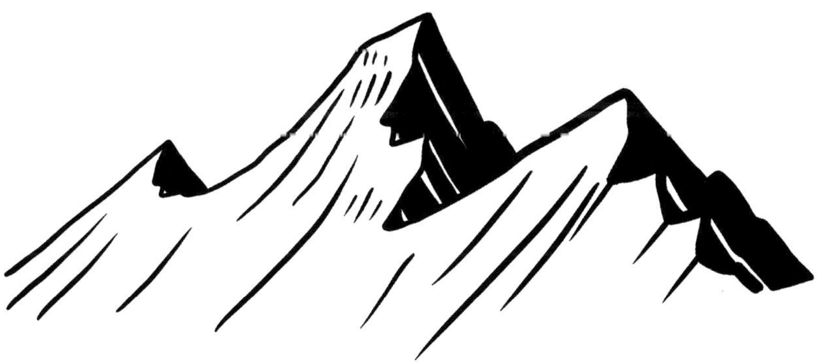

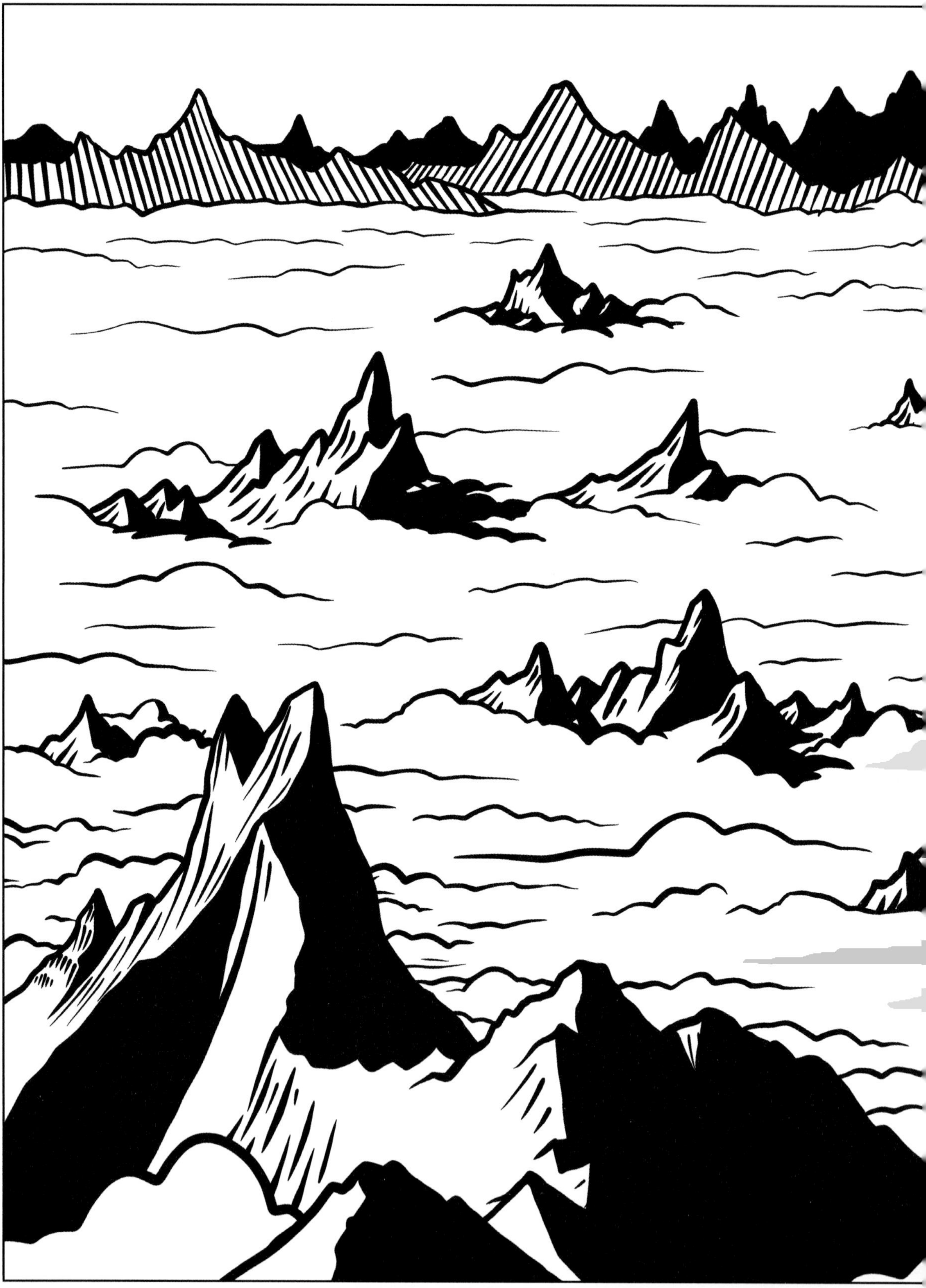

3. Mystic Pointy Peaks

Mountains have captivated humanity for centuries, their towering peaks a testament to the raw power of nature. In this tutorial, we'll guide you through the process of drawing these mystical giants, with a focus on capturing their sharp points and dramatic slopes. Forget gentle rolling hills—here, we'll delve into the world of jagged peaks, sculpted by millennia of erosion. We'll explore techniques to create those iconic, sky-piercing silhouettes that cast long shadows across the landscape. This step-by-step guide will equip you with the skills to create your own awe-inspiring mountain range, perfect for adding a touch of drama and adventure to your artwork. Get ready to embark on a journey of artistic exploration and conquer the challenge of drawing these majestic peaks!

Snow-Capped Peak

The undisputed ruler of the mountain range is the snow-capped peak! Its jagged form, a testament to time and nature's power, pierces the sky. We'll build this majestic feature step by step, starting with a simple jagged line that forms its silhouette. Get ready to illustrate the crown jewel of your mountain scene!

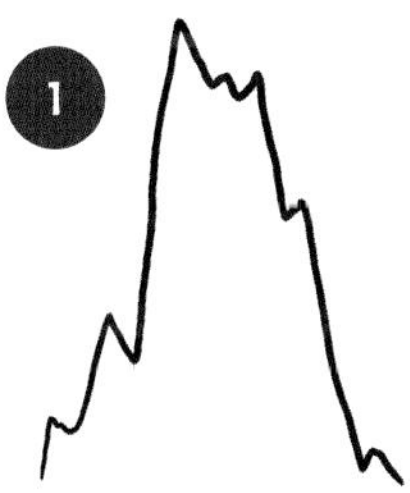

Begin with a jagged pointy line across the center of the frame.

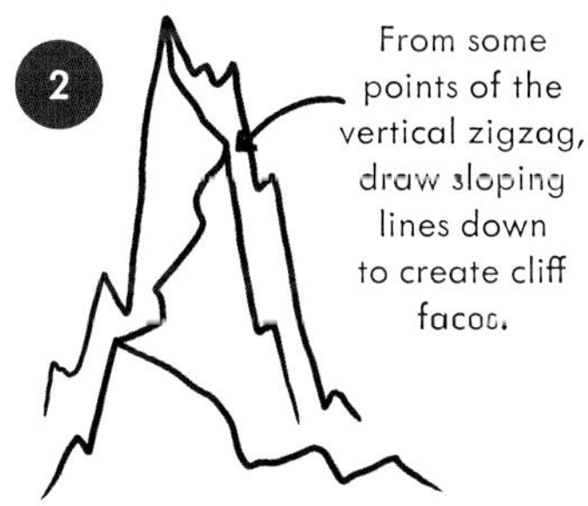

From the peak, draw a zigzagging vertical line going down the mountain.

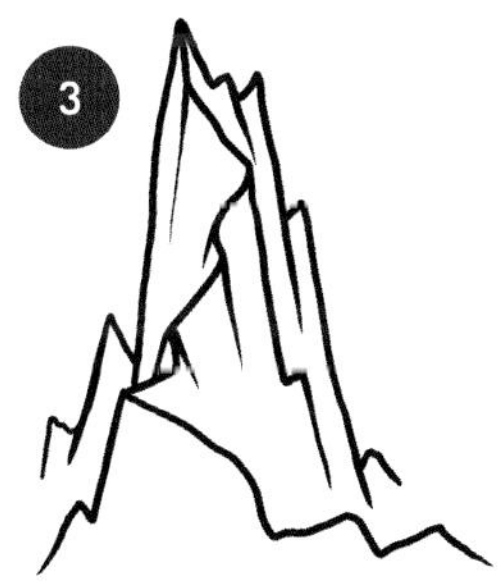

Draw some more vertical dashes down from the peaks of the mountain.

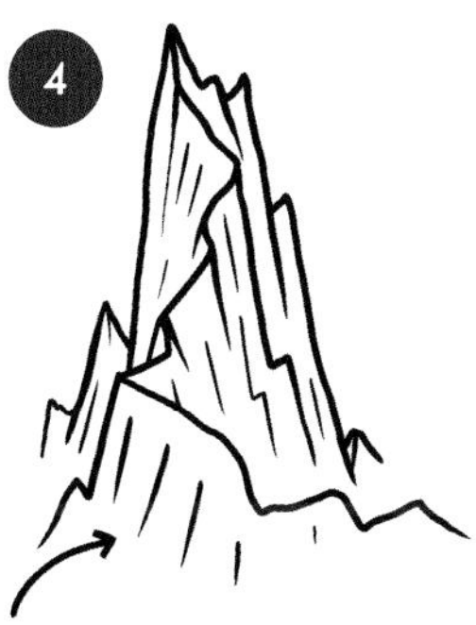

Add more small vertical dashes throughout the mountain.

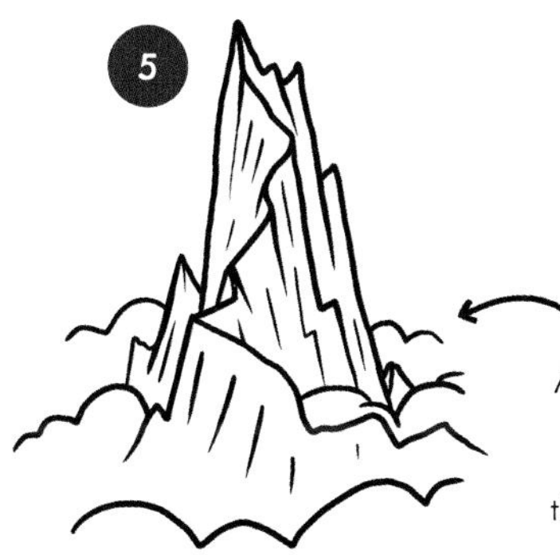

Add puffy lines Around the bottom of the peak to make it peek through the clouds.

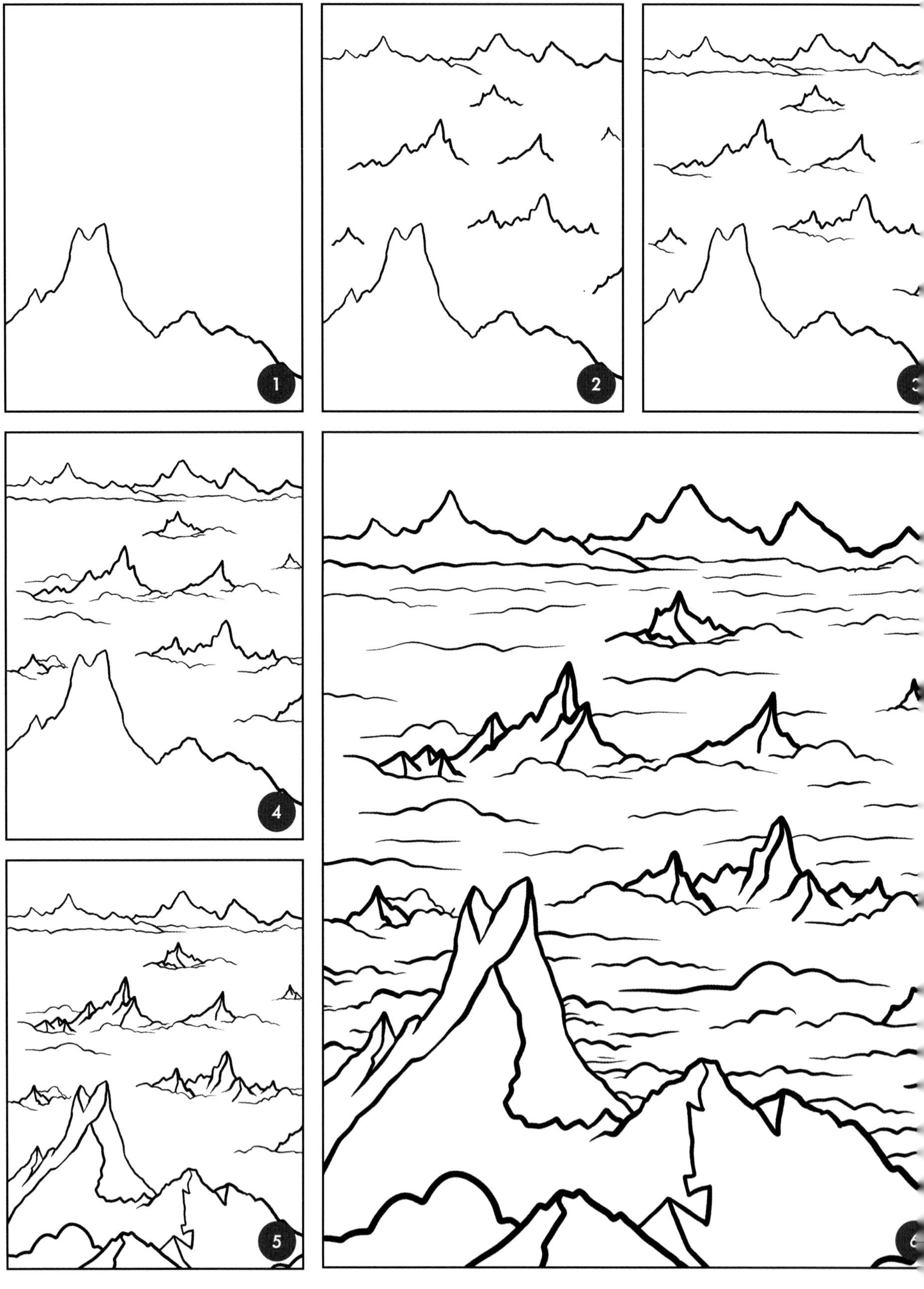
1
2
4
5

Now, Let's Draw the Scene

(See full image on page 64)

1. Begin your mountain by making a jagged line across the lower third of your frame; go wild with it, as some mountains have absurdly pointy shapes.

2. Drop in some more jagged peak lines behind your main mountain, ranging in size and shape. Add a long ridge line to the background with a slight overlapping area.

3. On the bottom left of each ridge line, add bumpy horizontal lines for the beginning of some clouds. These can be slight or reach all the way across the bottom of a range. Add in a wobbly horizontal cloud line underneath your mountain range in the background.

4. Let your clouds start to take shape by adding in more bouncy, bumpy lines along the bottom of your mountains and behind them. Let them overlap randomly while keeping a few spaced apart.

5. Now it's time for your mountains to come to life! From the top points of some peaks draw jagged lines that trail down towards the left. For the mountain in the foreground, create one wildly rugged range line that connects to another small peak created in the front. Add a final range line that swoops from the taller to the lower peak. Add one last big cloud shape to the front of your misty mountains.

6. Lay in some thin, bumpy cloud lines that are layered between your mountain peaks. Keep them concentrated in the foreground while leaving them sparse towards the background.

(continued)

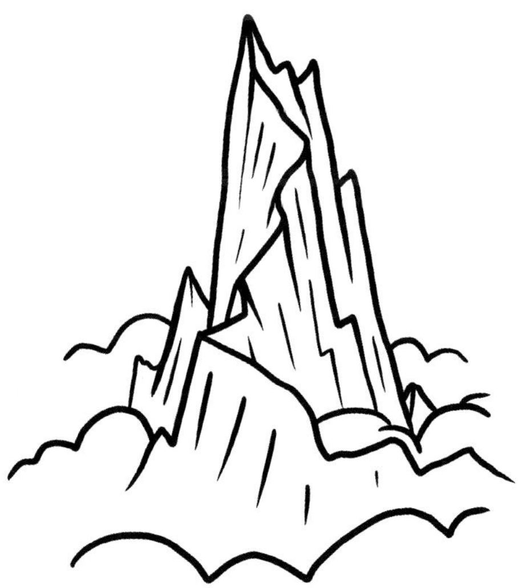

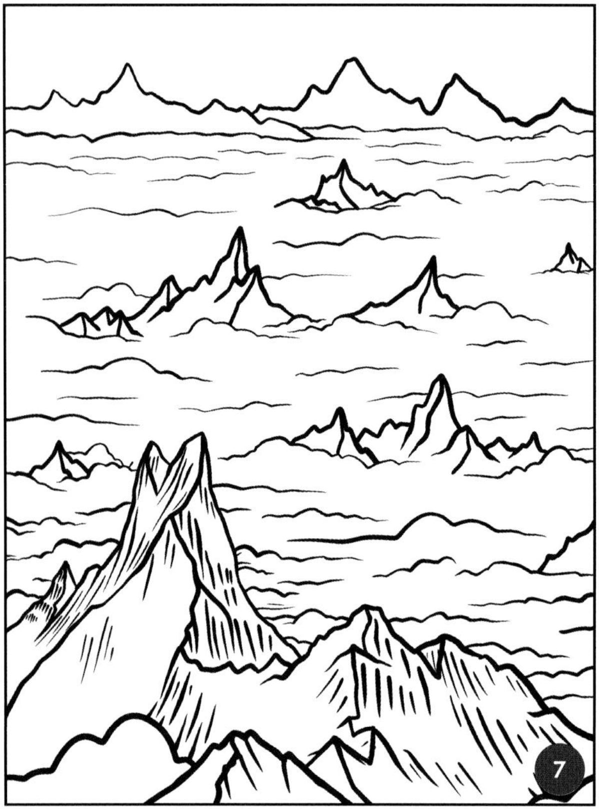
7
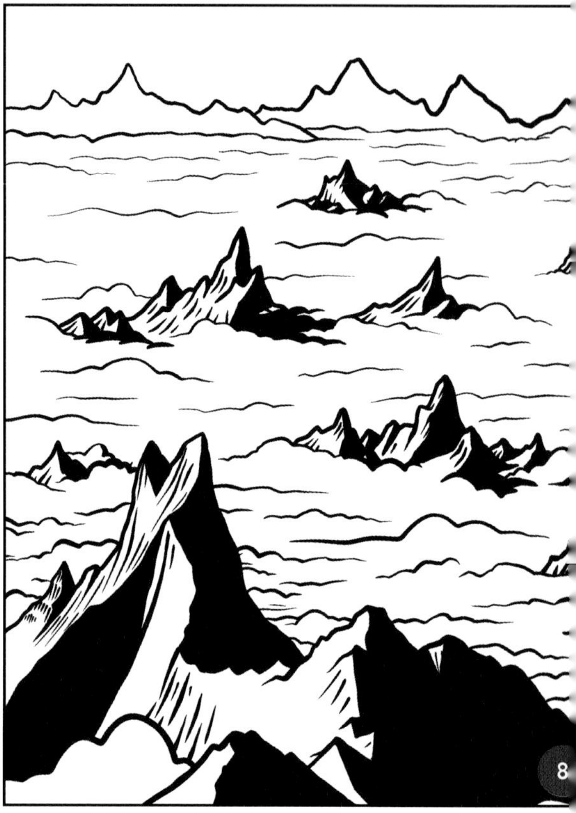
8
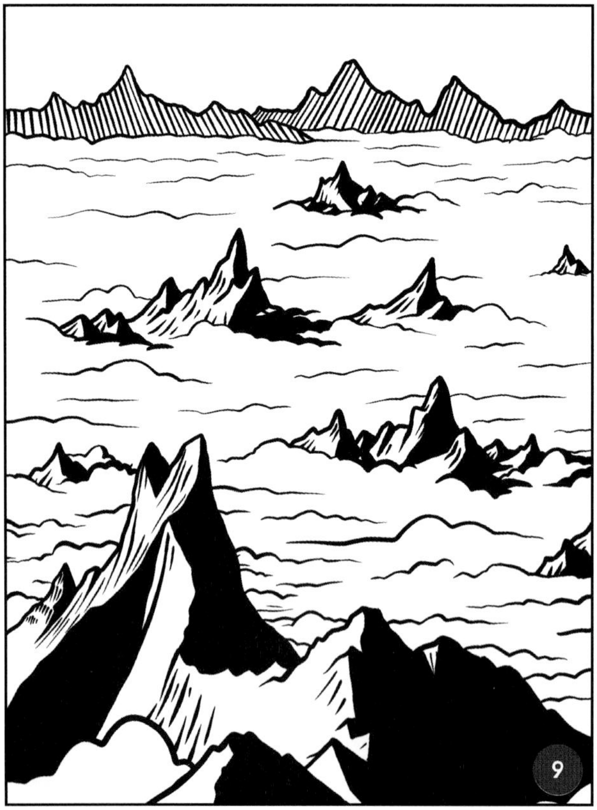
9
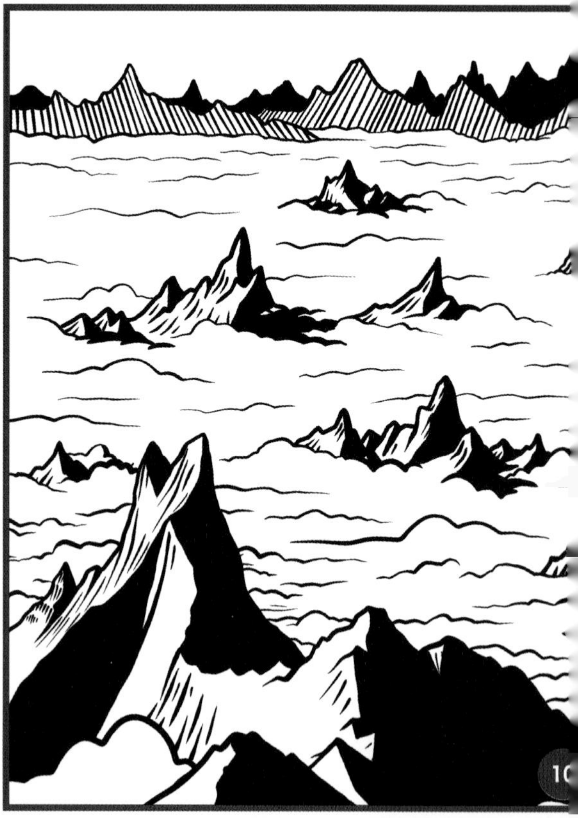
10

Now, Let's Draw the Scene (Final Steps)

7. Draw random rows of vertical dashes on the foreground mountains for bands of cliffs.

8. Add similar vertical cliffside dashes on the other mountains. Now it's time to create dramatic shadows! Shade in the right sides of each mountain range. (Think about the sun shining on your drawing from the left of the vertical ridgelines to figure out where exactly the shadows would fall!) Add shadowy clouds with some more bumpy lines that get similarly shaded in.

9. Fill in the mountain ranges in the background with diagonal lines. Create some intrigue with the left and right range's lines facing inwards toward each other.

10. To complete your drawing, add one more mountain range in the far distance with another jagged pointy line and shade it in.

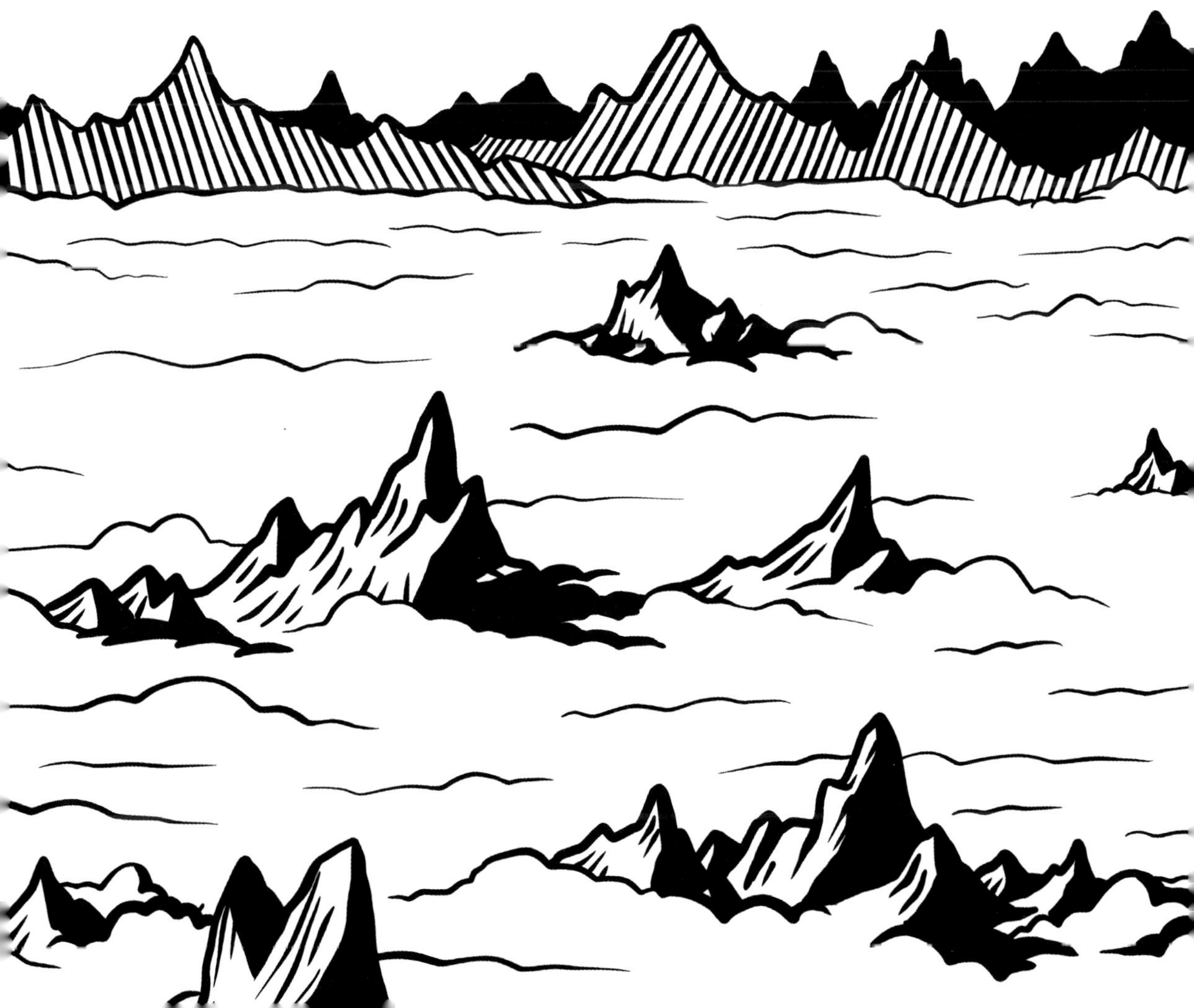

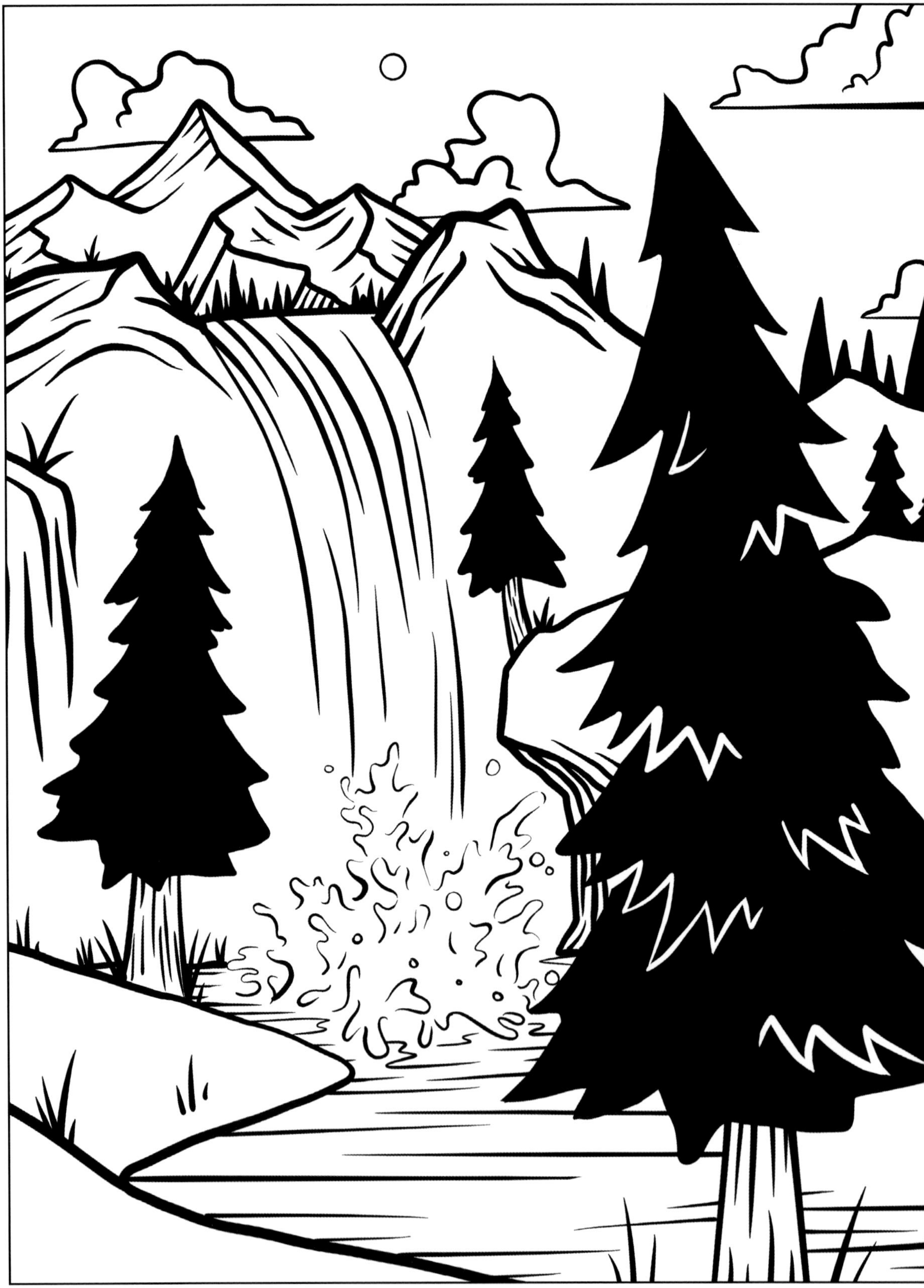

4. Cliffs and Rocky Ranges

Rugged cliffs and rocky ranges stand as testaments to the enduring power of nature. Their weathered surfaces, etched by wind and time, tell stories of geological transformation. Each crevice and crag holds a unique beauty, waiting to be reinterpreted on paper. But for artists, these landscapes offer more than just visual splendor—they present a thrilling challenge! In this tutorial, we'll guide you through the exciting process of translating these imposing formations into fascinating artwork. There is a certain satisfaction in using simple lines and shapes to recreate the textures of weathered rock. You'll learn how to strategically place pine trees to add depth and perspective, creating a scene that draws the viewer's eye into its majestic depths. The thrill doesn't stop there! We'll even explore how to create a cascading waterfall, bringing a touch of movement and life to your artwork. Think about the sense of accomplishment as you capture the dynamic flow of water thundering down the mountainside.

---

1. Draw three slightly curved Simple Pine Trees (page 58) with the largest in the front. Fill them in but leave some highlights on the largest one.

2. Add their trunks, then texture their bark with some thin vertical dashes throughout.

(continued)

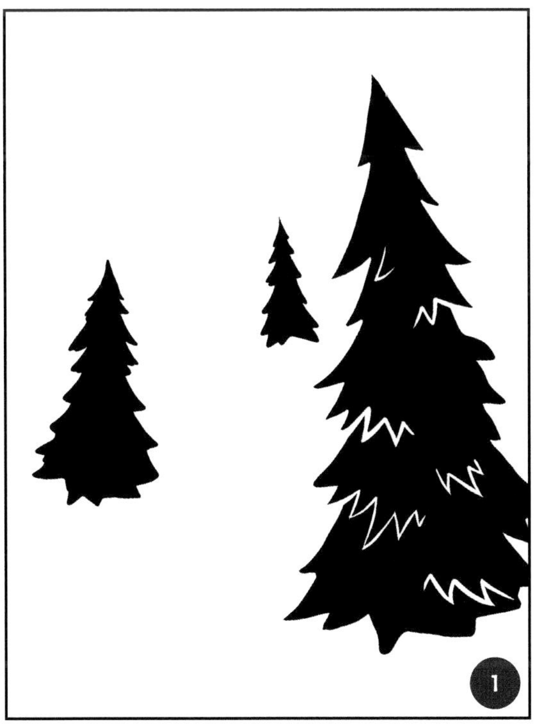

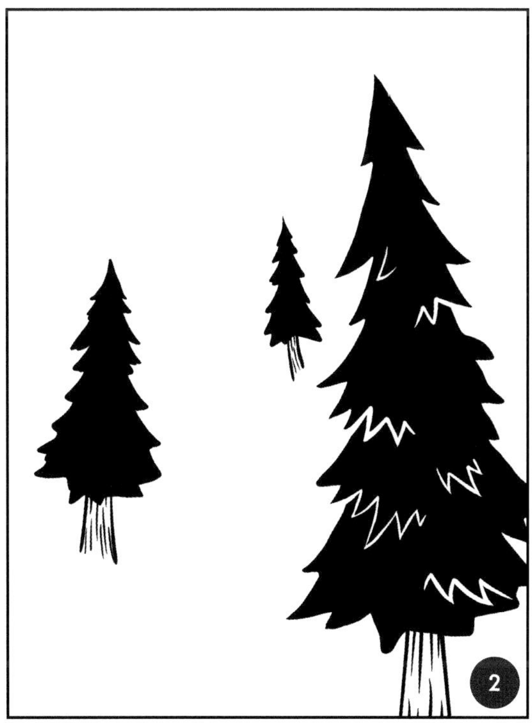

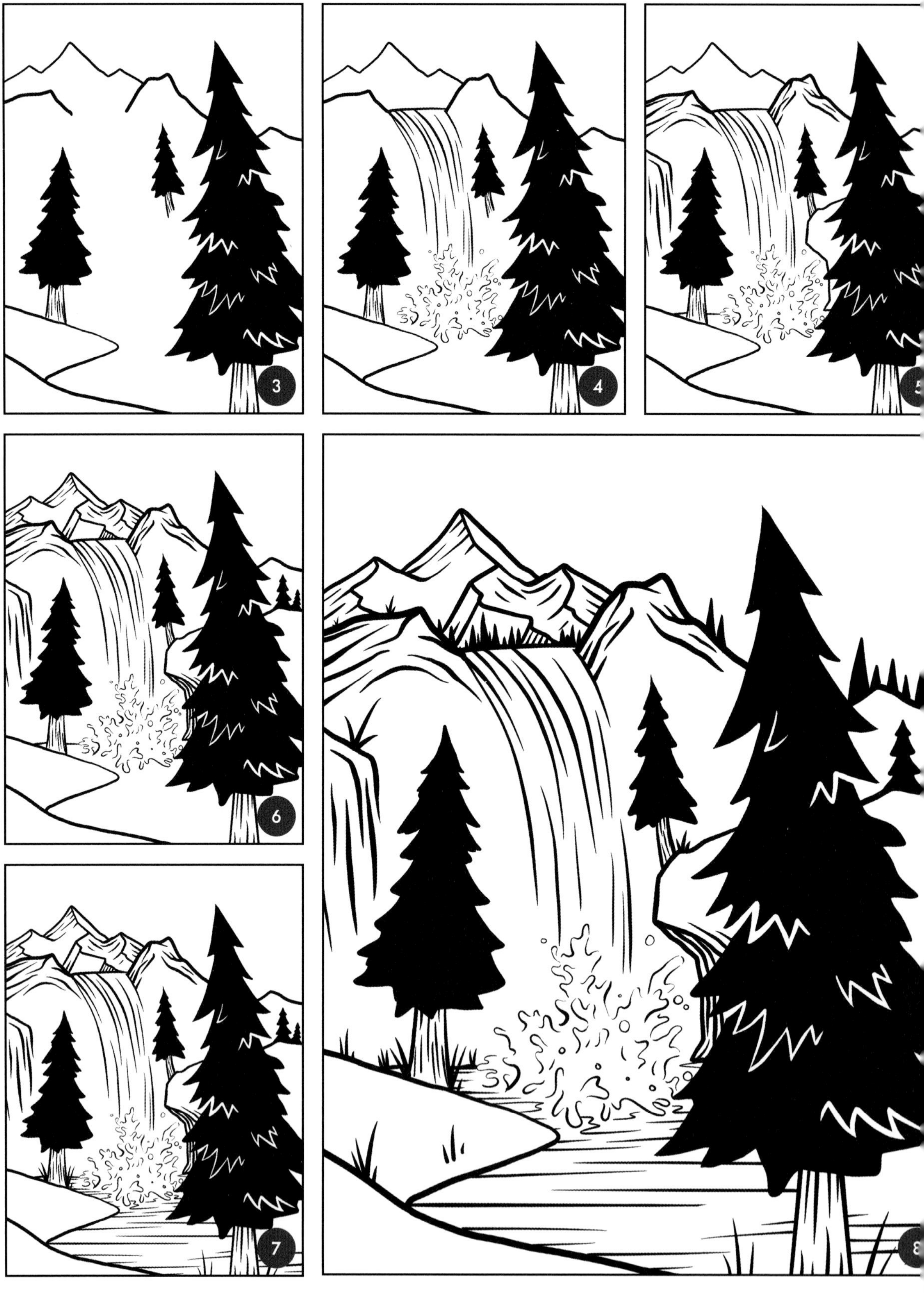
3
4
6
7

Cliffs and Rocky Ranges (Final Steps)

3. Add the outline of a jagged mountain range (page 59) in the distance, leaving a space between two for a waterfall. Then add a close shoreline on the bottom left of the frame with a simple Z shape.

4. Add your flowing waterfall with swooping lines coming down from the space you created that ends at the center of the frame. Make a splash at the bottom with lots of playful squiggly lines and small circles for splashing drops.

5. Draw some rocky texture on the tops of your mountains with lines following the direction of the rugged outline. Create another cliff face on the left side with some vertical lines and add a jagged line underneath the pine tree in the distance.

6. Make some more tiny pine trees on a mountain line in the upper right frame. Using what you've learned about drawing ridgelines and rock texture, add more detail to the mountains and cliffs in your scene.

7. Draw some grassy dashes along the bottoms of your closest pine trees. Create a refreshing pool of water with rippling horizontal lines in the space behind your closest tree and under the waterfall.

8. Add more vegetation with more grasses poking out randomly throughout and some simple narrow triangles for pine trees along the back-right ridgeline and top of the waterfall.

9. Finish your rocky range with a small sun and bountiful Cumulonimbus Clouds (page 56) in the sky, making their bottoms flat and their tops puffy and wiggly.

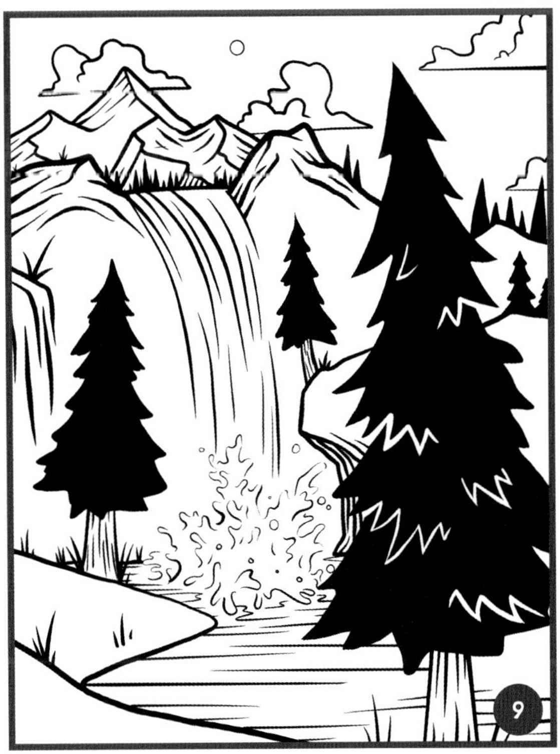

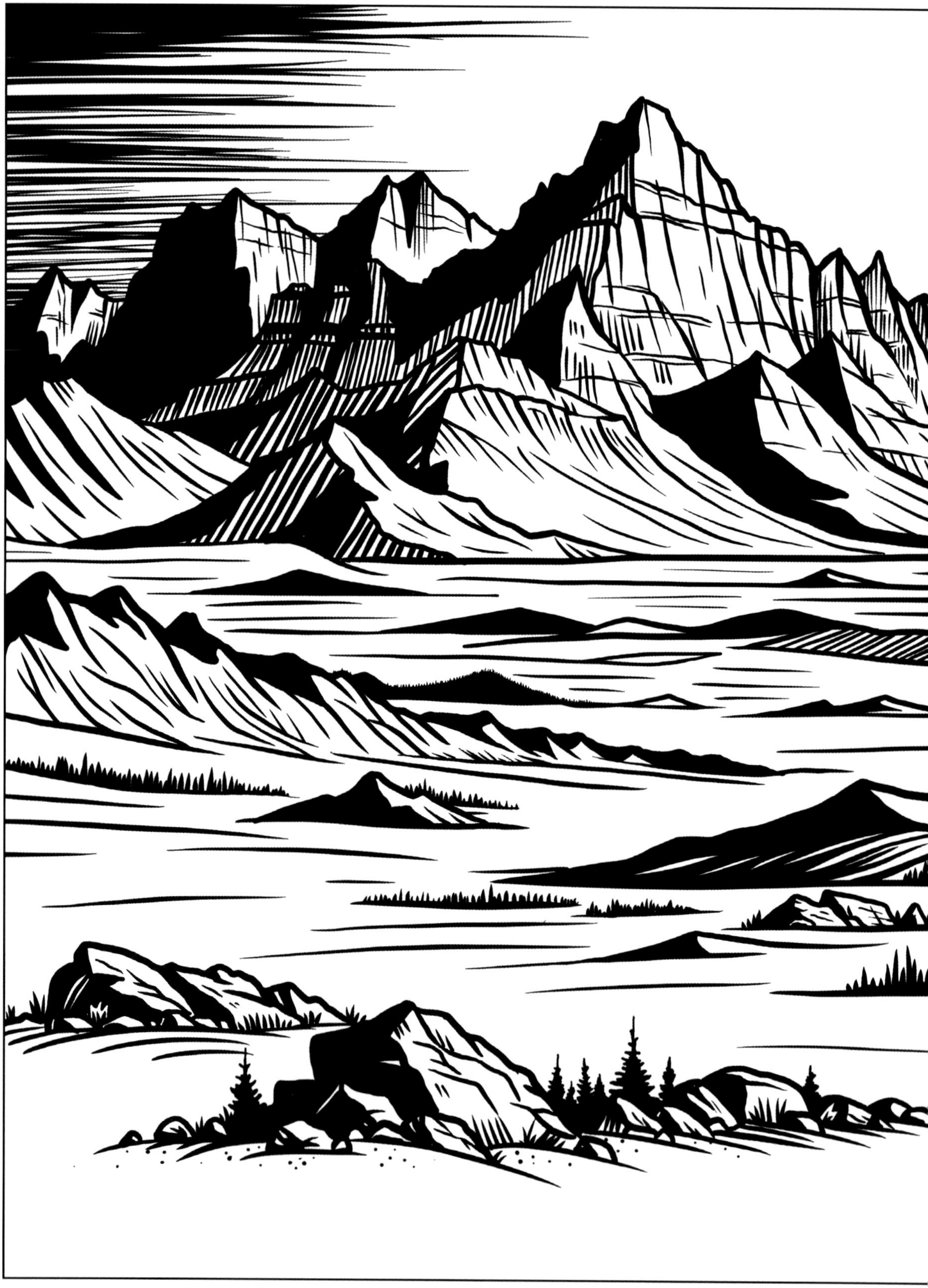

5. Battered Ancient Mountains

There's a certain magic in drawing a mountain range. These giants hold the history of bygone eras inside their rugged forms, and their immense grandeur has inspired artists for generations. These landscapes offer an excellent opportunity to practice your structure and form in a new way. You'll learn how to translate the textures of weathered rock, eroded slopes and dramatic peaks into simple lines and shapes. Don't be intimidated by the complexity of the scene! I've broken it down into manageable steps, empowering you to build depth and dimension with each stroke. By the end of this journey, you'll have transformed a blank page into a powerful work of art, where the timeworn beauty of ancient mountains reigns supreme. Get ready to unleash your creativity and conquer the artistic challenge of this epic scene!

---

1. Begin laying in your foundation with some eroded boulders in the foreground. Working left to right, start with a couple small half circles, then a larger irregular arc, followed by some medium sized overlapping arcs. Throw in a few upward dashes to signify some trees.

2. Build up the foreground with another bumpy arc behind the first. For extra realism, let some areas of the arc have some sharp angles as well as rounded slopes.

(continued)

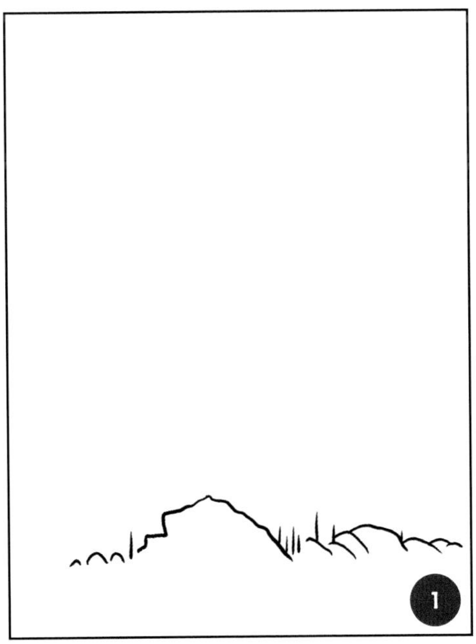

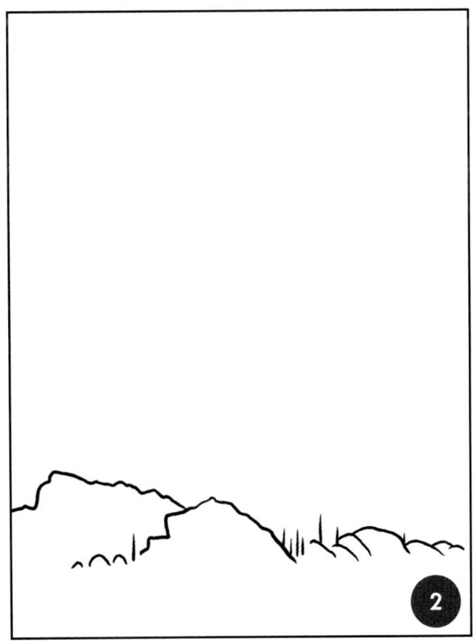

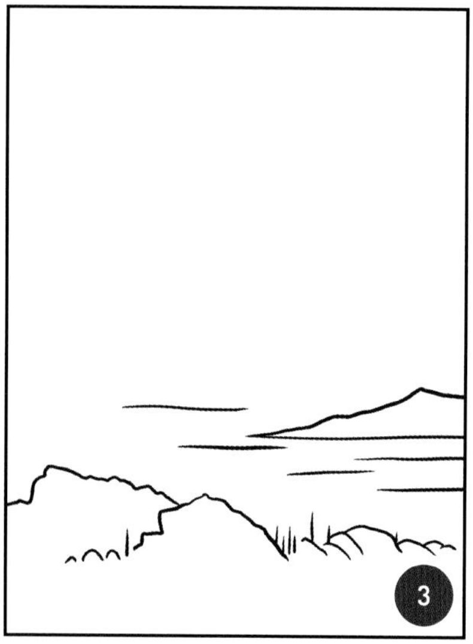
3

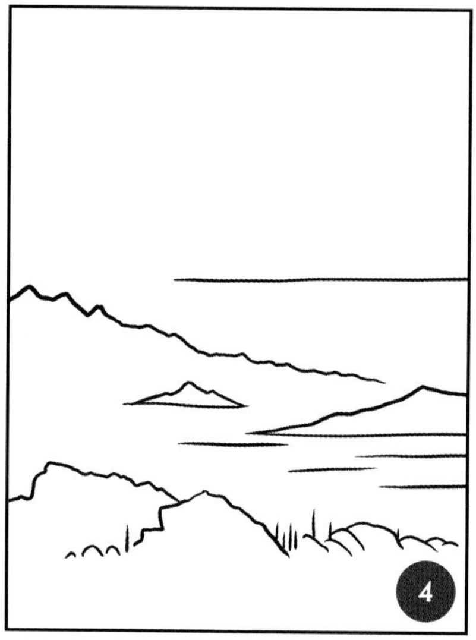
4

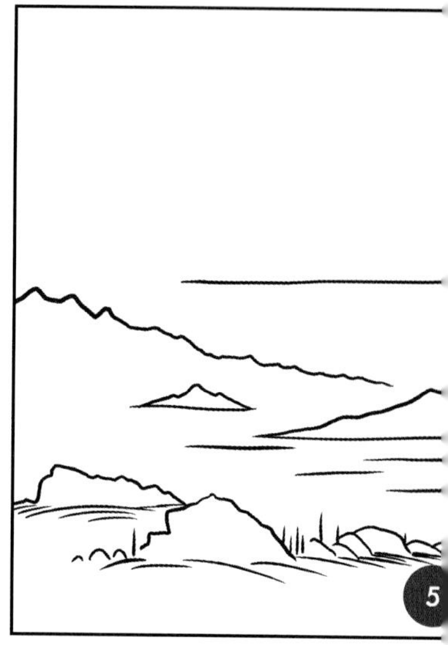
5

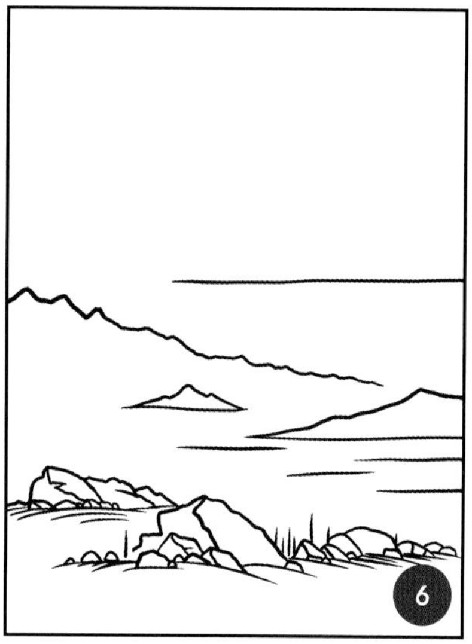
6

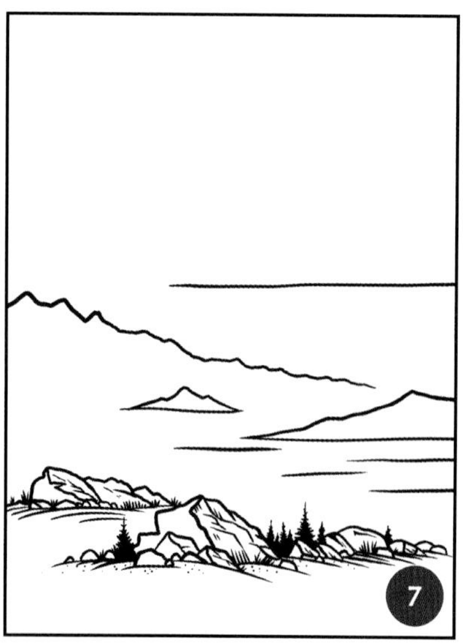
7

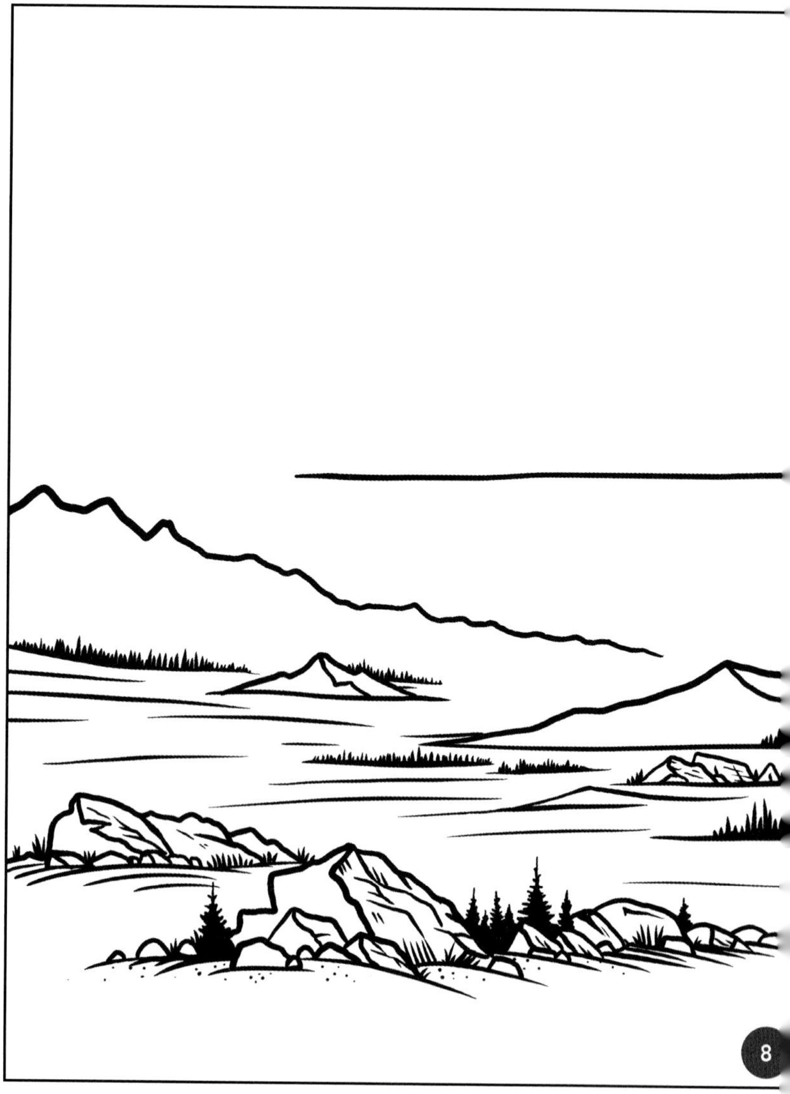
8

Battered Ancient Mountains (Continued)

3. Draw some parallel horizontal lines on the lower right and middle of the frame. Turn one long parallel line into a mountain by simply making it a triangle.

4. Add another small triangle to the middle of the frame, then draw a long, rugged line starting from the left side that ends trailing off lower than its peak. Add a long horizontal straight line on the right side, slightly above the mountain line you just created.

5. Let's go back to the foreground. Make low arcs underneath your boulders to create the sloping ground.

6. Begin adding some details to the foreground, adding clusters of small Rocks (page 13) atop the arcs. Add some small vertical dashes in the areas between the rocks.

7. Draw some more details to the ground by adding dots. Convert the vertical dashes from before into some scribbly triangular trees. Place some spiky little dashes sprouting from the ground for extra plant life. Draw sharp slants and vertical dashes on the right sides of the rocks to add jagged edges.

8. Create more depth in the middle ground by drawing some horizontal lines throughout and adding trees with thick vertical scribbles. Add a few more mountain and boulder shapes and draw jagged lines down the peaks of your small hills to add dimension.

(continued)

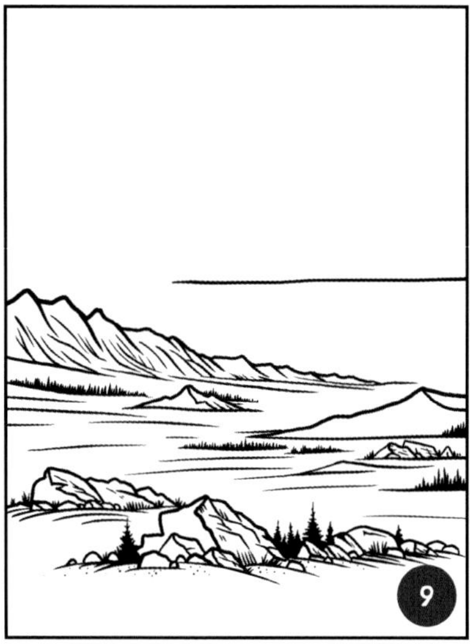
9
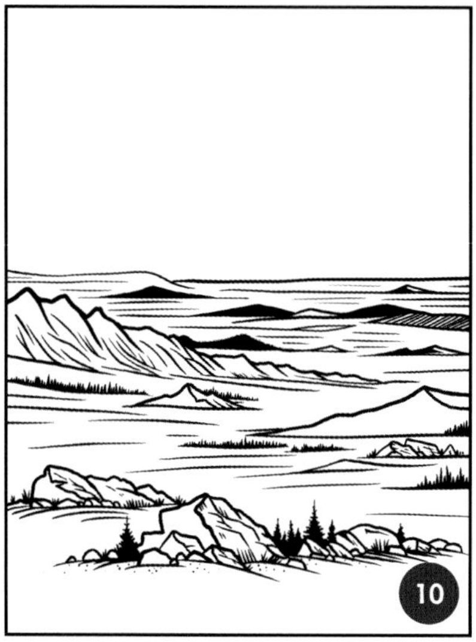
10
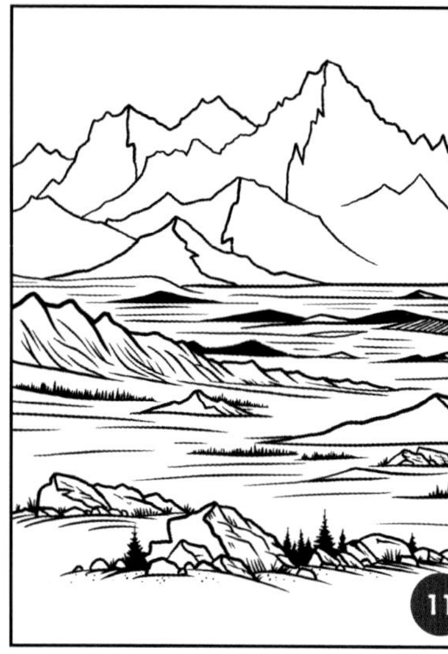
11
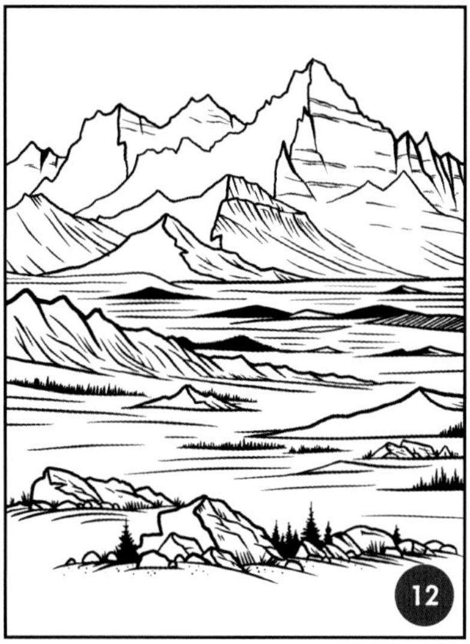
12
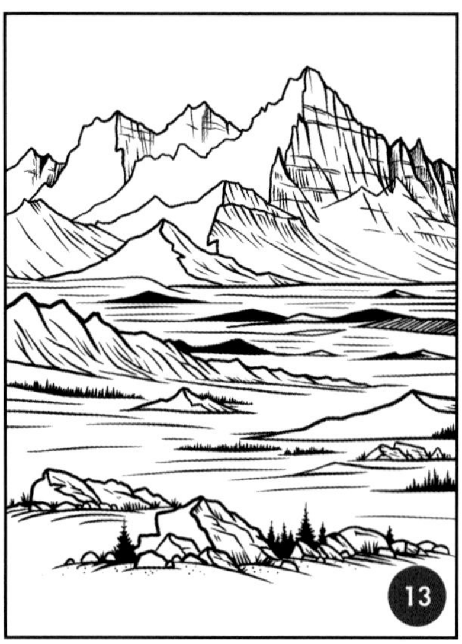
13
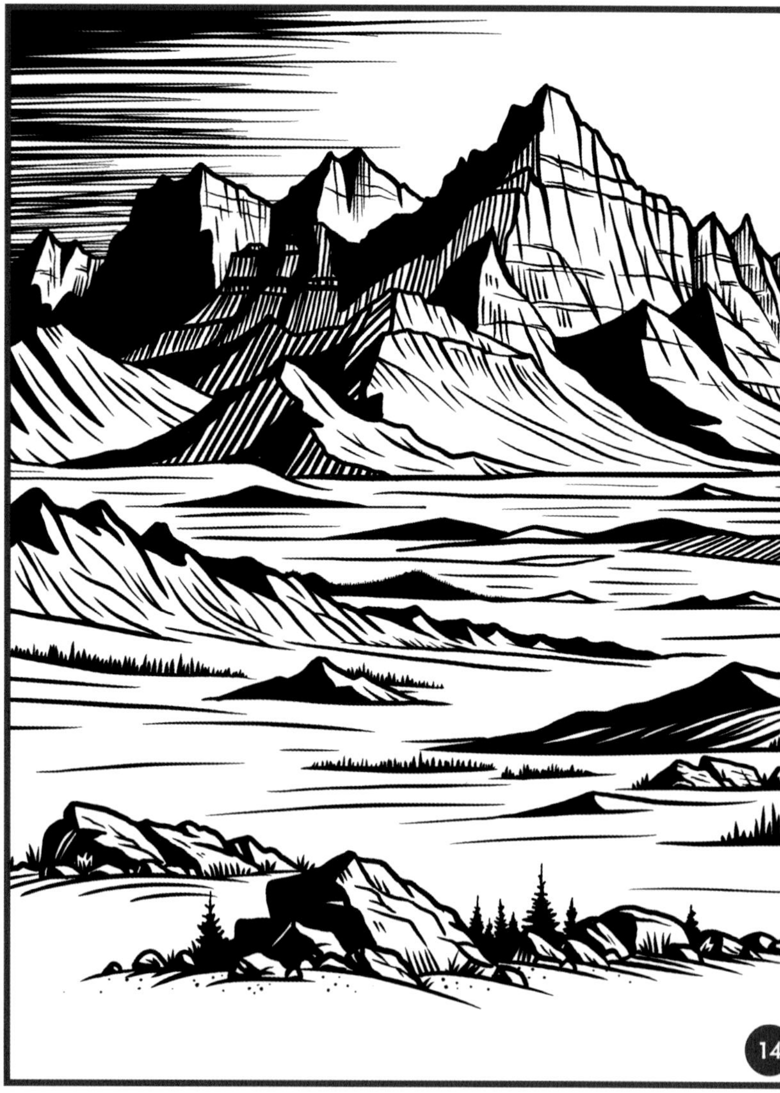
14

Battered Ancient Mountains (Final Steps)

9. Create etched cliffsides on your mountain with slanting strokes down the sides, leaving some areas blank and letting some connect to the ground lines below.

10. To begin adding more background, connect the right horizontal line to the left side of the paper with another hilly shape. Add more horizontal strokes below that vary in length. Add a few low triangular shapes to make small distant peaks and shade them dark or with diagonal dashes.

11. Make an impact in the background with some giant ancient mountains! Draw more jagged peaks that layer on top of each other. Be sure to make one mountain the tallest over the others to give the eye a focal point. Adding a focal point allows a place for the eye to rest in a scene with so much detail and shadow to come. Add some zigzag lines that trail down the highest points of these mountains, separating the ridgelines.

12. Create the illusion of erosion on your mountainsides with a few thin horizontal lines across only the right sides of the mountains. Draw some slanting strokes trailing down the peaks.

13. Continue building texture by adding some vertical lines over the horizontal ones to create steep mountain faces. Adding clusters of vertical dashes closer together creates areas of shadow; try to imagine the sun shining on the right sides of these mountains and adding shadows where it may not reach, such as behind the tallest peaks and in between ravines.

14. To add the shadows, envision the sun shining on your scene from the right side of your frame, then add shading to the areas on the left. This can be done with diagonal dashes to indicate a lighter shadow, or filled-in areas to indicate total darkness.

To finish, add a dramatic sky by making strokes from the left side of the page towards the center, keeping them clustered close together.

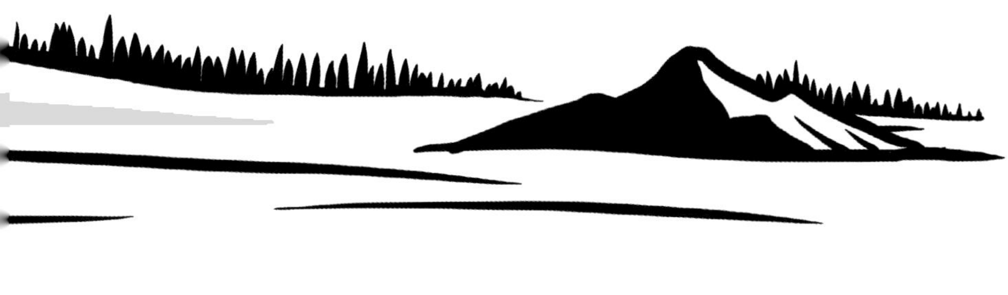

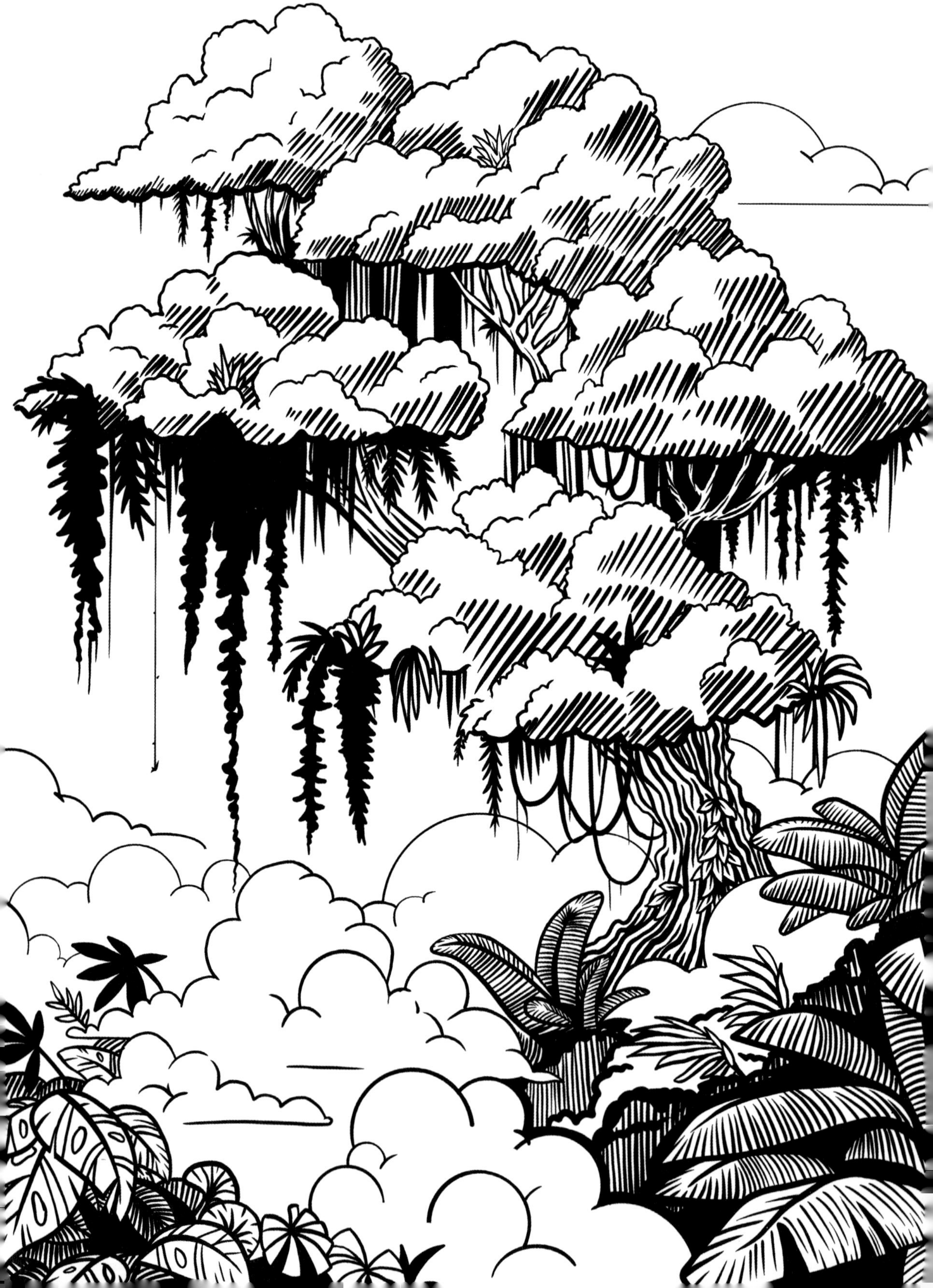

SPIRITED ARBOREAL PLACES

The majesty of trees is something that can't be overstated. They stand tall, reaching for the sky with their branches. Their roots run deep, anchoring them to the ground. Trees provide us with cooling shade, lifegiving oxygen and some of the tastiest foods. They are also home to a wide variety of wildlife. In some places, it seems that trees are more than just trees. They are sacred and are revered by the people who live near them. These special locations are known as spirited arboreal places.

Spirited arboreal places are found all over the world. Together we'll explore the immense old growth forests of California, cloud forests of South America, the ancient oak forests of England, the interconnected aspen forests and the rainforests of Southeast Asia. These places are special. It is as if the trees themselves have a wisdom of their own.

This chapter is your personal guide to translating the soul of these mystical landscapes onto the page. I'll break down the artistic process step by step, from rendering the textured bark of Ancient Redwood Giants (page 87)—get ready for some bark love!—to the feathery fronds of Ferns that dance in the breeze (page 87)—those ferns are fire!—and even tropical Jungle Leaves that bring rainforests to life (page 96).

By the end of this journey, you'll have transformed a blank page into a celebration of spirited arboreal places, where the magic and wonder truly come alive. So grab your pens and pressed tree pulp (more commonly known as paper) and let's get to creating.

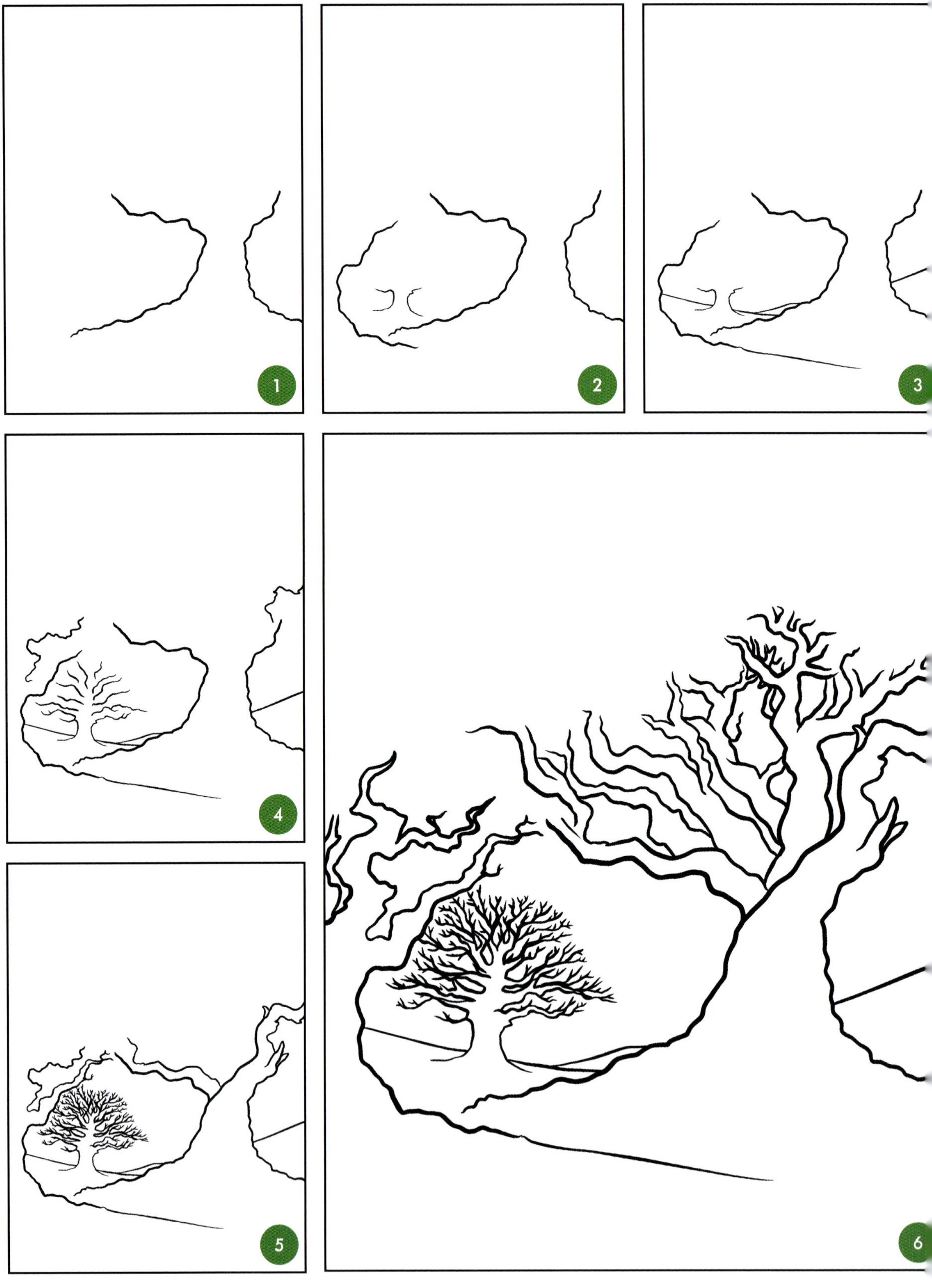
1
2
3
4
5
6

1. Gnarled Oak Tree Mystery

Deep within the heart of an English woodland, a sense of awe-inspiring history unfolds. Gnarled oak trees, some estimated to be over a thousand years old, stand as silent sentinels. Their twisted branches, reaching in every direction, have witnessed centuries pass. Weathered bark, etched with the passage of time, whispers secrets of a bygone era. These majestic giants embody the enduring resilience of nature and stand as testaments to a rich ecological tapestry.

But capturing these ancient wonders on paper isn't just about replicating their form—it's about elevating your artistic skills and embarking on a meditative journey. Here, we'll delve into the world of linework, using a technique that's almost like artistic zen. We'll master the fundamental art of the "wiggle," a key to creating the gnarled branches and weathered trunks that define these ancient oaks. With each repetitive stroke, you'll not only build texture and depth, but also find yourself falling into a calming rhythm.

This chapter will also include a dedicated component tutorial focusing on these astounding branches. We'll use wiggly lines throughout the scene as an easy technique to show the essences of these timeworn giants. So, grab your pencils, artists! Let's embark on a journey to unveil the Gnarled Oak Tree Mystery, one artistic stroke and meditative moment at a time. We'll learn to evoke the spirit of these living legends, ensuring their stories continue to inspire for generations to come.

---

1. Start with a large wiggly outline of a trunk that will become your focal point.

2. Add the side of another trunk on the left with another arcing wiggly shape. Draw a similar trunk shape to the first that is smaller and inset between the two trunks.

3. Make sloping lines out from the bottom of your trunks to create the ground.

4. Create some gnarled branches coming out of your distant tree trunk by drawing sporadic wiggly lines and adding a few wiggles to your trees in the foreground.

5. Continue to develop your distant tree with lots of wiggly Y-shaped branches coming out of one another. Then, start building your foreground tree branches with thick wiggly lines and narrow ends and a few short branches here and there.

6. Add layers of these rugged branches above the others, letting them overlap and intertwine. Don't feel the need to follow a specific pattern and instead work on layering them one at a time, going back into sparse areas and adding smaller branches towards the tops.

(continued)

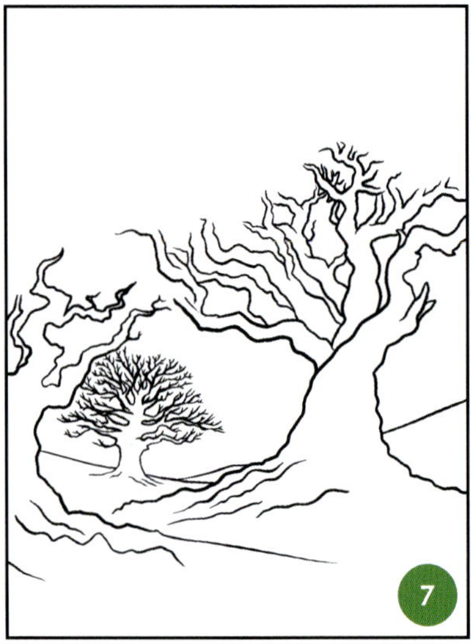
7

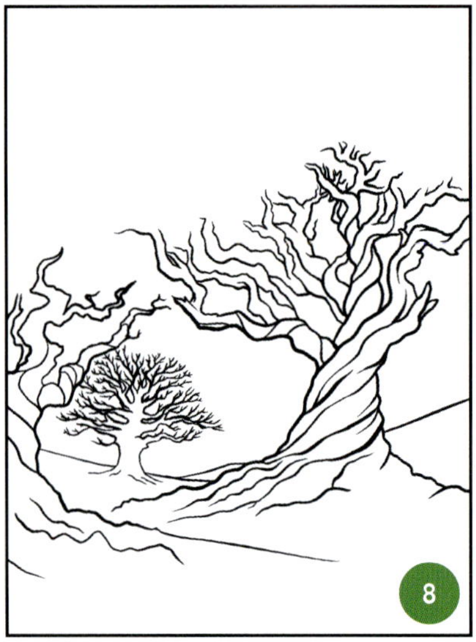
8

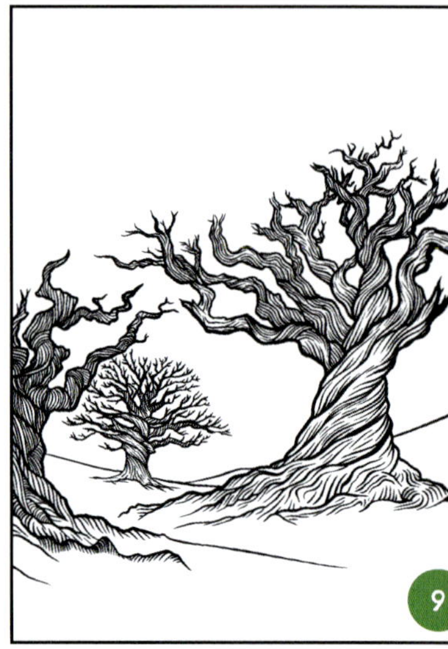
9

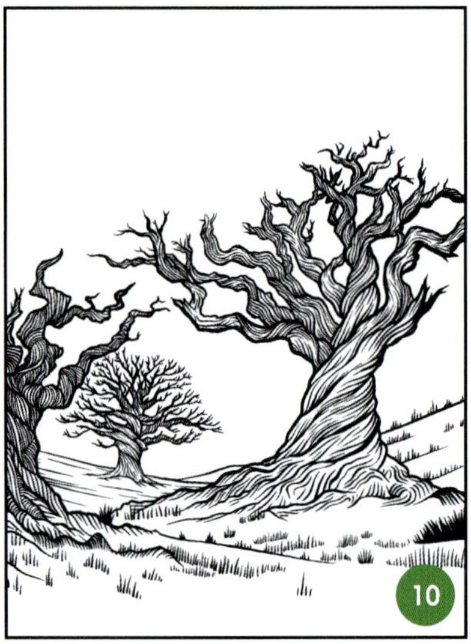
10

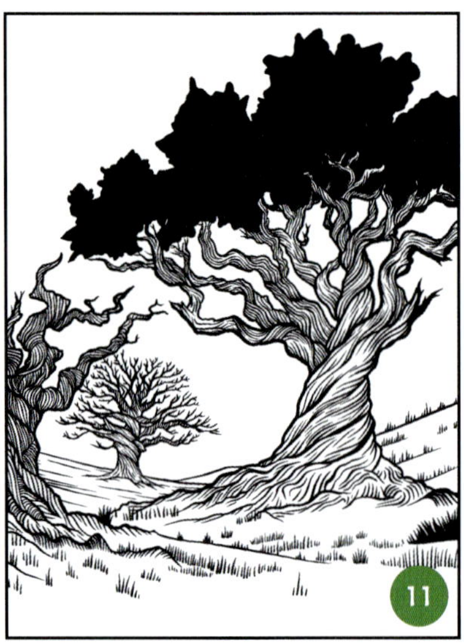
11

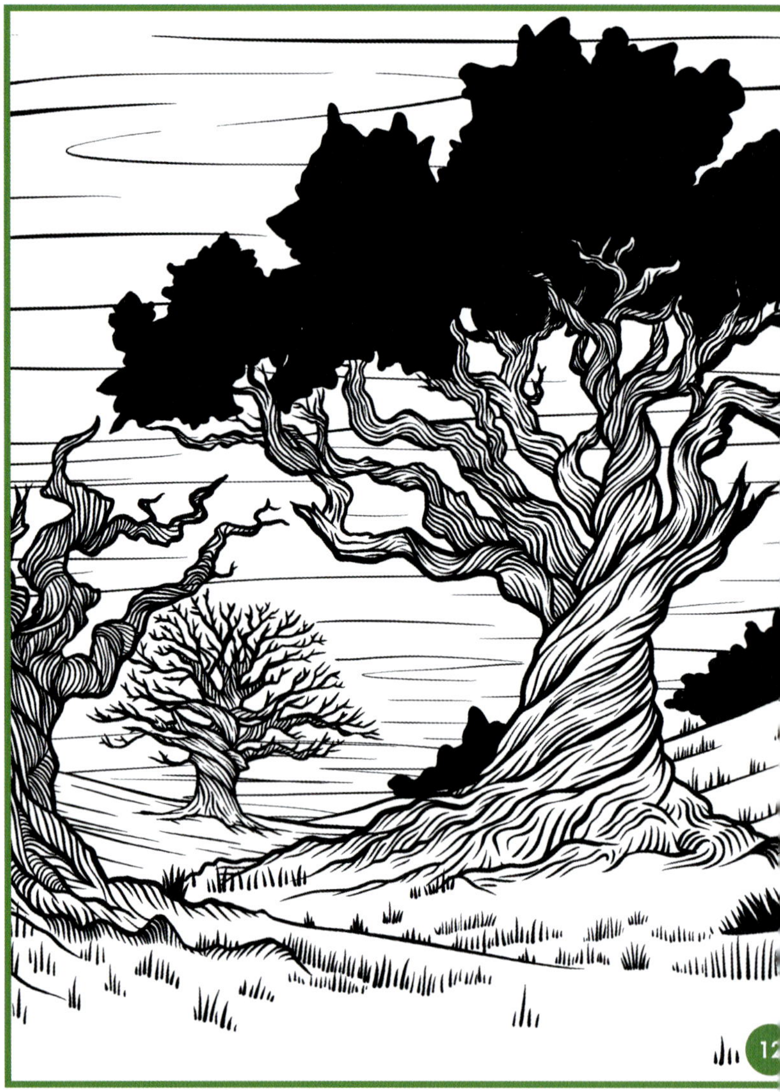
12

Gnarled Oak Tree Mystery (Final Steps)

7. Draw gnarled roots coming out the bottom of the trunks.

8. Begin to create a twisting effect in your trees by making diagonal sloping lines going across the trunk and branches.

9. Create bark texture with thin lines throughout the trees following the curves and twists. (See the below image for a close up example.)

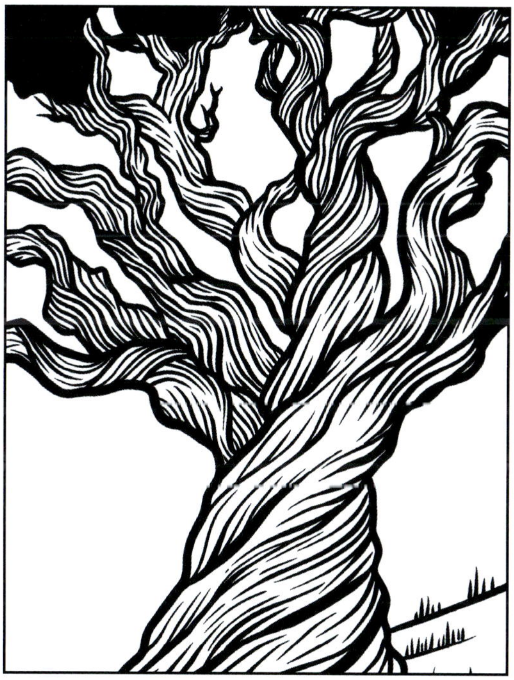

10. Add a grassy ground with short vertical dashes in small lines and bunches.

11. Draw a leafy treetop above your biggest tree's branches with a spiky jagged shape and fill it in. The key to keeping this realistic is by letting parts of the branches and sky peak through the foliage with gaps; the canopy top is never a perfectly round shape but has high and low points too.

12. Then add similar shapes on the ground behind the tree to make faraway foliage.

Now, finish your drawing with some wispy horizontal lines throughout the sky.

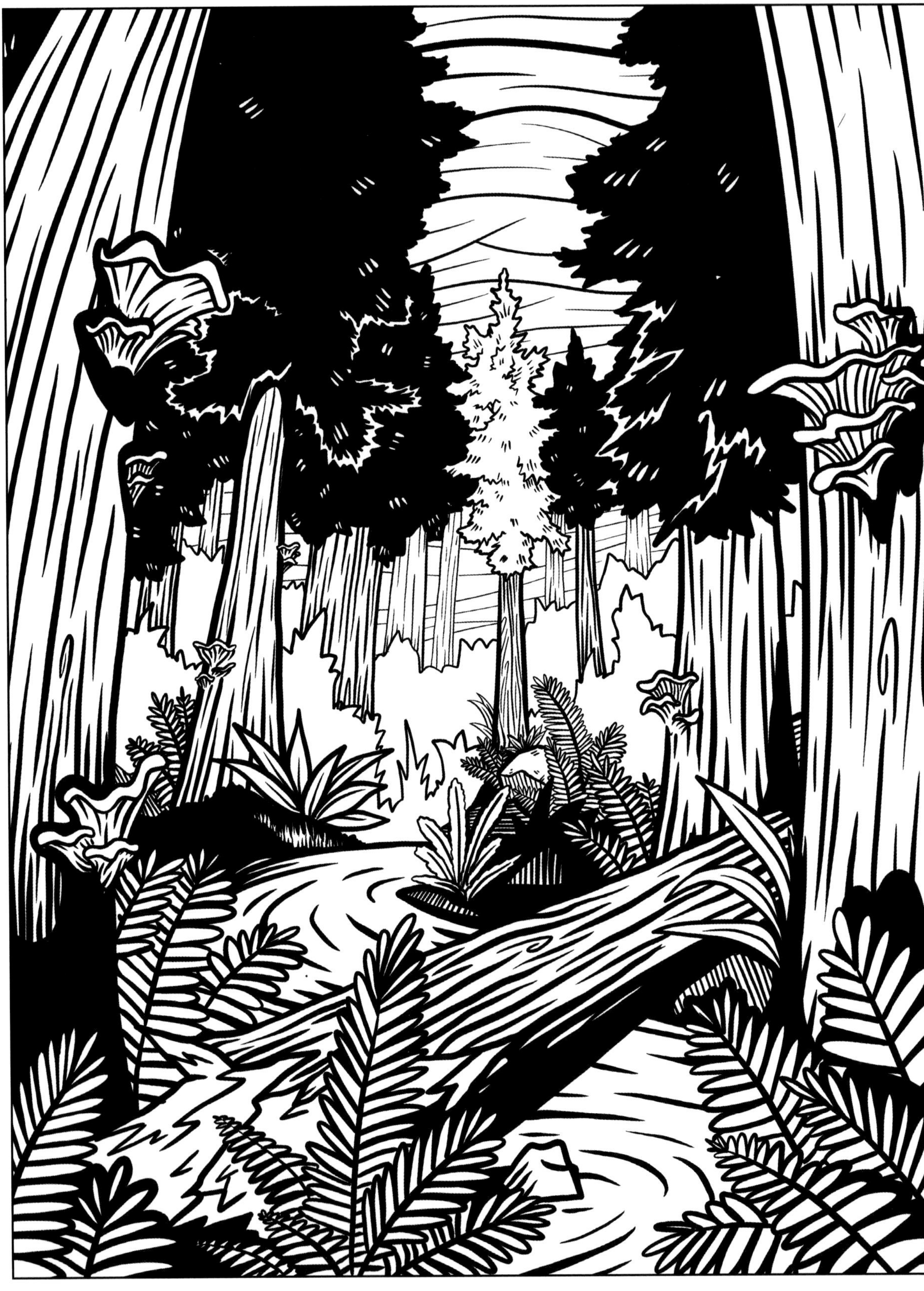

2. Ancient Redwood Giants

Alright artists, let's delve into the towering realm of the redwood forest! These ancient giants pierce the sky with their burnt umber trunks, whispering tales of a bygone era. Each gnarled form and fiery scar tells a story, a testament to the resilience of these titans. But our mission isn't just to draw their physical presence—we're here to bottle their soul on the page.

Here's the key: The scene breathes life from the forest floor upwards. We'll start by establishing a base layer of lush Ferns (page 87). Envision these unfurling outwards, creating a natural pathway that guides the eye towards the heart of the composition.

Now, the real fun begins—the mushrooms! Picture these vibrant Oyster Mushrooms (page 88) bursting forth from the damp earth, their varied sizes adding a touch of whimsical chaos. Let them be your guiding lights—use their placement to dictate where the redwood giants will rise. Remember, these aren't mere decorations; they're integral storytellers, hinting at the hidden life teeming beneath the towering canopy.

As you sketch those majestic redwood trunks, allow them to organically sprout around the vibrant mushrooms. Don't be afraid to experiment with perspective! Maybe a fallen giant lies in the foreground, its diagonal form drawing the viewer deeper into the scene.

Fern

Before the towering redwoods steal the show, let's establish the lush life blanketing the ground. Ferns are our first step! These graceful plants unfurl from central points, with smaller fronds flanking them on either side. We'll build on these basic shapes next to create a realistic and textural base for your redwood masterpiece.

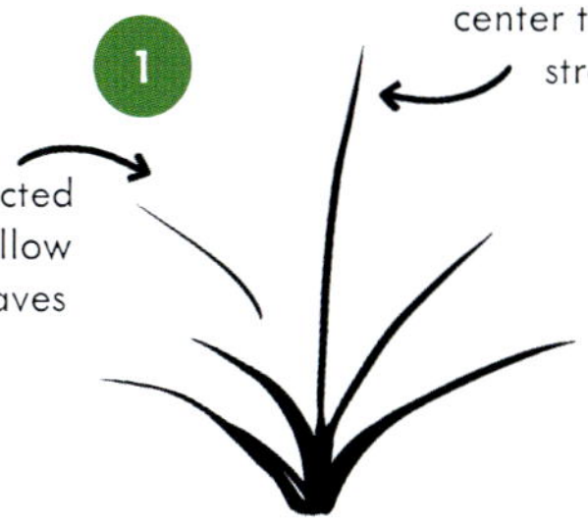

Begin with arching dashes that sprout from a center point on the ground.

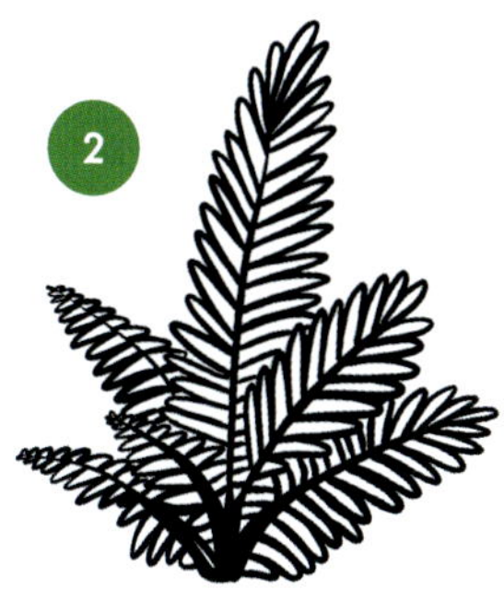

Make narrow round arches along each side of the dashes following their angles.

Oyster Mushrooms

The damp embrace of the redwood forest floor fosters a unique branch of life, and the oyster mushroom is a prime example. These fungi come in fascinating shapes and sizes. Here, we'll use them to hone our line control. We'll start with loose, wiggly lines to establish the base of each mushroom, then refine them into the smooth, undulating curves that define these essential redwood residents. Get ready to explore the subtle variations in form and size that make oyster mushrooms so visually interesting!

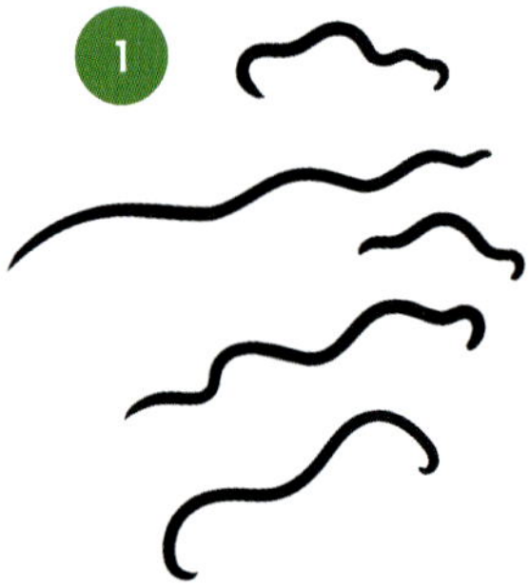

Start with some wiggly lines of different lengths in a stack, leaving space between them.

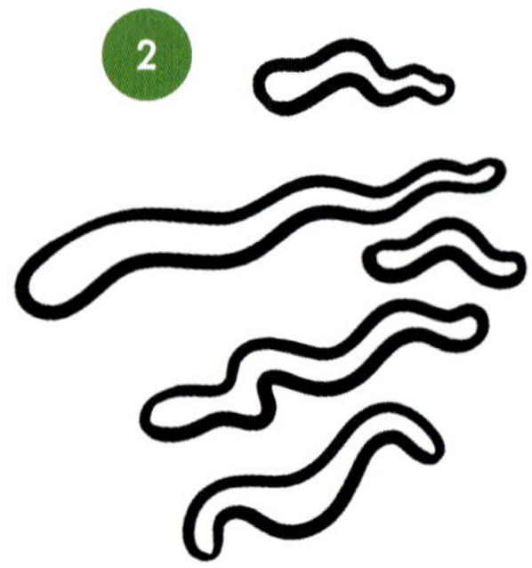

Turn those lines into wormlike shapes.

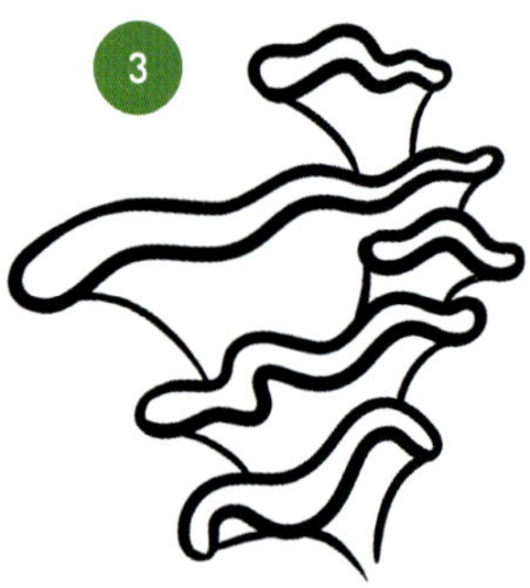

Draw sloping vertical lines down from each end of the worm shapes that narrow and connect to the ones below. Make the bottom lines narrow to a point.

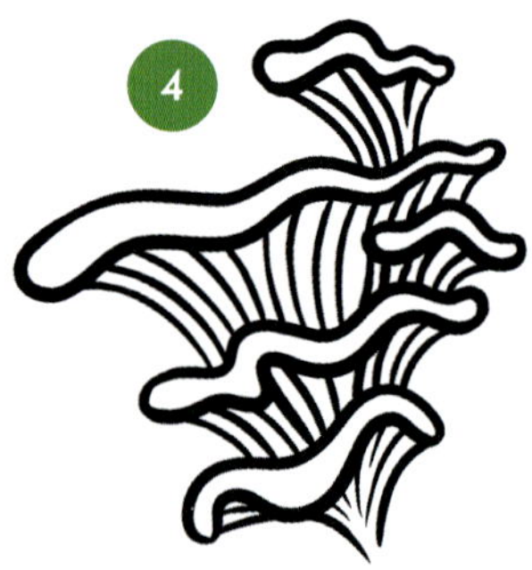

Add gills with lines throughout the shapes you just created.

Leafy Plant

The redwood forest floor isn't just about towering giants—a vibrant undergrowth is home to a variety of small leafy plants. These plants add texture and life to the scene. Leafy plants, in all their diverse forms, play a crucial role in this ecosystem. Here, we'll focus on capturing their essence rather than a specific species and honing your layering skills.

1. Draw a teardrop shape.
2. Draw two more sideways teardrop shapes coming out from each side of the first.
3. Continue to layer your leaves that sprout between your initial shapes and the center point.
4. Draw a central line through the middle of each leaf.

Sword Fern

Sword ferns add a touch of drama to the redwood understory. Their distinctive form, with fronds rising from a central point, creates a dynamic element in our scene. We'll replicate their essence with a few simple steps. Get ready to add a touch of elegance to your redwood masterpiece!

1. Draw upward strokes that shoot out from a central point on the ground.
2. To create the leaves, simply draw frilly arches around these lines that connect at the central ground point.

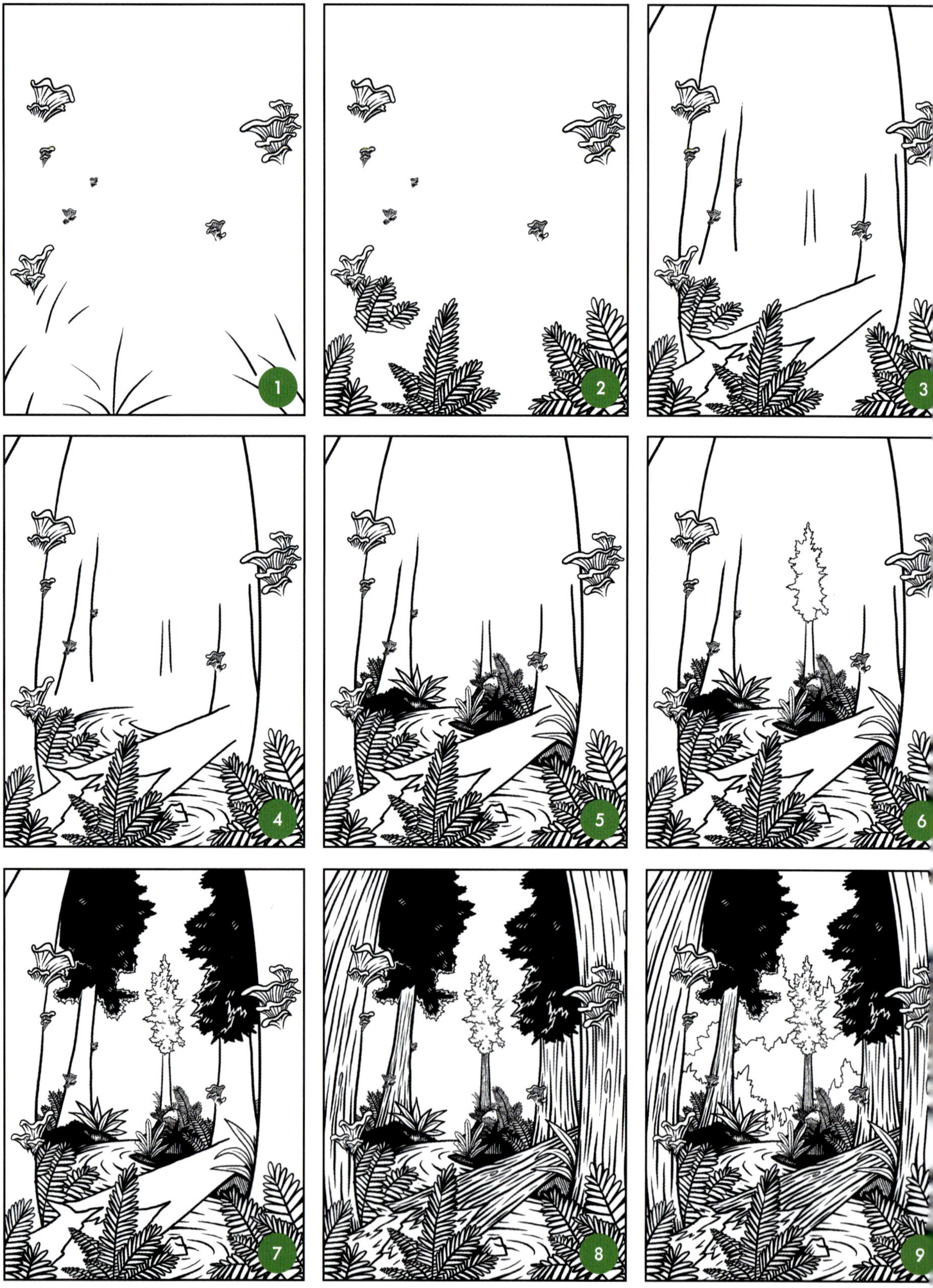
1
2
3
4
5
6
7
8
9

Now, Let's Draw the Scene

(See full image on page 86)

1. Mushrooms are bountiful in the redwood forest, so let's start with some Oyster Mushrooms (page 88) of various sizes in the upper two thirds of your page! Draw some dashes sprouting outwards around the bottom of your frame as well. Just make sure you leave enough space in the center to draw your main focal point in later.

2. Turn your dashes into Ferns (page 87) along the bottom of your forest.

3. Use your mushrooms as a guide to decide where you'll draw some trees. Use parallel lines that narrow at the top. Then make a smaller trunk in the focal point of your frame. Add a fallen tree in the foreground with a diagonal trunk to give the scene a sense of action; after all, the forest is a place of growth *and* decay!

4. Starting at the bottom of your frame, draw a winding stream following an imaginary S-like shape that narrows towards the center of the frame. Add small dashes throughout to indicate running water.

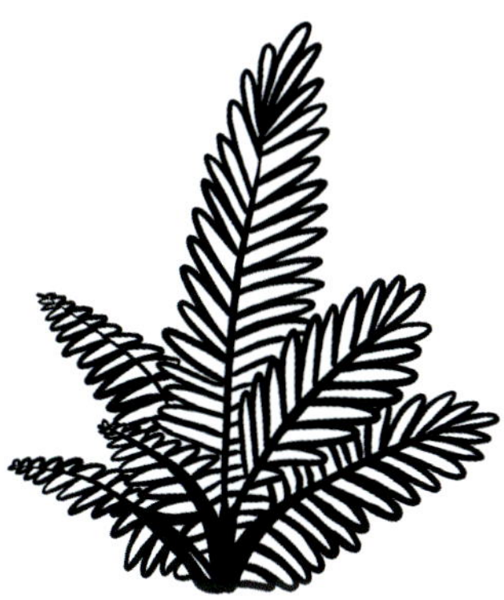

5. Build your forest floor with some Leafy Plants (page 89) and Sword Ferns (page 89) growing along the river as well as some Rocks (page 13) and ground shapes which can be shaded completely or with diagonal lines.

6. Finish your focal young redwood tree by drawing jagged foliage on the top of the smaller center trunk.

7. Finish the redwood foliage on either side of the young tree by drawing jagged outlines then shading them, leaving small dashes of white throughout to add highlights. Add small clusters of dashes throughout the young redwood for its own spiky pine needle texture. This technique creates a more intense contrast between the focal tree and the surrounding forest.

8. Draw lines of various lengths vertically along the trunks to add in a simple bark. To create more depth, make sure to add lines that come from behind trees, ferns or other elements. Some simple spirals add knotty texture to the bark as well.

9. To start creating your background forest, add three rough jagged horizontal lines behind your trees. Be sure to give enough space between them to allow more details later.

(continued)

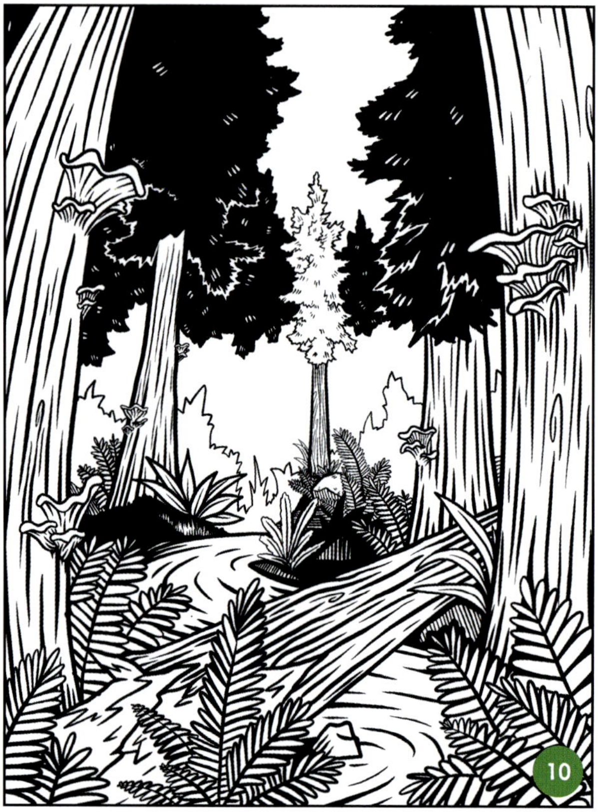
10
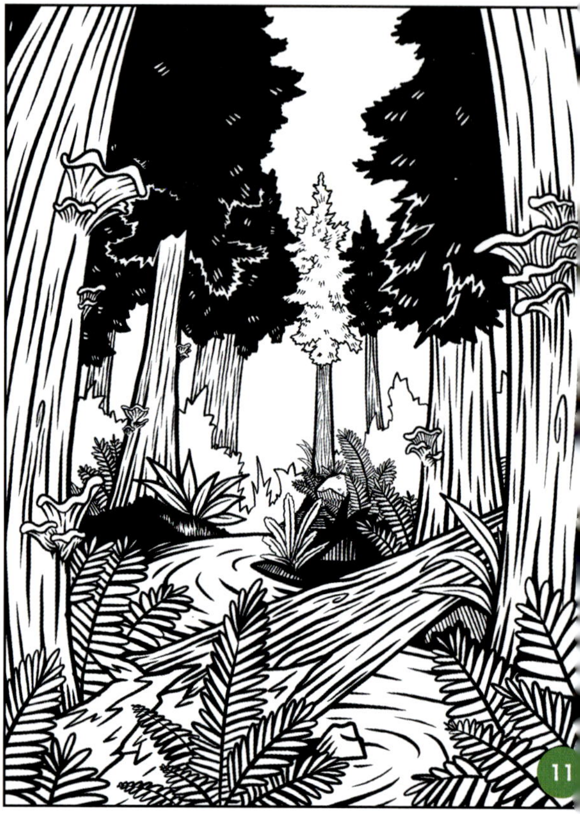
11
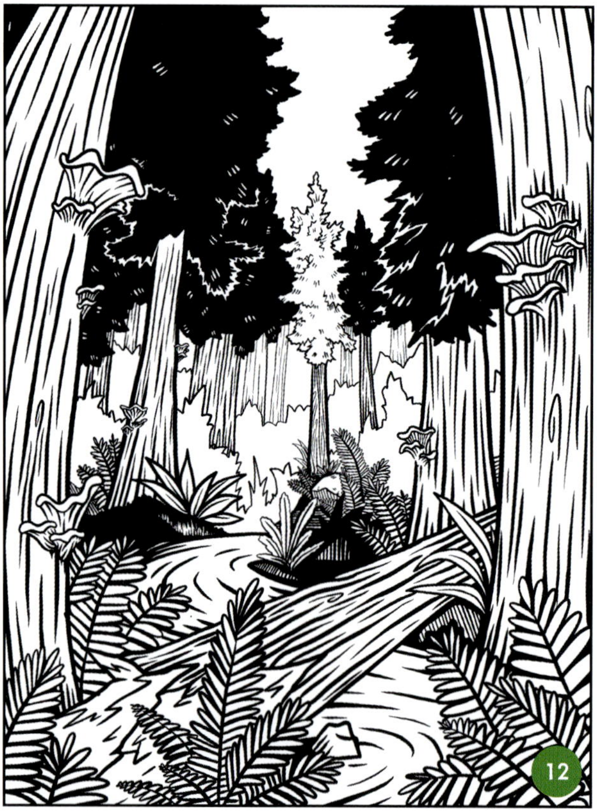
12
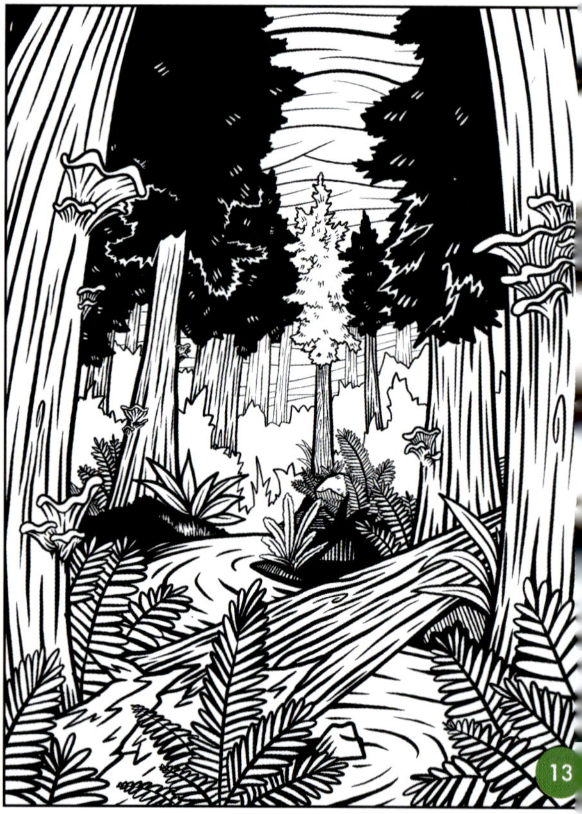
13

Now, Let's Draw the Scene (Final Steps)

10. Use the top jagged horizontal line from step 9 as a guide to shade in more treetops. Remember to add more dash highlights for every new layer.

11. Under those treetops, place some more trunks that disappear behind the bottom jagged horizontal line. Then add more bark texture using thin lines to create depth.

12. Add another jagged horizontal line behind those trees and add even more distant smaller trunks above the line.

13. Create a sky with some waving lines behind your trees.

14. Make a final impact and draw shadows by adding dark areas to the underside of the fallen tree, along the bottoms of the foreground trunks, behind and below the mushrooms and on the right side of the ferns in the foreground.

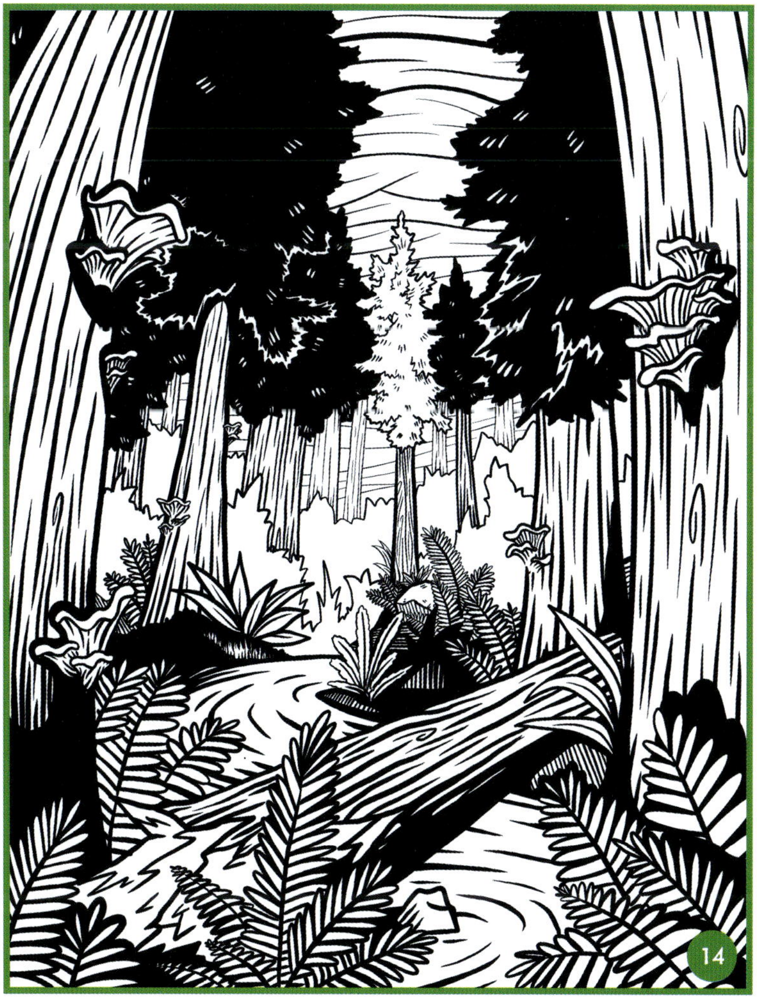

3. Cloud Canopies

Deep within the heart of the rainforest, sunlight filters through a breathtaking spectacle—the canopy embraced by the clouds. Here, a vibrant tapestry of life unfolds. Towering giants stretch skyward, their branches adorned with an incredible diversity of leaves. From broad, waxy fronds to delicate, needle-like points, each leaf plays a vital role in this verdant ecosystem. But capturing this scene isn't just about replicating details—it's also about understanding the essence of the canopy. The key lies in layering these diverse shapes, creating a sense of depth and immersion. By strategically placing clouds alongside the lush foliage, we'll transform our composition into a enchanting dance of texture and form. Their ever-changing shapes and textures offer an entrancing spectacle, transforming the landscape into an ever-evolving canvas.

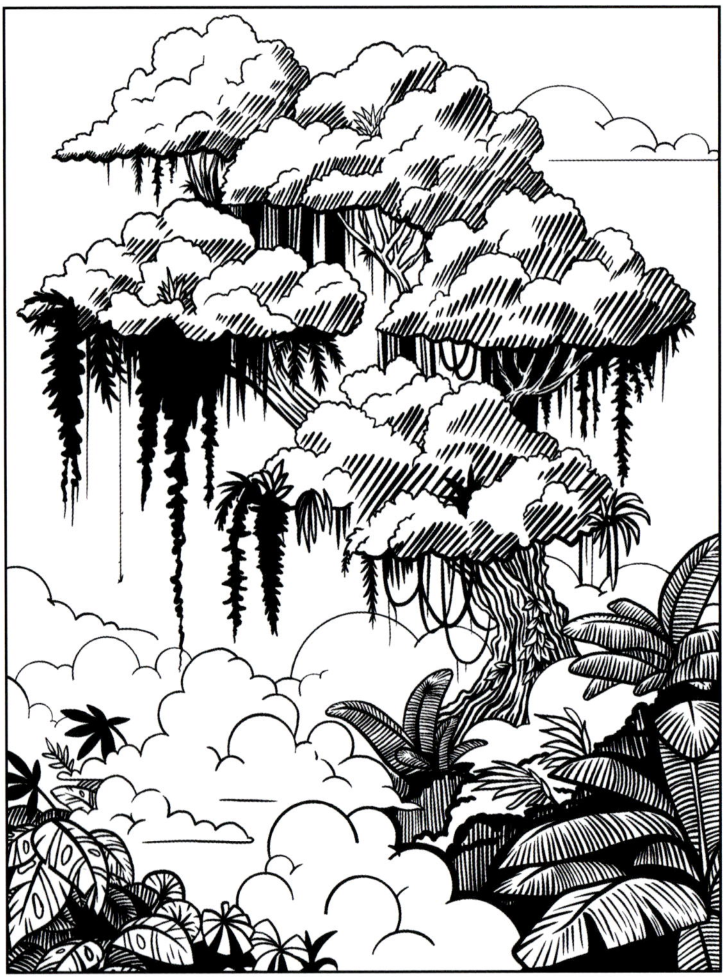

Plantain Plant

Thriving amongst the layered foliage, the plantain plant stands out with its unique adaptation to the cloudy realm. Its broad, waxy leaves, perfect for capturing even the faintest sunlight, unfurl from a central stalk. Here, we'll hone our line control by rendering these broad leaves with confident strokes and learn to recognize structure by building the plant around its central stalk, adding depth with each layer. Get ready to depict this fascinating resident of the rainforest canopy!

1

Begin with a wider U shape with an arc on the top.

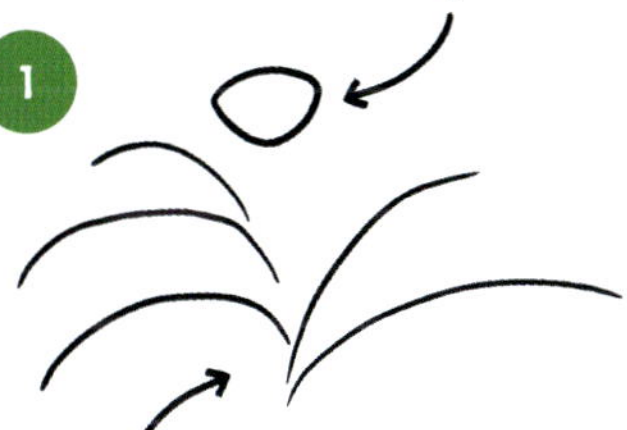

Add some swooping arch lines underneath this shape that slightly stack on top of each other.

2

Draw two lines coming down from the first U shape.

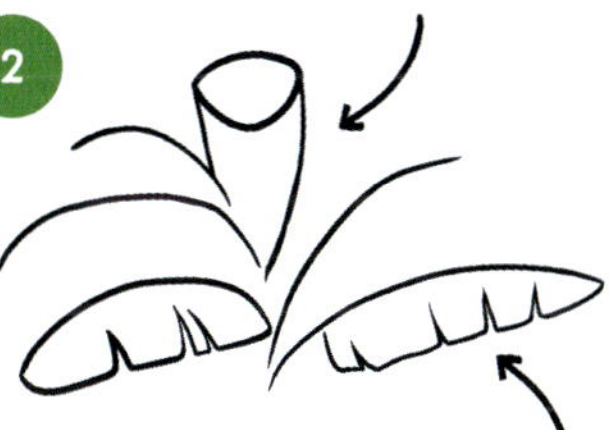

Draw a connecting line on the bottom of the lowest two arch lines. Use sharp upside-down V shapes to create breaks in the leaves.

3

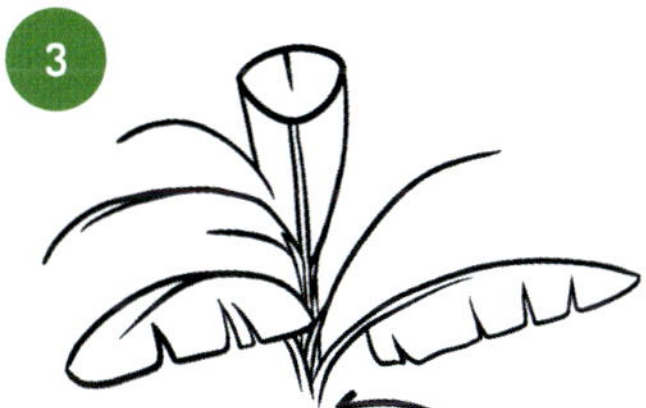

Create central stems for your plantain with some thin lines in the center of your leaves.

4

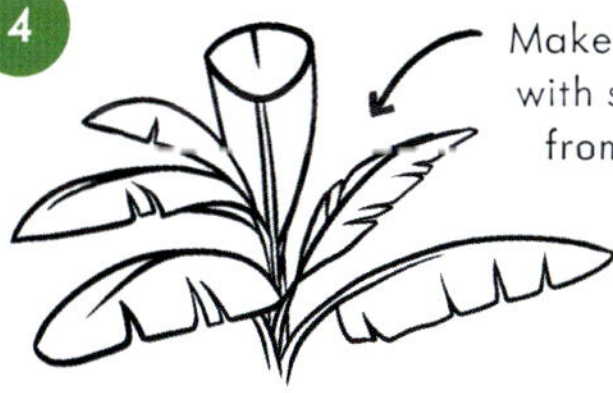

Make more leaf shapes with small cuts in them from the other arch lines.

5

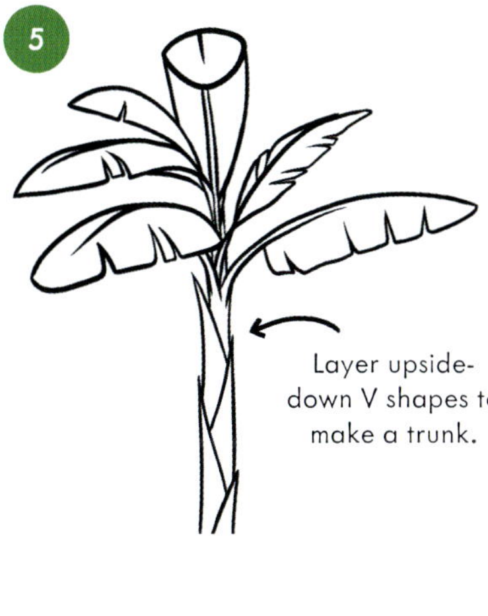

Layer upside-down V shapes to make a trunk.

6

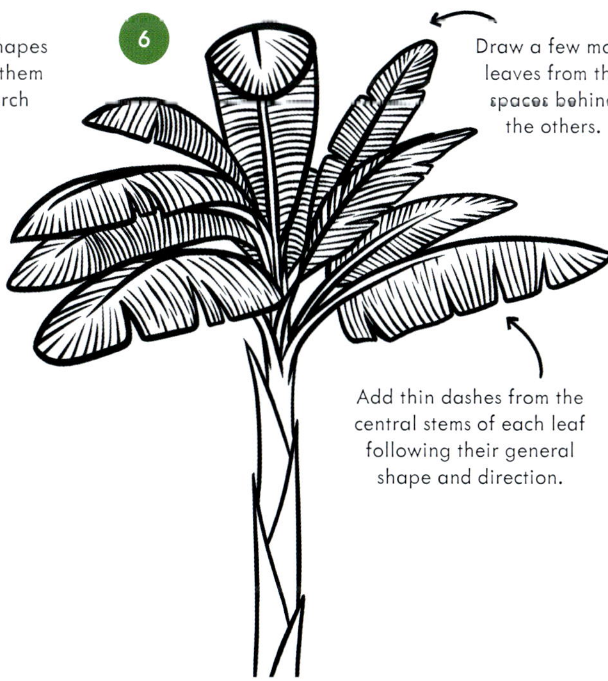

Draw a few more leaves from the spaces behind the others.

Add thin dashes from the central stems of each leaf following their general shape and direction.

Jungle Leaves

Imagine a cornucopia overflowing with an assortment of foods that range in shape, size and flavor—that's the essence we're aiming for! By combining these unique leafy forms, we'll build a more visually stunning scene. We'll explore three such "jungle leaves," each with its own distinctive character. Through the art of layering, we'll learn to create depth and dimension, bringing these fascinating rainforest residents to life on the page!

Pothos Leaves

1

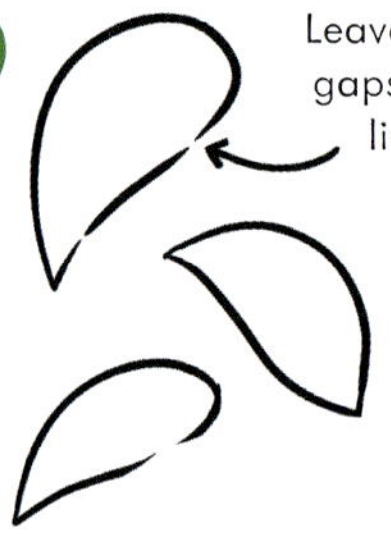

Leave a few gaps in the lines.

Draw a few teardrop leaves in a group.

2

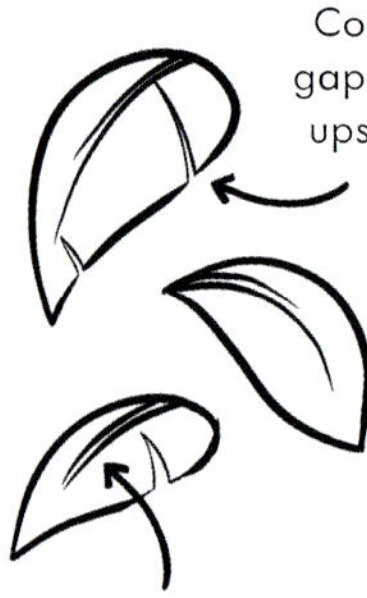

Connect the gaps with thin upside-down Vs.

Add center lines down the middle.

3

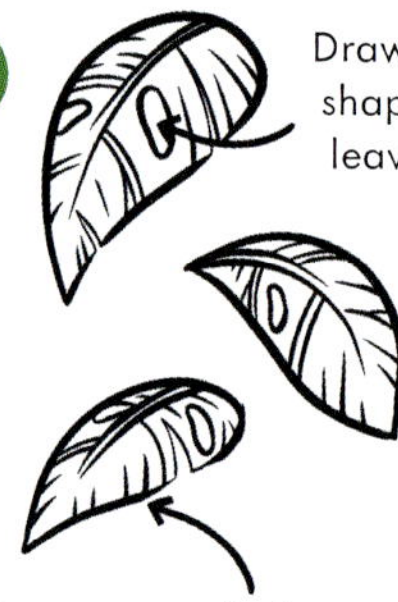

Draw a few round shapes inside the leaves for holes.

Add veins with dashes coming from the sides of the leaves and the center lines.

Fan Leaves

1

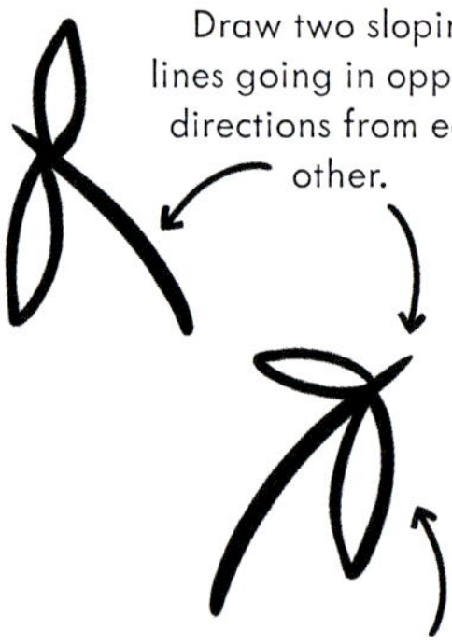

Draw two sloping lines going in opposite directions from each other.

Add two small pointy oval shapes opposite each other near the top of each line.

2

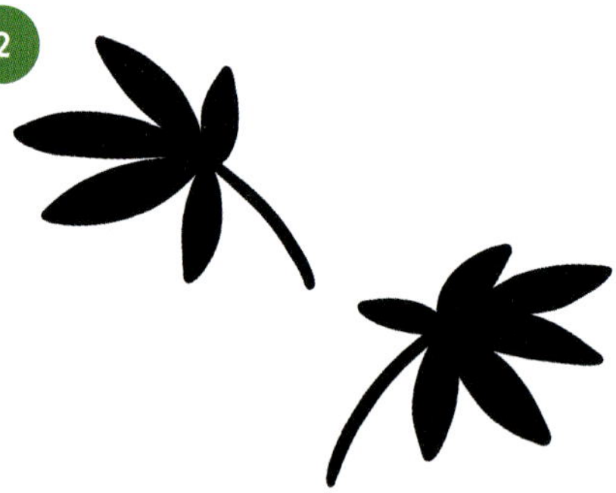

Draw more pointy leaves coming out the top of each line creating a fan shape, then shade them in.

Half Moon Leaves

1

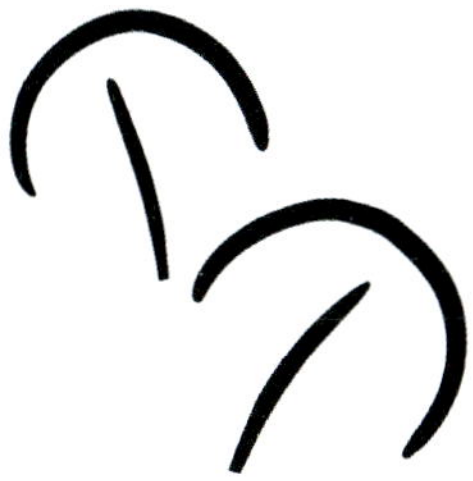

Start with two half circles. Draw a line down the center.

2

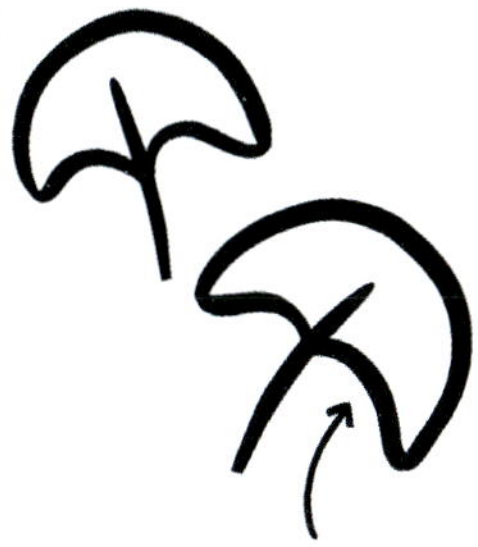

Create an umbrella-like shape at the bottom.

3

Draw some dashes that come out around the center line.

Compound Leaves

1

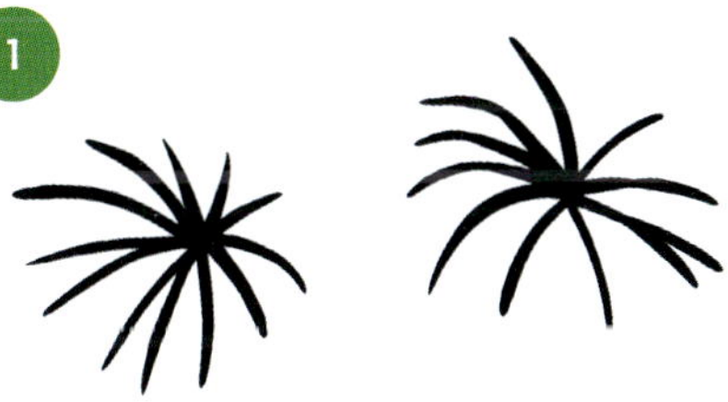

Draw a cluster of V shapes sprouting randomly from a center point.

2

Connect the bottoms of the V shapes with some lines.

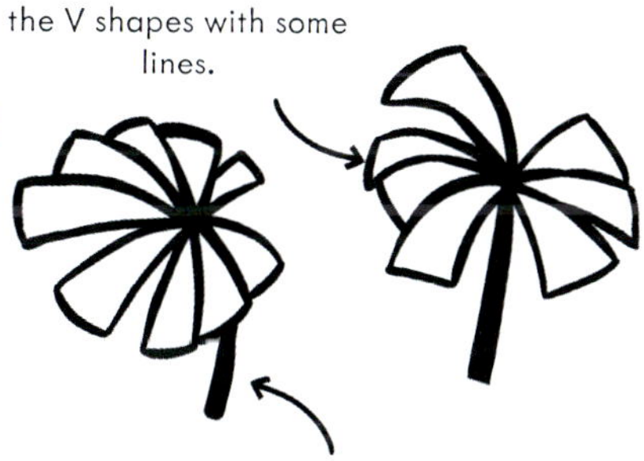

Add thick stems coming out of the bottom.

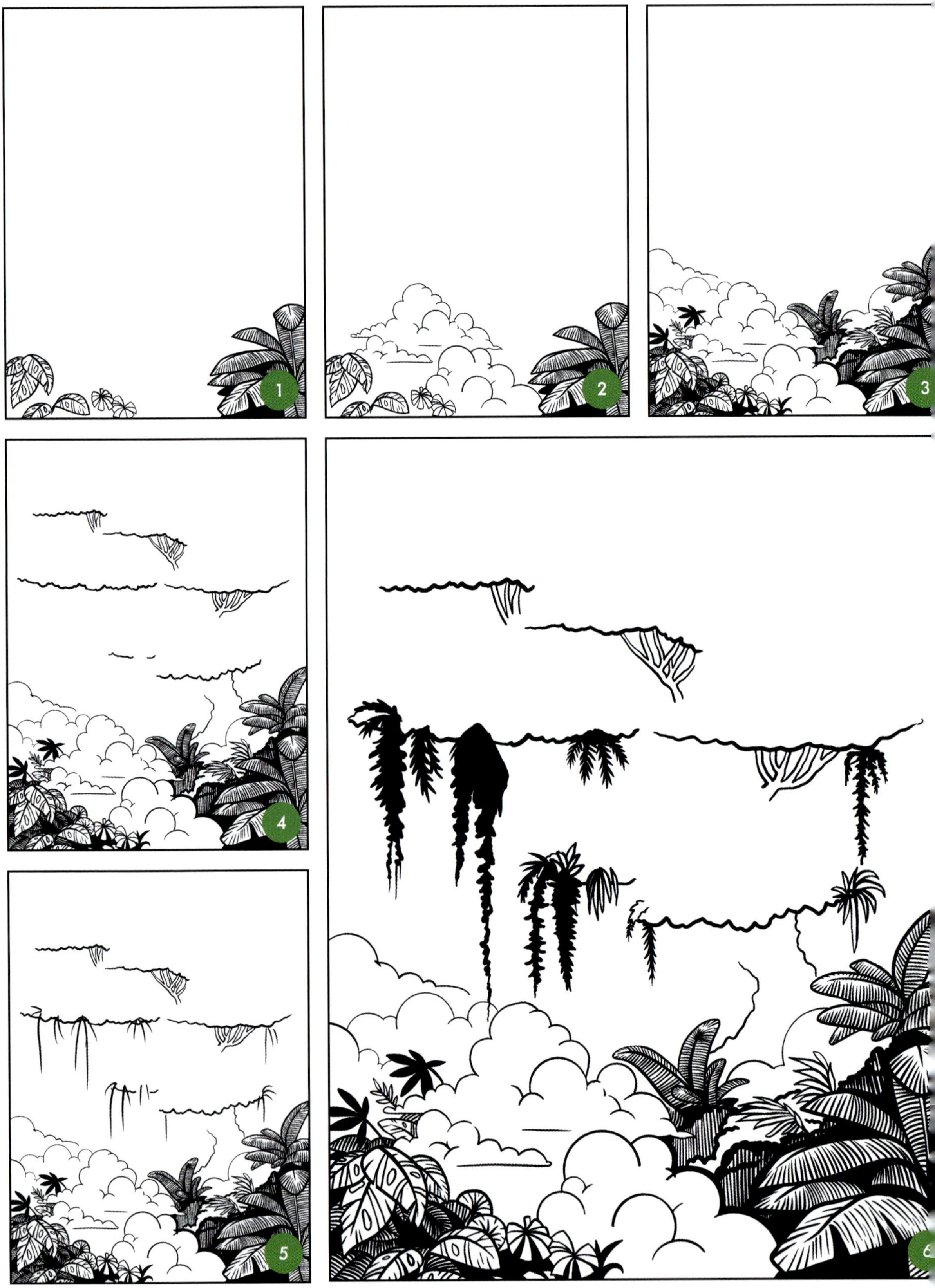
1
2
3
4
5
6

Now, Let's Draw the Scene

(See full image on page 94)

1. Start with a Plantain Plant (page 95) on the right and some Jungle Leaves (page 96) at the bottom of your frame.

2. Create some bubbly Cumulonimbus Clouds (page 56) on the bottom third of your frame. You don't even have to draw a line for the bottom to make your clouds extra wispy and light!

3. Build up the forest around these clouds with more plantains and different types of jungle leaves. Layer in a few more puffy round cloud tops above the others on the left and right side of the frame.

4. To begin your tree canopies, start with wiggly horizontal lines in the center of the frame and add a gnarled trunk out of the bottom of the lowest wiggle on the right. Add branches out of the bottom of a few other canopy bottoms that angle toward the central trunk.

5. Begin to add hanging plants from the tree bottoms with a few clusters of downward strokes.

6. Get creative with your hanging plants with some scribbly shapes around these clusters! Fill them in or make broad leaves that droop downwards.

(continued)

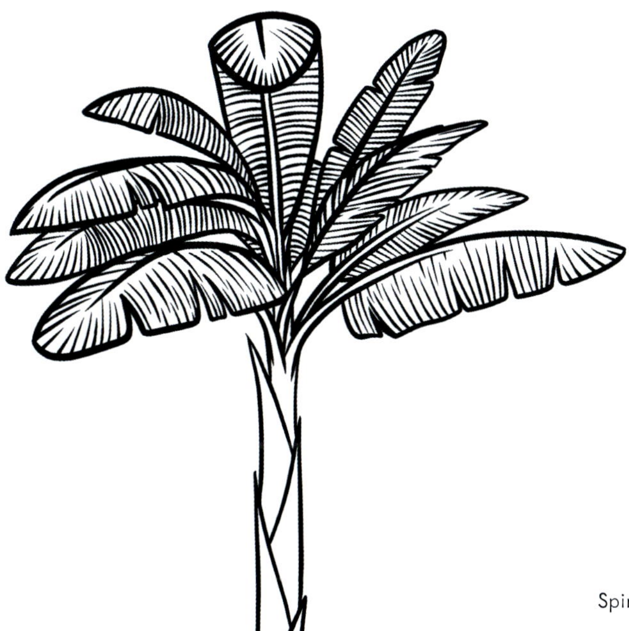

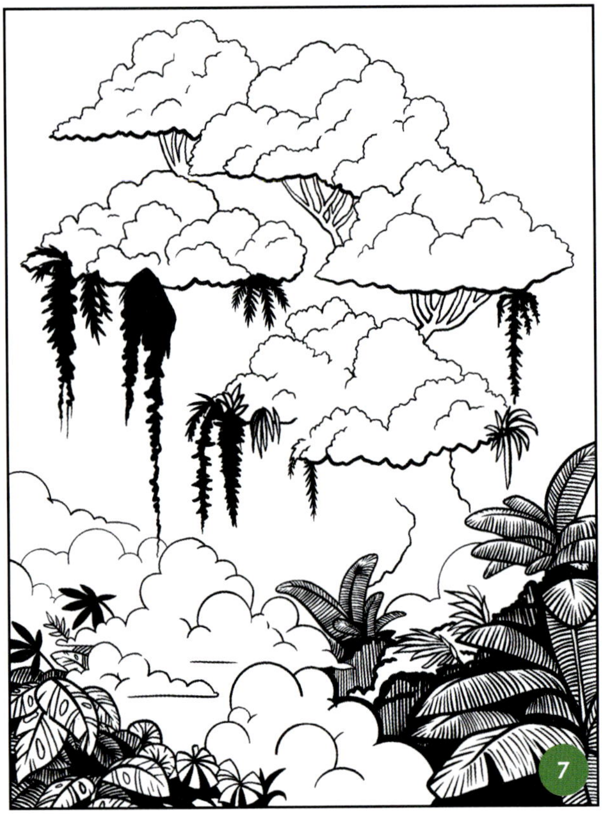
7

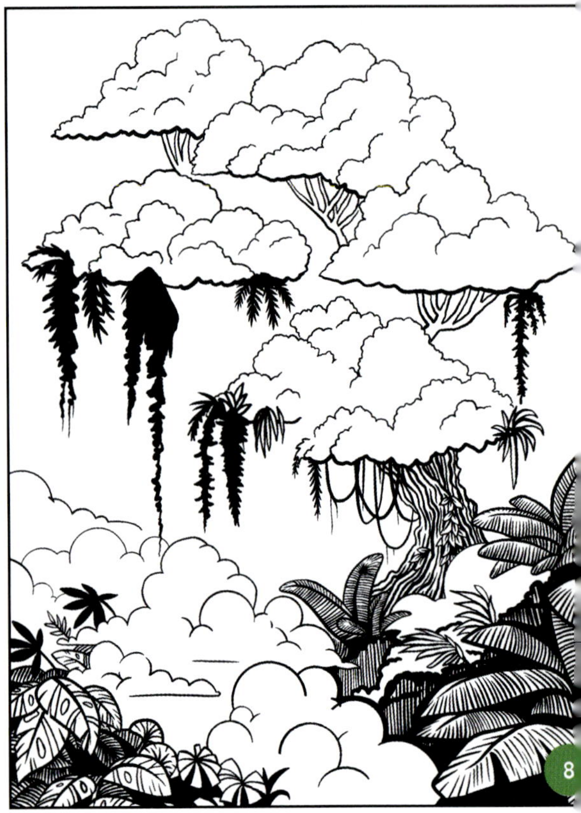
8

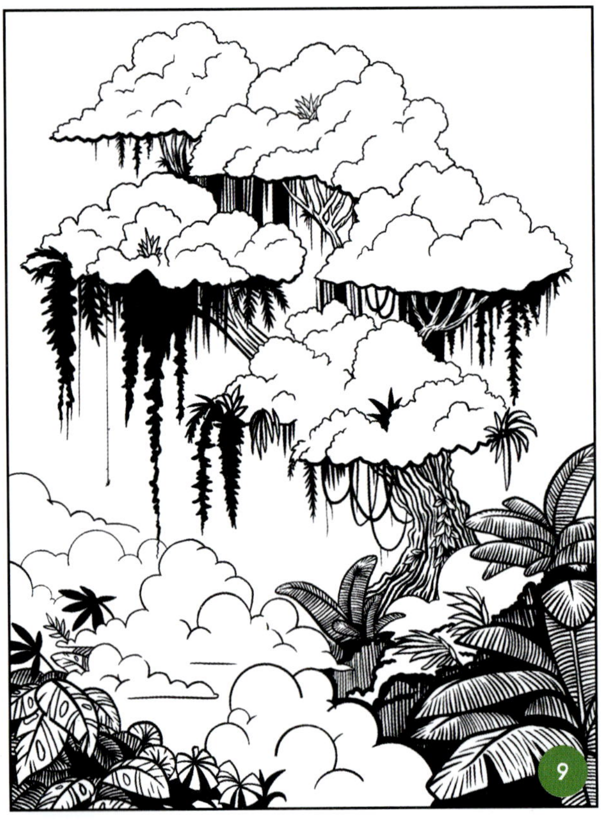
9

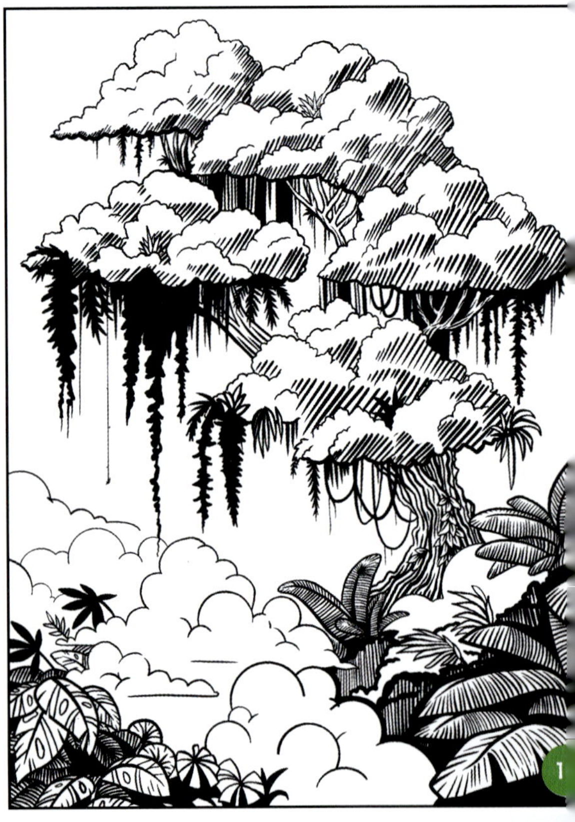
1

Now, Let's Draw the Scene (Final Steps)

7. Making the tree canopies is remarkably similar to drawing clouds. Instead of smooth round tops, make them wobbly and add small edges for more leafy texture.

8. Add texture to the tree trunk by filling it in with lines of various lengths. Add small leaves in a trailing bunch down the trunk as well as some looping vines with U shapes underneath the tree canopy.

9. Draw more foliage underneath each tree canopy with more clusters of hanging plants, looping vines, or just simple vertical strokes shaded in. Add a few random Air Plants (page 39) inside the canopies as well.

10. To shade the canopies, add diagonal dashes to the bottom and right sides of the rounded treetops.

11. Add a few last clouds behind the trees to complete your Cloud Canopies!

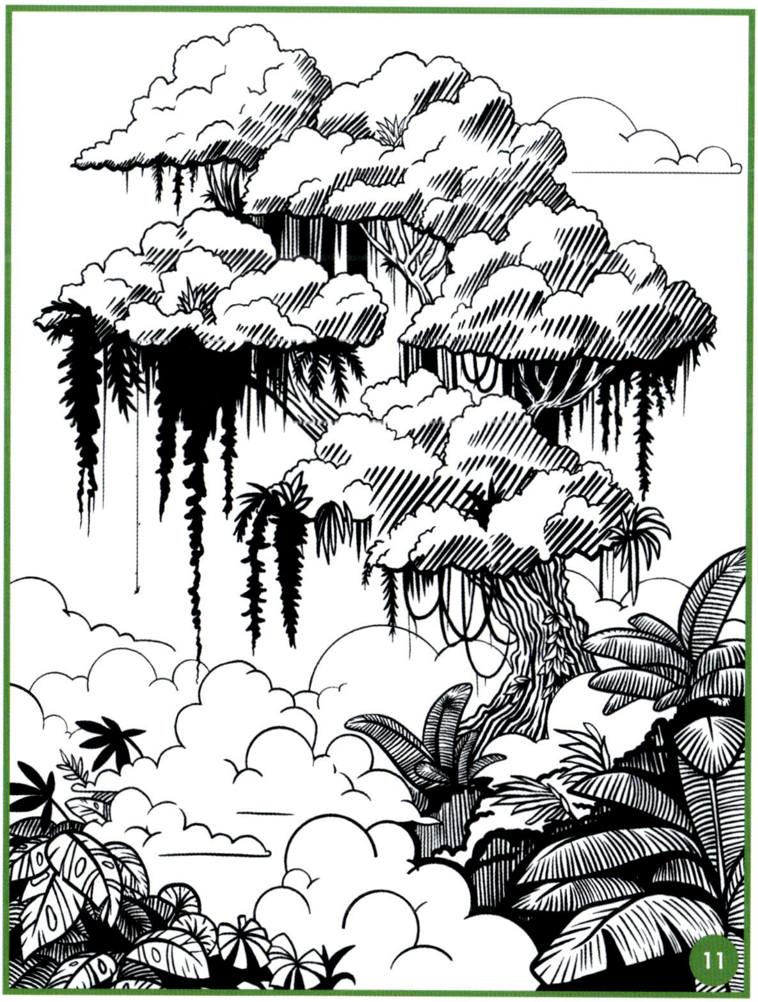

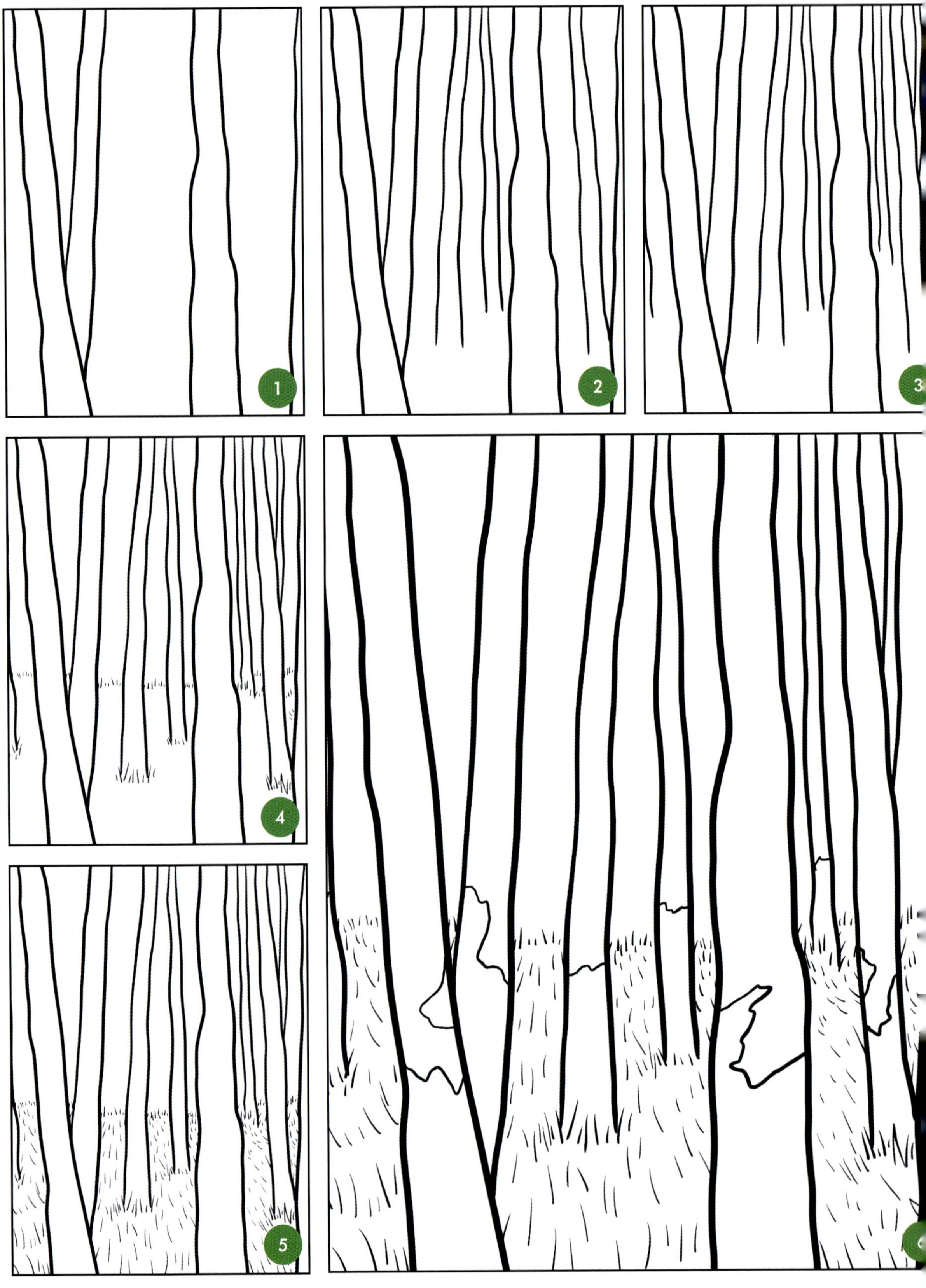
1
2
3
4
5

4. Aspen Forest

Deep within a realm of hushed whispers and sunlight filtering through trembling leaves lies the Aspen Forest. Here, a hidden truth awaits to be unveiled—these seemingly individual trees harbor a remarkable secret. Unlike their solitary counterparts, the aspens are not separate entities, but rather a single, vast organism. Their roots, woven together in an intricate network, form a singular life force that pulses beneath the forest floor.

Capturing this calming ecosystem on paper becomes a journey of revealing the essence of unity and interconnectedness. The artistic challenge lies in portraying this unique characteristic visually. We'll learn how to create the illusion of individual trees while subtly hinting at their subterranean connection. Through strategic placement and clever linework, we'll build a scene brimming with texture and depth.

---

1. Begin with some long trunks in the foreground. Let two of these trunks overlap in a Y-like shape.

2. Add three thinner tree trunks in between the others; make the bottoms of these trunks end slightly higher than the bottom of the frame to create some perspective.

3. Draw even thinner trunks in the spaces between and allow parts of these trunks to be hidden slightly behind the others.

4. Make a horizon line of grassy dashes across the bottom third of the frame and add some more grass under the bottoms of the trunks.

5. Fill out the rest of the ground with more sporadic grassy lines.

6. Create some aspen bark texture with squiggles along the lower parts of the trunks.

(continued)

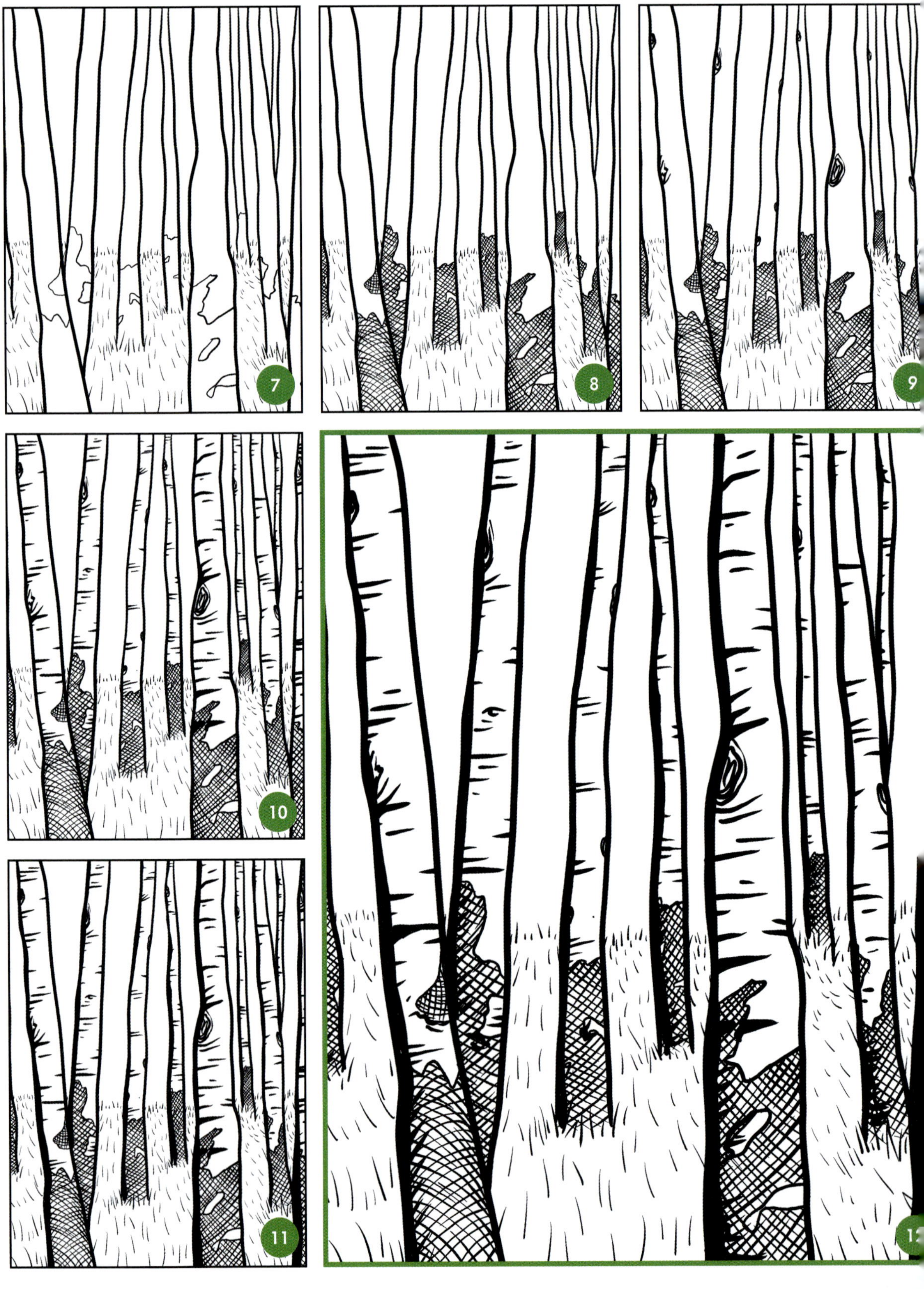
7
8
9
10
11

Aspen Forest (Final Steps)

7. Continue to develop the bark along the bottom with some more squiggly shapes.

8. In the area underneath these squiggles, draw some shading with cross hatching lines; these are easily done with diagonal lines in each direction that overlap.

9. Add knots in the wood along the sides of the trunks with some scribbly ovals, letting them fall wherever there is a slight bump or irregularity on the side of the trunk.

10. Draw thick horizontal dashes coming from the sides of the trunks for more bark texture.

11. Thicken the trunk lines, making the left sides slightly thicker than the right.

12. Add more shading with horizontal dashes to the bottoms of the trunks in the cross-hatching areas.

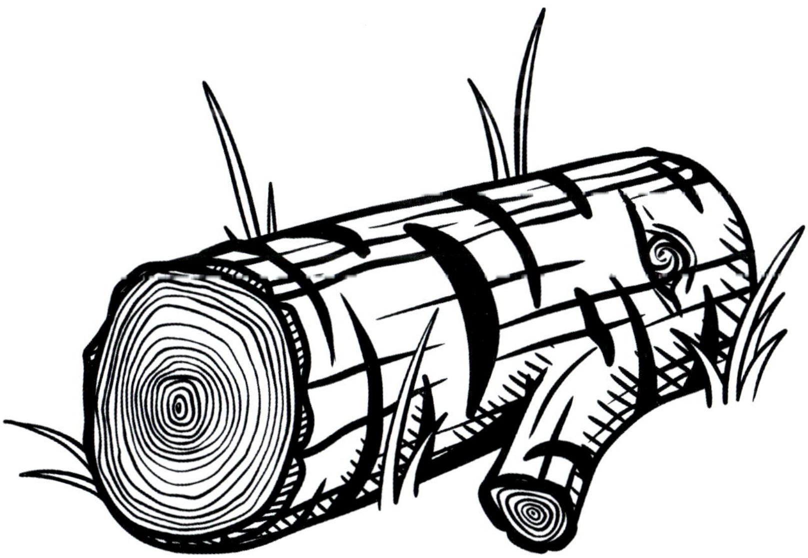

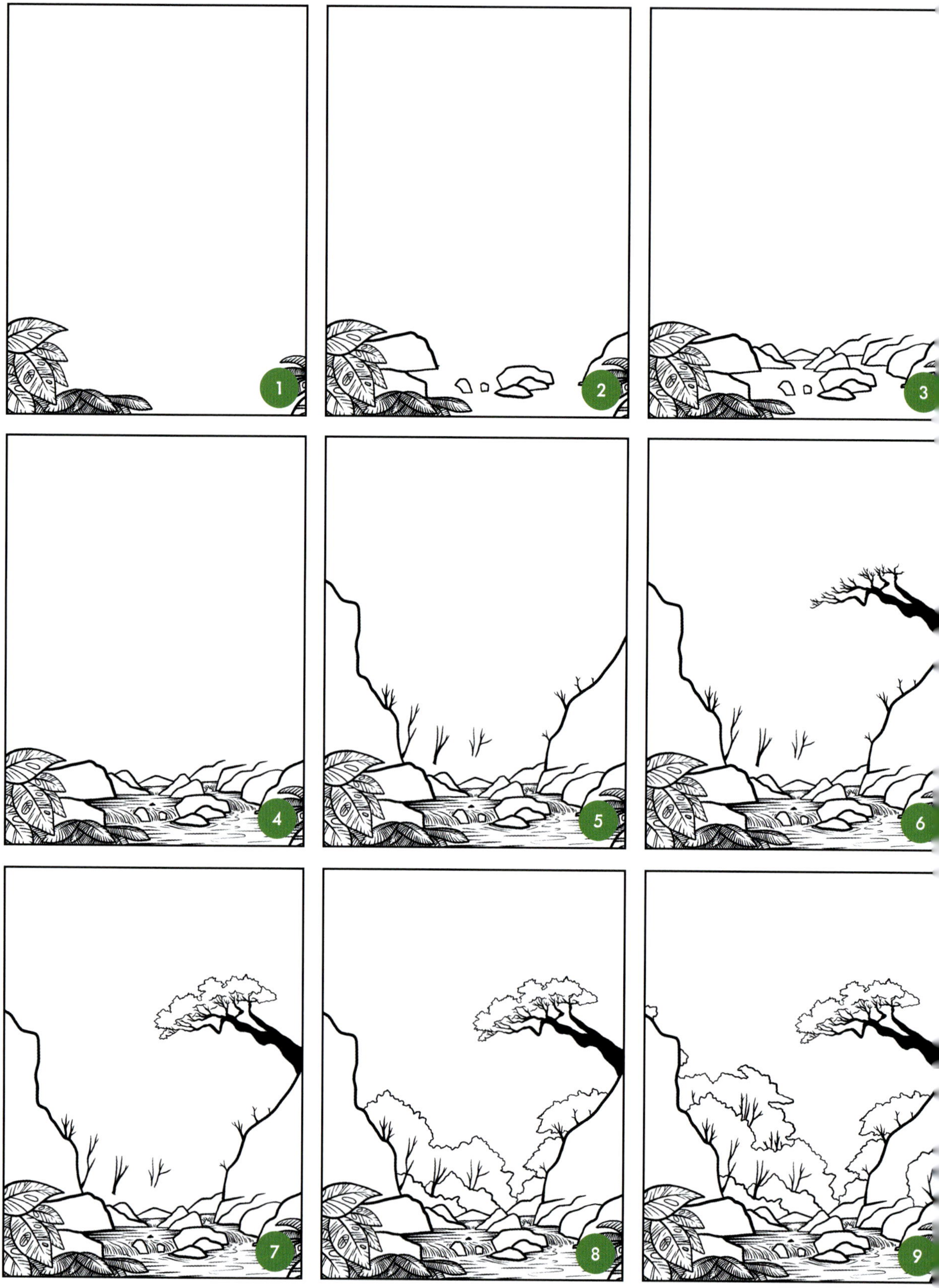
1
2
3
4
5
6
7
8
9

5. Rugged Rainforest

Welcome to the heart of the rainforest, where the moon casts shadows on a dramatic canyon filled with damp undergrowth. Cascading waterfalls thunder down moss-covered cliffs, their roar echoing through the verdant expanse. Exotic birds, hidden in the foliage, announce their presence with vibrant calls. Capturing this imposing scene in black and white might seem like a challenge, but fear not, aspiring artists!

By strategically placing a few well-defined lines, we can bring this vibrant ecosystem to life. We'll learn how lines of varying thickness and direction can create the illusion of cascading waterfalls, towering cliffs and lush foliage. With each stroke, the familiar shapes and textures of plants from previous chapters will emerge, transformed by the nighttime shadows. So, grab your pencils and prepare to be amazed at how line art, combined with strategic shading, can bring the rugged rainforest to life in a lush black and white landscape!

---

1. Start with some bunches of Jungle Leaves (page 96) along the bottom of the frame.

2. Add some Rocks (page 13) along the bottom fourth of the frame.

3. Build the scene with more rocks encircling a main area at the bottom of the frame which will become a stream.

4. To create a small pond, fill in this main area with horizontal ripple lines, and using what you've learned from drawing waterfalls (page 45) add curved lines to show water cascading down the rocks.

5. Add two large, rugged rock lines on each side to start building a frame. Draw spindly tree trunks and branches in between and behind the rock lines.

6. Make a larger wiggly tree trunk hanging over the edge of the rock line on the right and add some branches.

7. Make a tree canopy with a squiggly organic shape around the tops of the branches. The lines don't have to connect perfectly at the bottom where the branches meet the foliage.

8. Add layers of more squiggly foliage lines around the background trunks you created.

9. Keep expanding your rainforest by making more layers of spindly trunks and leafy treetops throughout the landscape.

(continued)

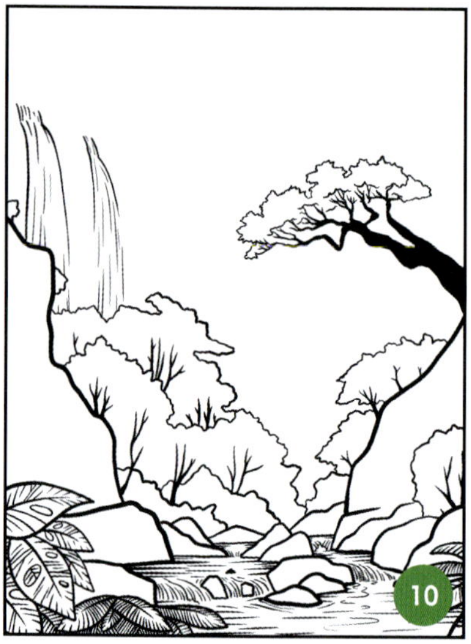
10
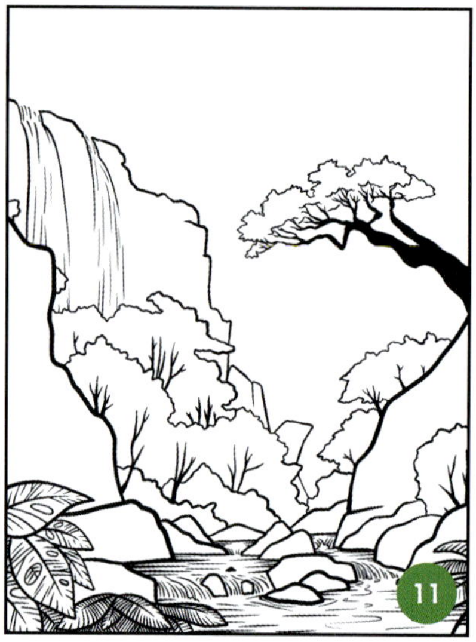
11
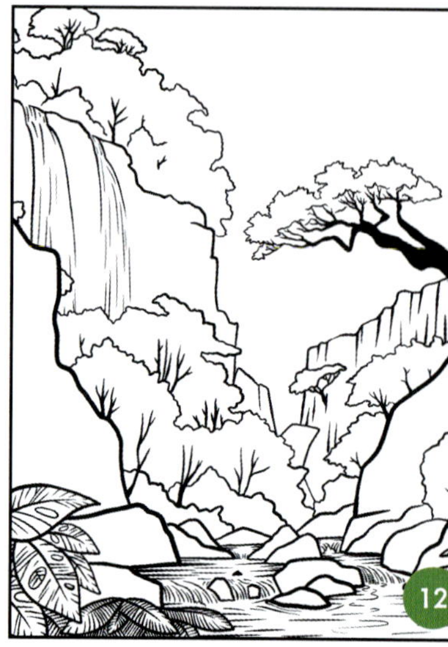
12
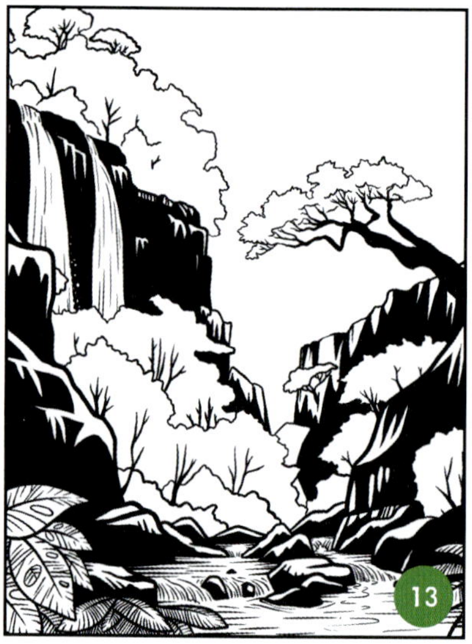
13
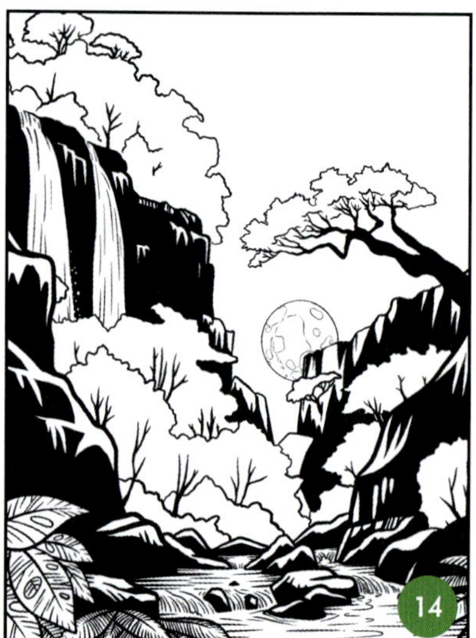
14
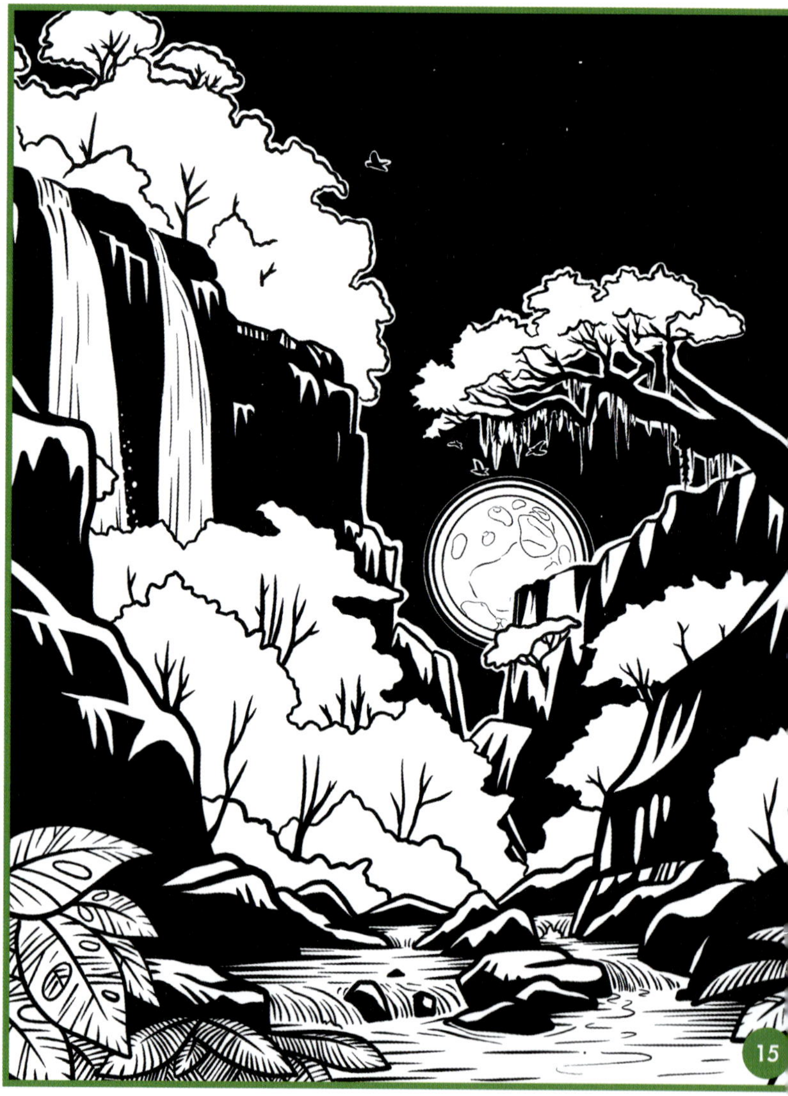
15

Rugged Rainforest (Final Steps)

10. Begin to make a large waterfall on the upper left side of the frame with some lines that swoop down behind the tops of your trees.

11. Draw a rugged line similar to step 5, using a mix of sharp edges and flatter areas to create a cliff the waterfall cascades over.

12. Add another jagged cliff on the right side with a line across and vertical dashes down. Put some trees behind the waterfall and coming off the cliffside. By leaving a gap in the center area, these elements seem to converge towards the vanishing point of an unseen horizon.

13. Put shadows on the rocks. Leave some horizontal highlights on the top edges of the cliffs and rocks and vertical highlights on parts of the cliffsides.

14. Draw a full Moon (page 25) in the low center of the frame.

15. Add some Flying Birds (page 112) and Vines (page 40) hanging down from the overhanging tree to complete your rainforest scene!

Finish it off by filling in the night sky to match your moon. To really let your features stand out, leave a small outline of light around everything in the background, and leave a few light circles around the moon for glowing moonbeams.

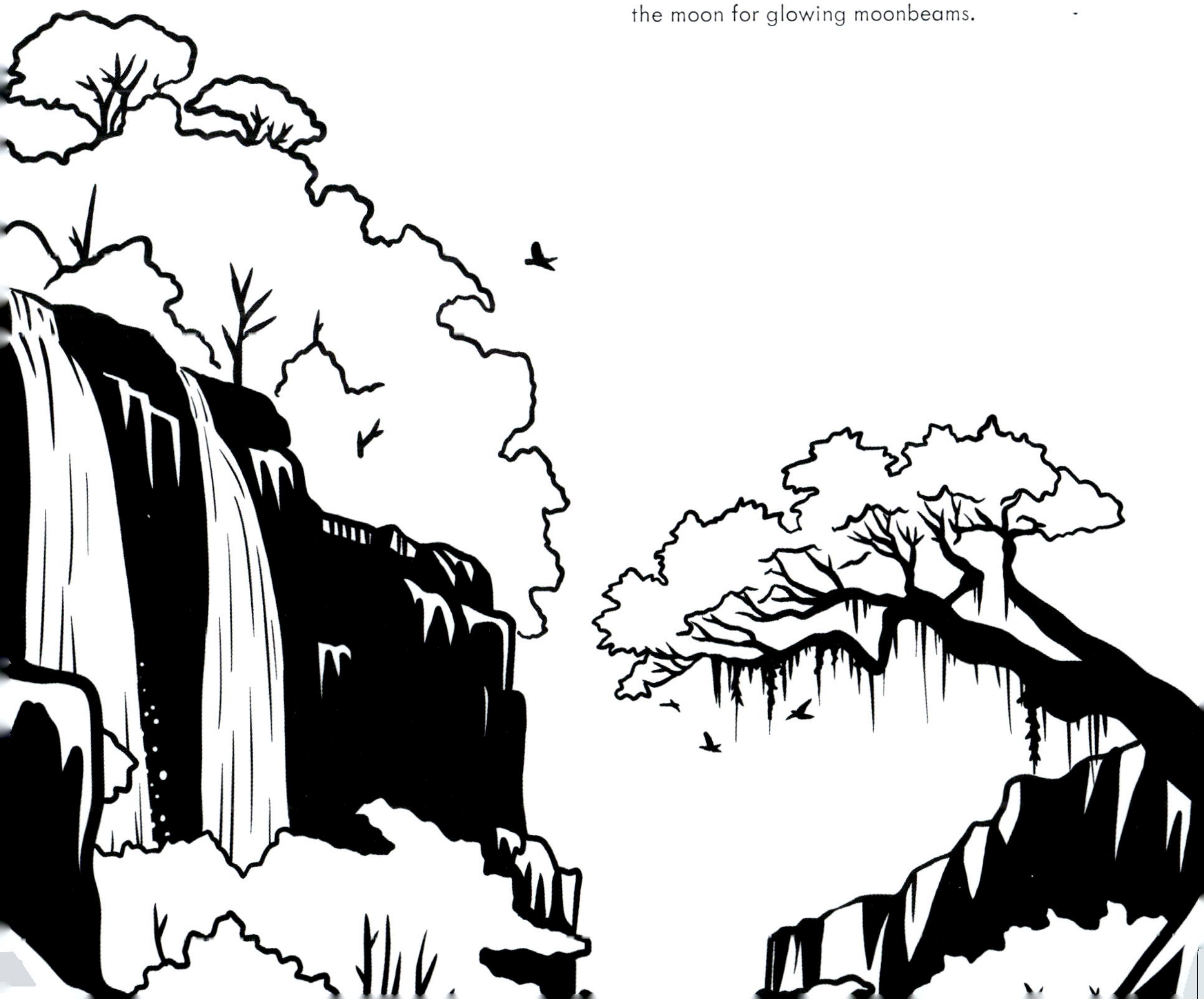

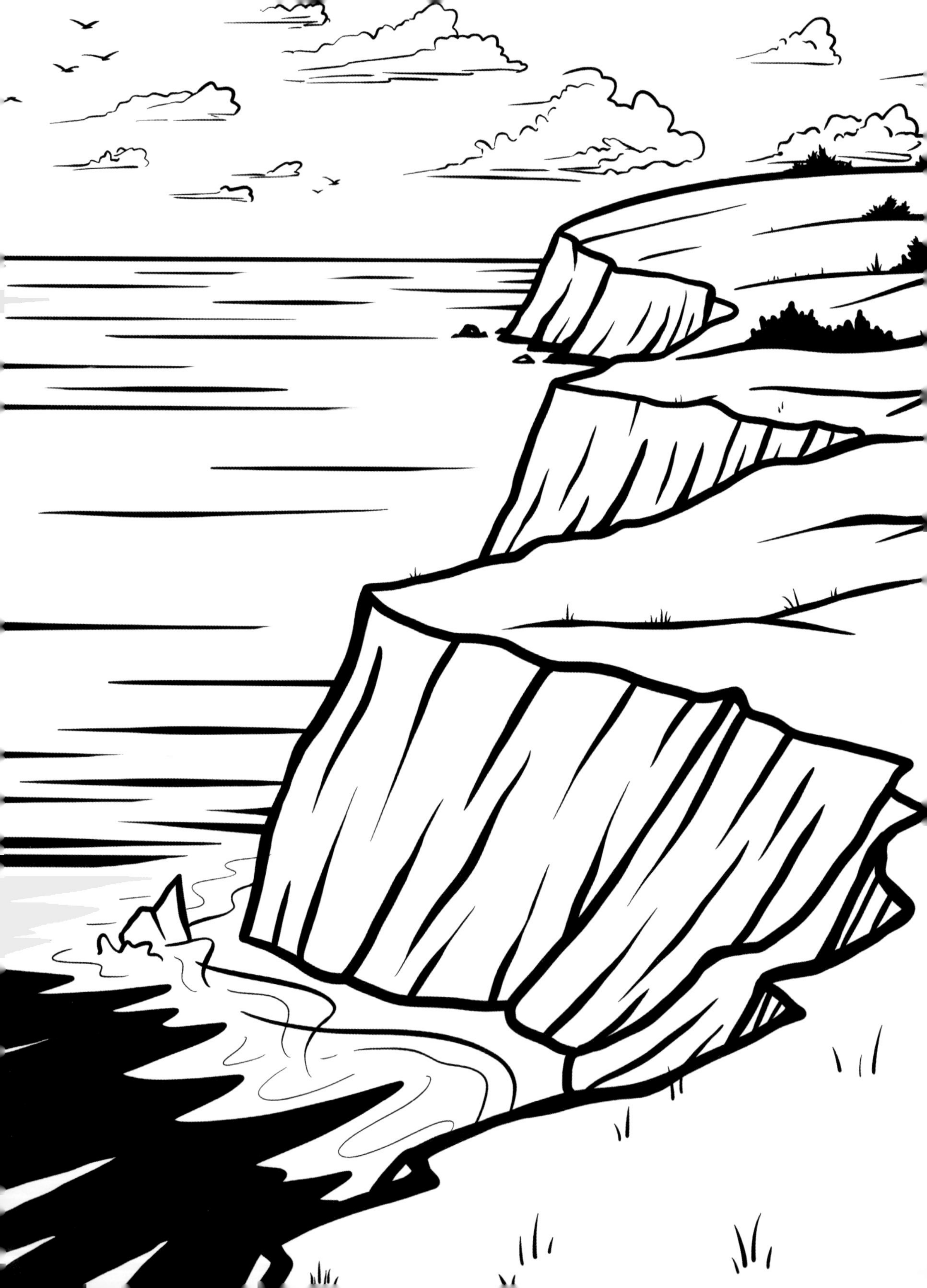

SHIFTING COASTAL SEASCAPES

Anywhere the ocean and land meet, you can find intertidal zones. Together we'll explore the immense variety: otherworldly tide pools, a foggy northern lighthouse, tropical beach paradise, treacherously steep ocean bluffs and even thriving shallow reefs. These coastal places are special. They are where the world's most fascinating flora and fauna hide in plain sight. Don't be fooled by the initial stillness, artists! The rhythmic hush as the tide recedes slowly reveals a hidden world. Here, land and sea converge in a dynamic embrace, a vibrant tapestry woven by the constant dance of the waters. This stunning realm is a kaleidoscope of marine creatures, each uniquely adapted to this ever-changing environment.

This isn't just about replicating what you see—it's about capturing the essence of this dynamic world. We'll learn how to translate the ever-shifting textures of wet and dry rock, the playful dance of light and shadow on tide pools, and the loose forms of sea creatures clinging to life in the shallows. This dynamic realm offers a glimpse into the wonders of the marine world, reminding us of our own interconnectedness with the vast expanse of the oceans. I can't wait to show you!

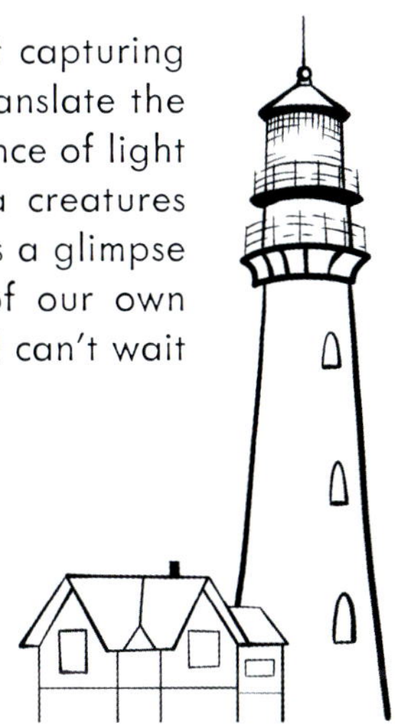

1. Jagged Coastal Bluffs

The salty tang of the ocean air hangs heavy; a symphony of crashing waves and screeching gulls fills your senses. Towering cliffs, weathered and majestic, stand as silent sentinels against the vast canvas of the sea. These coastal bluffs, their faces etched with the relentless sculpting of wind and waves, rise dramatically from the shoreline. Layers of sediment, exposed in the rugged cliffs, speak of a long and dynamic history. In some places, the bluffs crumble at the water's edge, sending plumes of mist skyward with each crashing wave. In others, vegetation clings precariously to the slopes, adding a touch of life to the stark landscape.

In this lesson, we'll unveil the secrets of these coastal giants. We'll focus on the power of simplicity, demonstrating how a few well-placed lines can evoke their grandeur. We'll also explore basic techniques for drawing birds gliding on the wind and wispy clouds dancing across the sky, all elements that will complete our dramatic coastal scene.

Flying Birds

No scene of a dramatic coastline is complete without the soaring silhouettes of birds against the vastness of the sky. These feathered inhabitants effortlessly ride the wind currents, their forms adding a sense of freedom and movement to our coastal artwork. With just a few simple shapes, we can preserve the essence of these birds in flight, adding a touch of life to our majestic bluffs. Let's explore how to bring these avian companions to life!

1

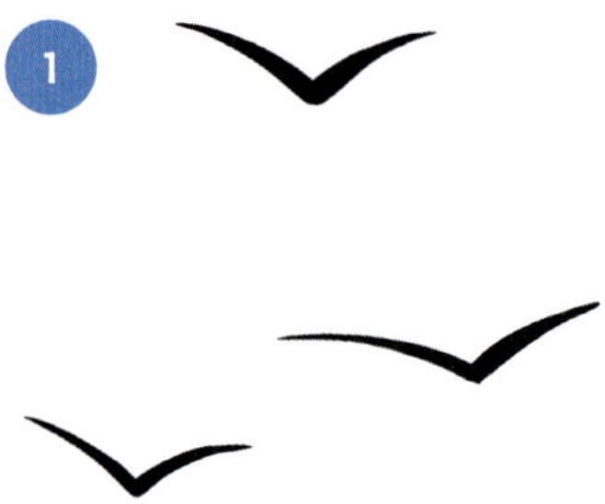

Start with a few V-like shapes with rounded sides to create the wings.

2

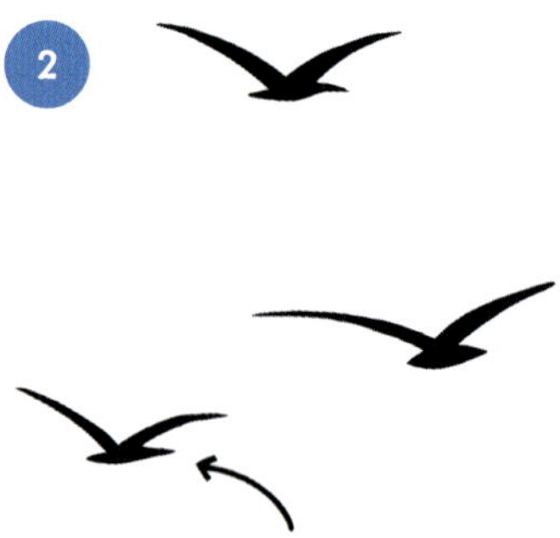

Draw bird bodies out of small, pointed ovals on the bottom of the wing shapes.

Windy Stratus Clouds

High above the coastal drama, the sky isn't simply a passive backdrop. Here, wispy stratus clouds, stretched thin by the wind, become active participants in the scene. These clouds, like brushstrokes across a canvas, hint at the unseen power of the wind whipping across the landscape. We'll capture their essence using just a few simple lines, adding another layer of dynamism to our coastal masterpiece.

1

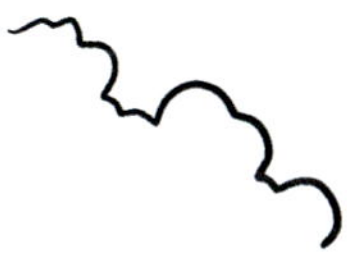

Draw a slanting line made of puffy arcs.

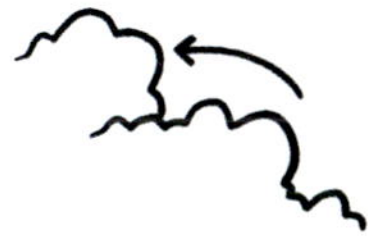

You can also add a smaller arc of puffy cloud tops above the first to create a layered look.

2

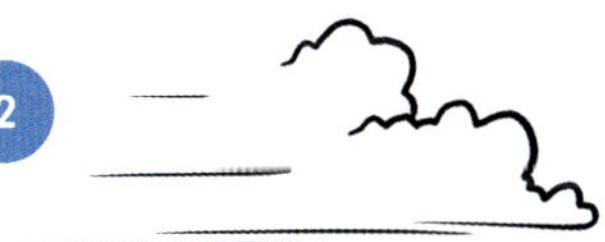

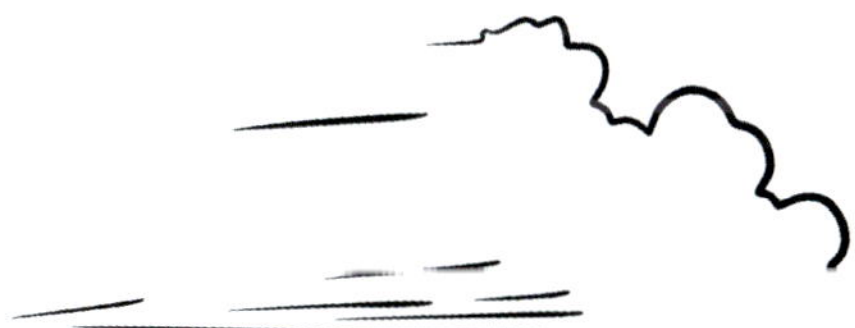

Draw horizontal wispy strokes underneath the tops. Make them thinner to the left side of the clouds for a windblown effect.

3

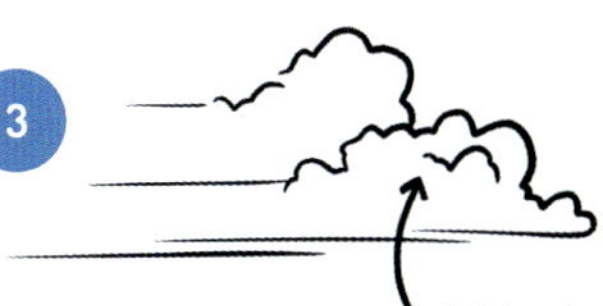

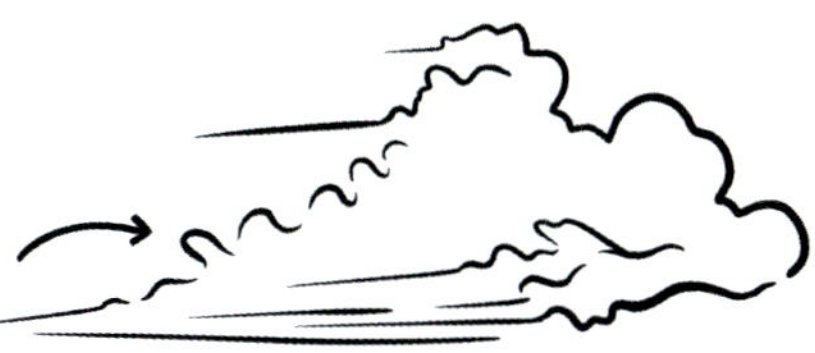

Add a few smaller layers of puffy lines to finish the clouds.

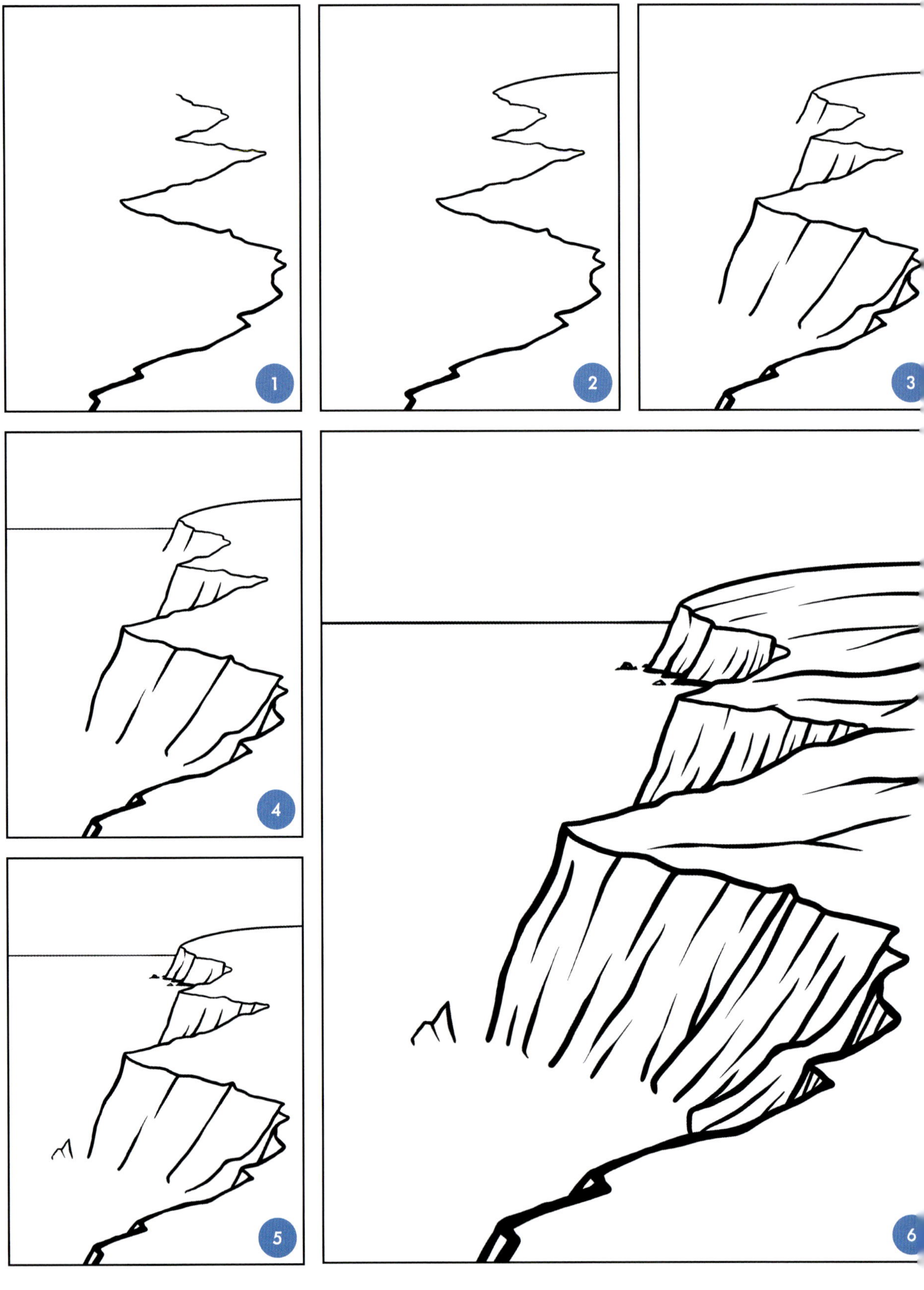
1
2
3
4
5
6

Now, Let's Draw the Scene

(See full image on page 110)

1. Begin your bluffs with a rough zigzag line down the center of your frame. Widen the zigzag and make the line thicker toward the bottom of the frame to create the illusion of perspective.

2. Add a slightly rounded line from the top of the zigzag that connects to the right side of the frame.

3. To create cliff faces, draw lines down from the peaks of the zig zag, making sure these vertical lines do not go past the following zigzag peak.

4. Draw a horizon line in the top third of the frame, connecting to the top of the cliffside.

5. Finish the bottoms of the distant cliffs. Put some small rocks around the bottom of the bluffs.

6. Add slanting strokes to the tops of the bluffs for texture. Draw vertical strokes along the cliffsides in varying lengths, letting some overlap with each other.

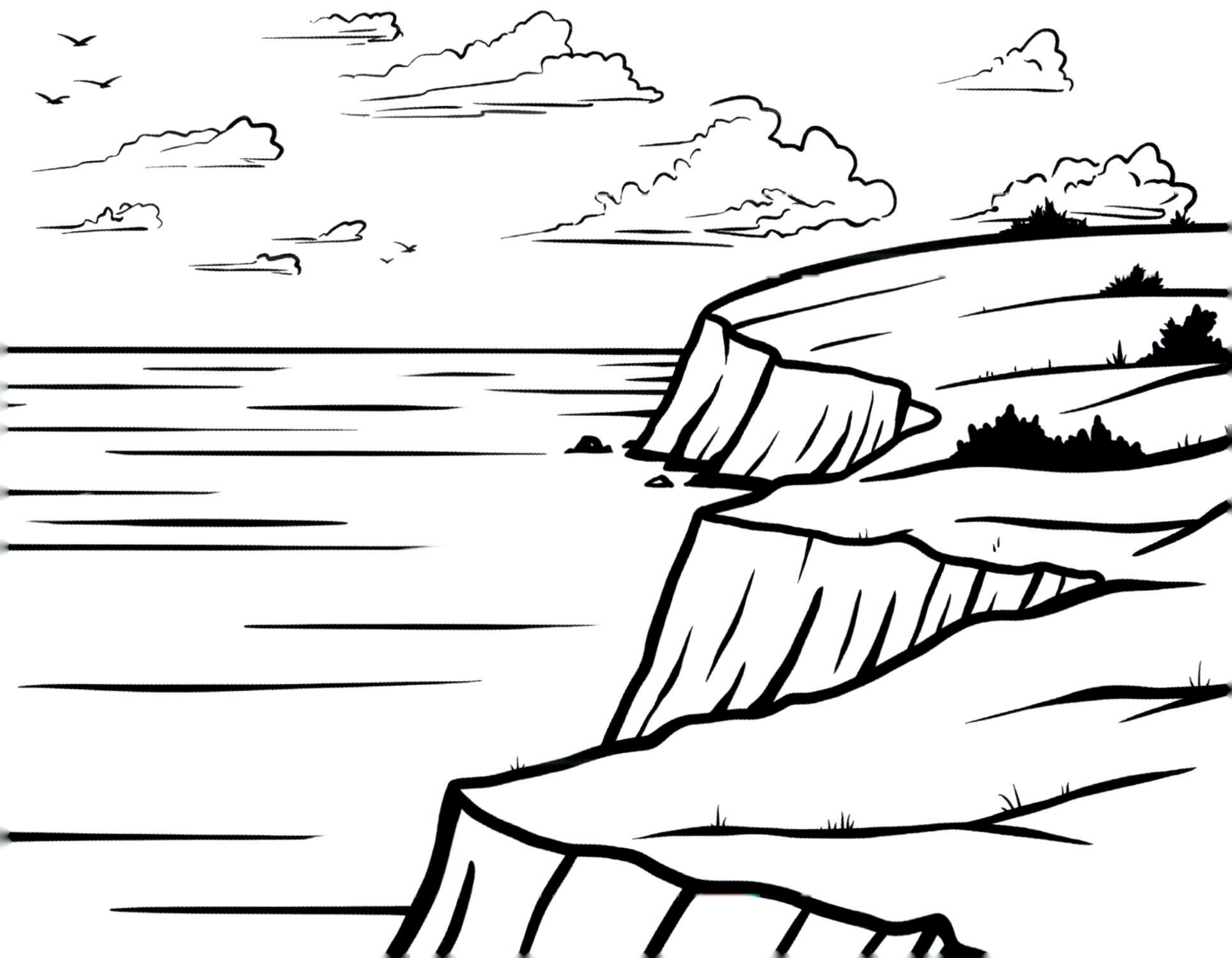

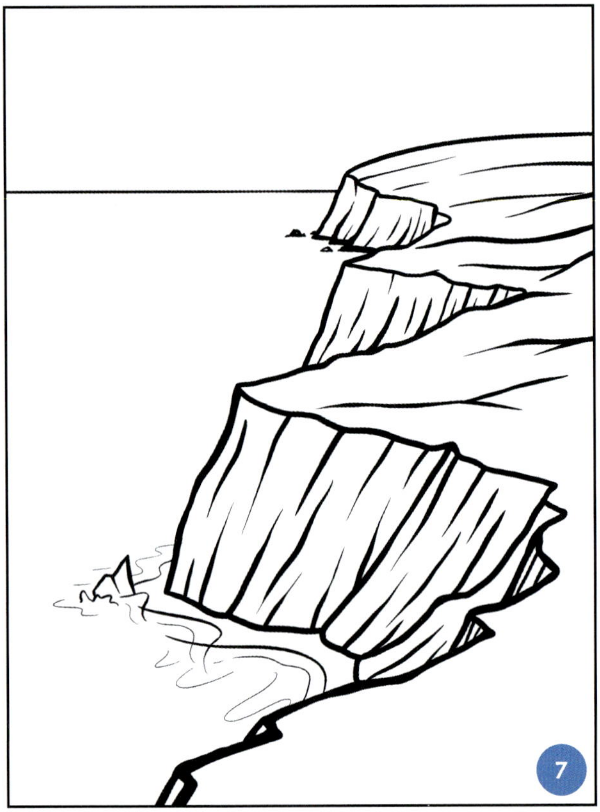
7

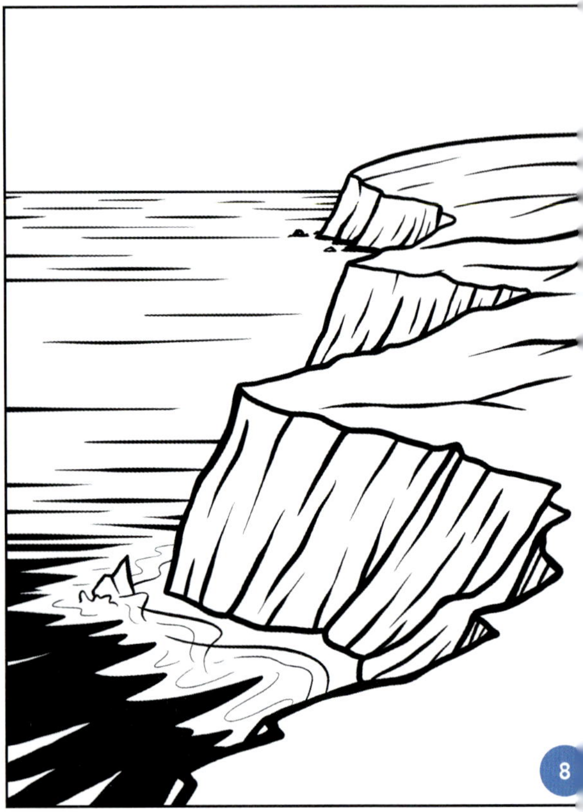
8

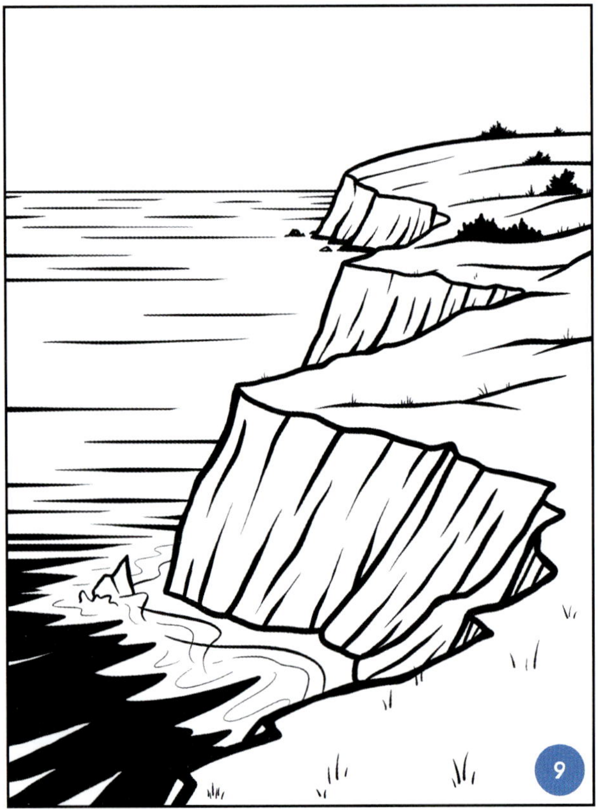
9

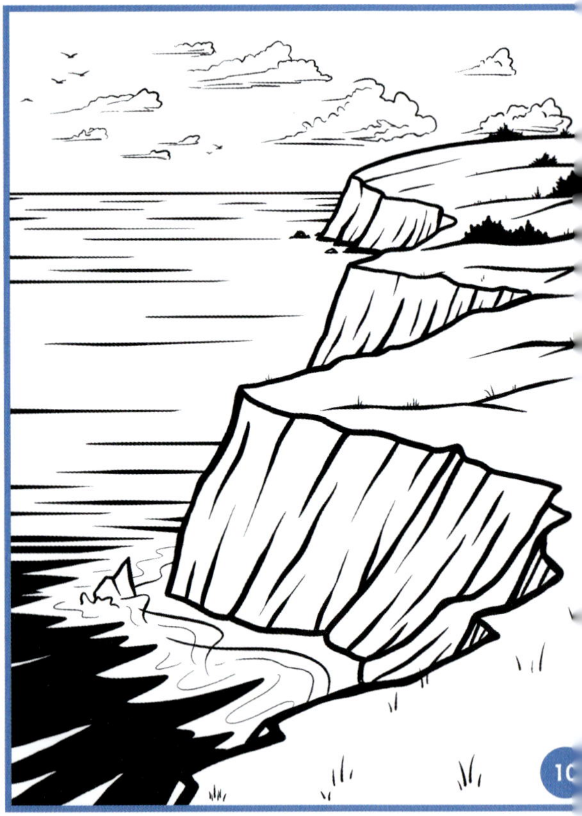
10

Now, Let's Draw the Scene (Final Steps)

7. Begin to add your coastline with some thin crashing waves that surround the bottom of the bluffs in the foreground.

8. Add horizontal strokes throughout the water to create distant waves and reflections. Make them smaller and closer together when they are nearest to the horizon line. To draw crashing waves, start with some wavy lines pointing towards the cliff-side in the foreground then shade them in.

9. Draw some small grassy dashes on the top of the bluffs and some scribbly bushes in the distance.

10. Draw some Windy Stratus Clouds (page 113) along the sky and a few Flying Birds (page 112).

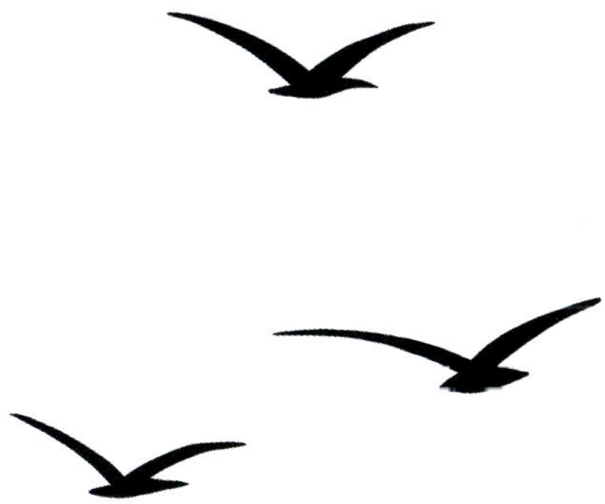

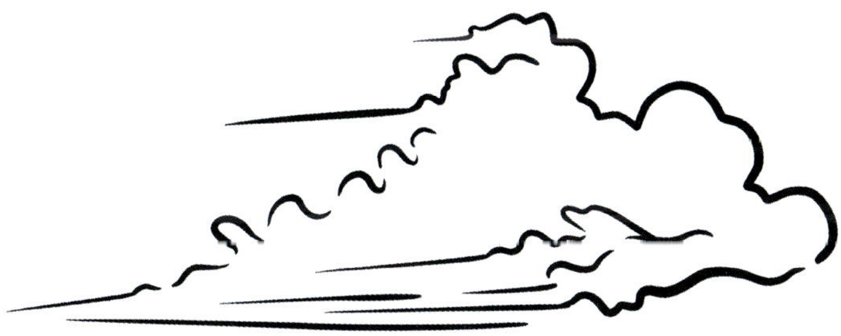

2. Tropical Beach Bliss

Ever dreamt of escaping to a place where worries melt away and the only sound is the gentle rhythm of waves? Tropical beaches offer such a haven, a paradise where turquoise waters shimmer under the sun and swaying palm trees provide cool, leafy shade. In this lesson, we'll embark on a journey to capture this blissful escape, not with a burst of colors, but with the simple elegance of line art. We'll learn to translate the essence of the beach: the graceful curves of palm fronds, the vast expanse of the ocean and the soft texture of the sand, all with the power of a few simple lines. Get ready to unleash your inner artist and bring the tranquility of a tropical beach to life.

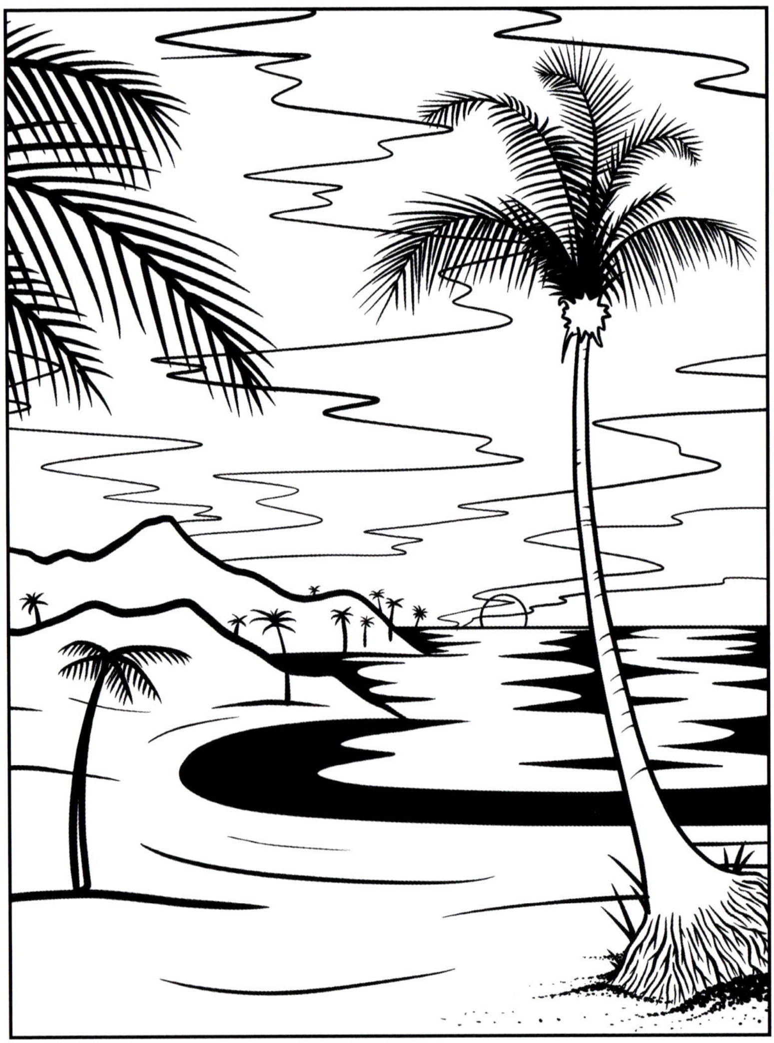

Realistic Coconut Palm

These iconic trees are the ultimate symbol of the tropics, but did you know they're also one of the most versatile plants on Earth? They provide us with delicious coconuts, strong building materials, and even shade from the scorching sun. The best part? Drawing a coconut palm is easier than you think! In this tutorial, we'll show you how to capture their graceful lush leaves with just a few simple steps.

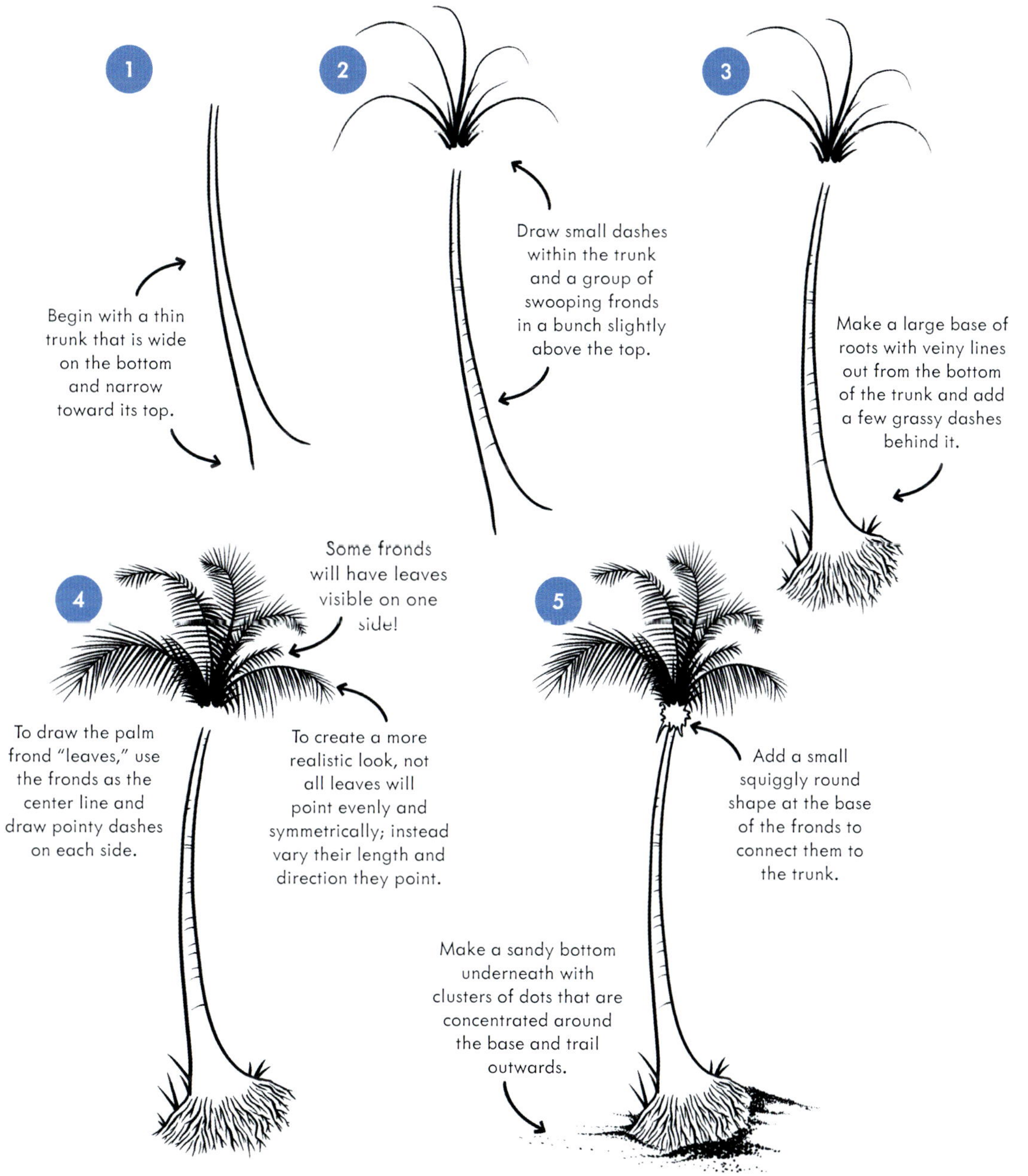

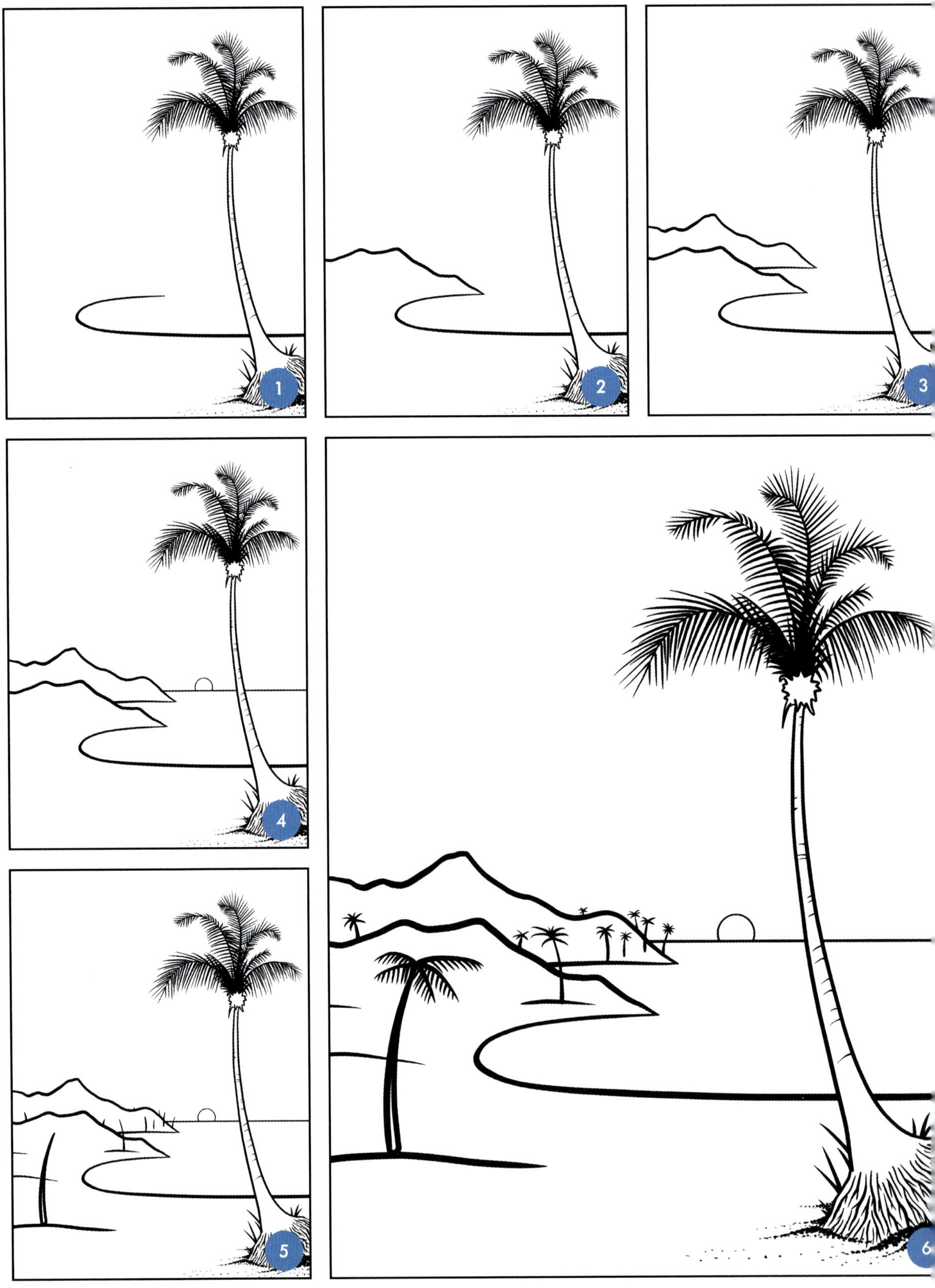
1
2
3
4
5
6

Now, Let's Draw the Scene

(See full image on page 118)

1. Start by drawing a Realistic Coconut Palm (page 119) on the bottom right of the frame. Draw a long swooping C shape behind it.

2. Add a squiggly line down to connect to the C's point.

3. Draw another squiggly line above this shape that connects to a flat line underneath it.

4. Draw a horizon line. Make a semi-circle on top of the horizon for a setting sun.

5. Create some more palm trees with trunks that get smaller as they go into the distance. Add horizontal lines underneath them.

6. Draw arches out of the tops of the trunks to make palm fronds. Add frond leaves to the closest trees but less detail to those in the background.

(continued)

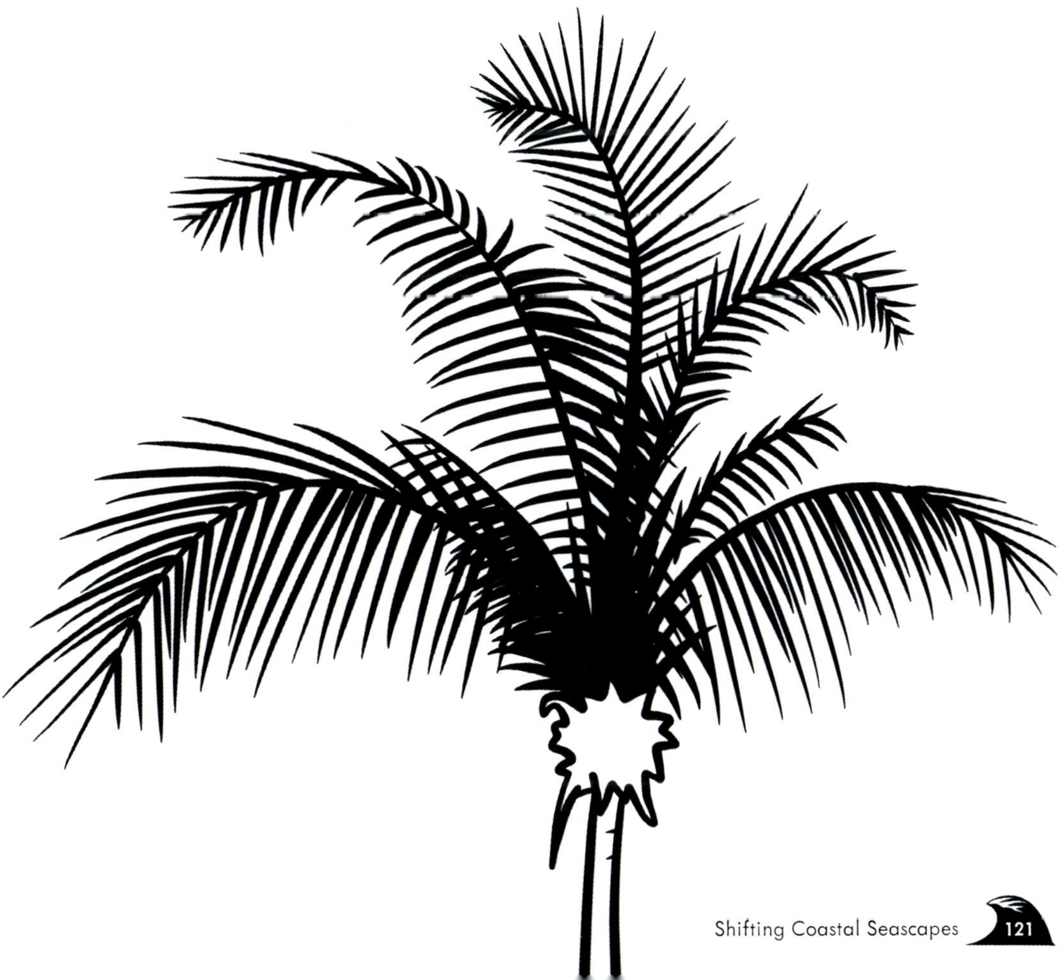

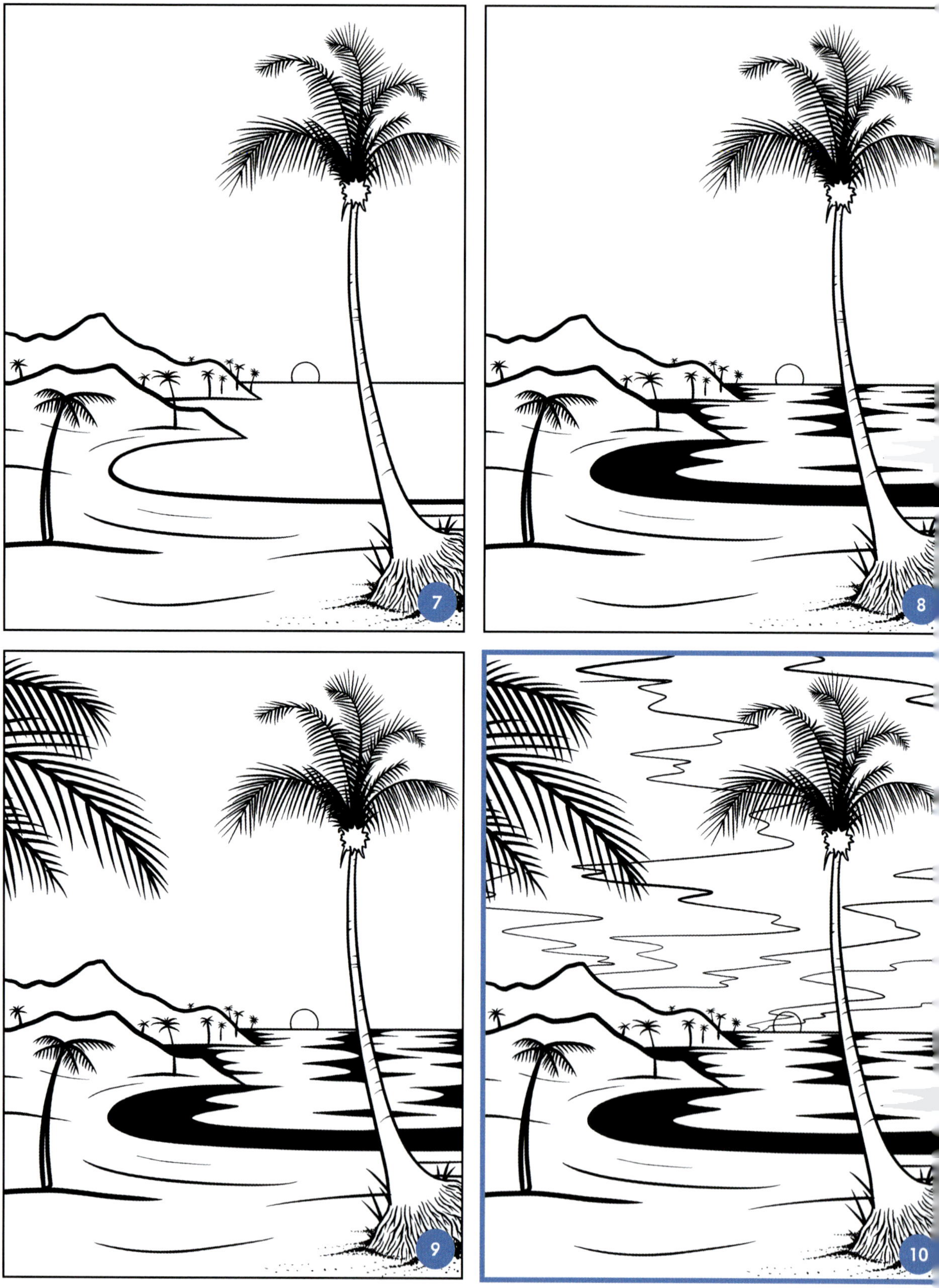
7
8
9
10

Now, Let's Draw the Scene (Final Steps)

7. Make a sandy beach with a few swooping lines.

8. To add shading to the water, draw horizontal arches from the left and right sides of the ocean and behind the palm tree. Make them point toward the center, which is left lighter where the sun is shining. Shade these areas and the front coastline in dark.

9. Take your drawing to the next level by drawing some large palm fronds coming in from the upper left of the frame.

10. Finish your tropical beach with some wavy lines through the sky.

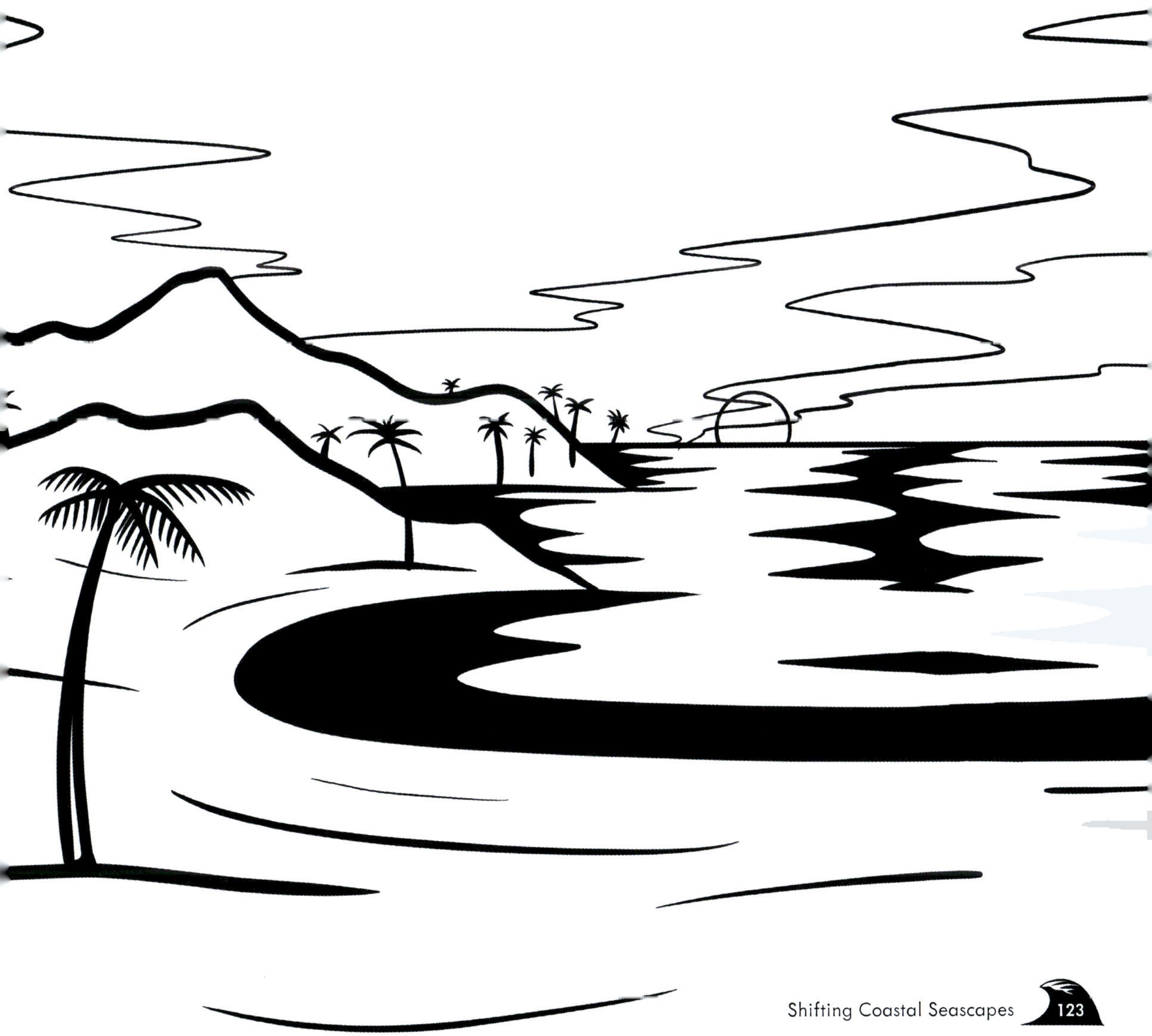

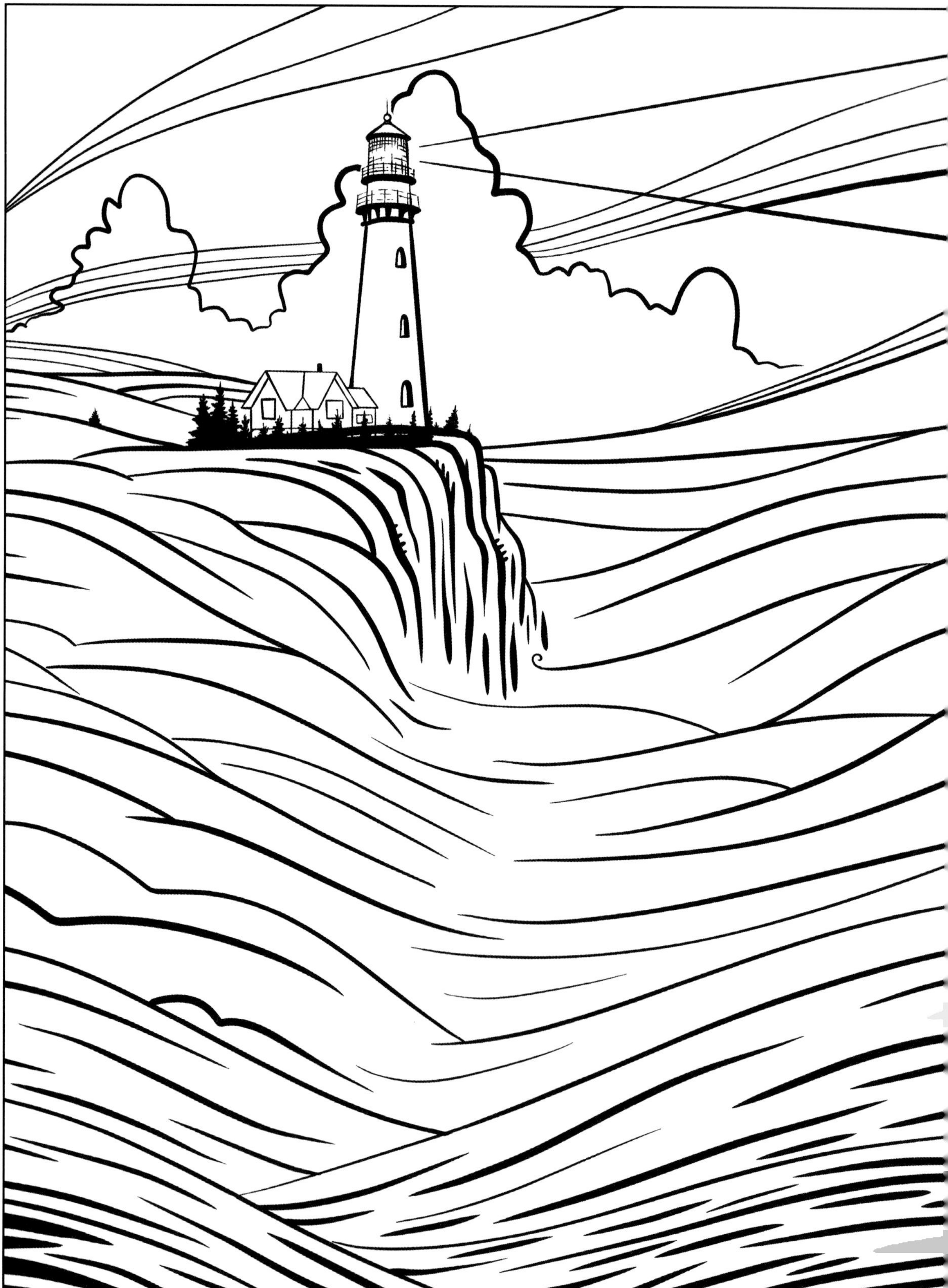

3. Foggy Lighthouse

The ocean roars, a symphony of crashing waves and swirling mist. A veil of fog, like a watchful curtain, obscures the coastline, leaving only hints of what lies beneath. Yet piercing through this ethereal shroud, a solitary lighthouse stands sentinel. Its sturdy form, a beacon of hope and resilience, reaches skyward, a silent promise of guidance in the face of uncertainty. In this lesson, we'll embark on a journey to capture this scene of veiled beauty. We'll translate the drama of the ethereal fog and the resolute form of the lighthouse using just simple strokes and shapes. With a focus on simple shapes and repetitive line, you'll learn to create a piece that evokes both mystery and tranquility.

Lighthouse

This iconic structure may guide ships through the treacherous waters and through dense storms, yet it must first be brought to life on your page. In this section, we'll break down the process of drawing this classic symbol of safety and resilience into a series of simple steps.

We'll begin with basic shapes, transforming them with a few well-placed lines into the sturdy form of the lighthouse. With each step, you'll add details—windows, a rooftop and a powerful light beam—to complete this guardian of the coast. So, grab your pencil, unleash your inner artist and let's embark on building our very own watchful sentinel.

1

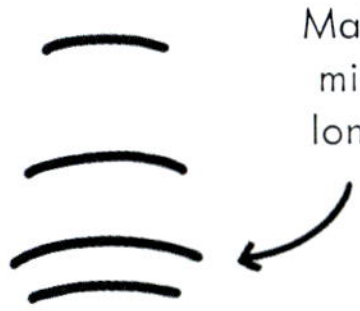

Make one in the middle slightly longer than the others.

Begin your towering lighthouse with some small gentle arcs in a vertical stack.

2

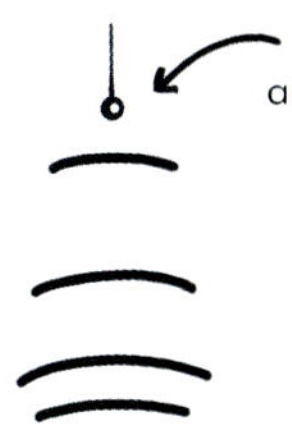

Add a little circle above the top arc with a thin point coming out the top.

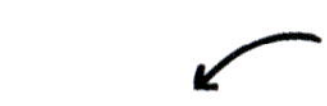

Add a small horizontal line on the bottom left

Lighthouse (Continued)

3

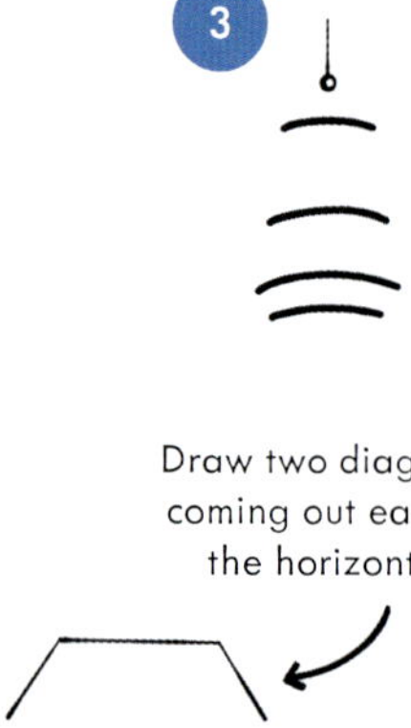

Draw two diagonal lines coming out each side of the horizontal line.

4

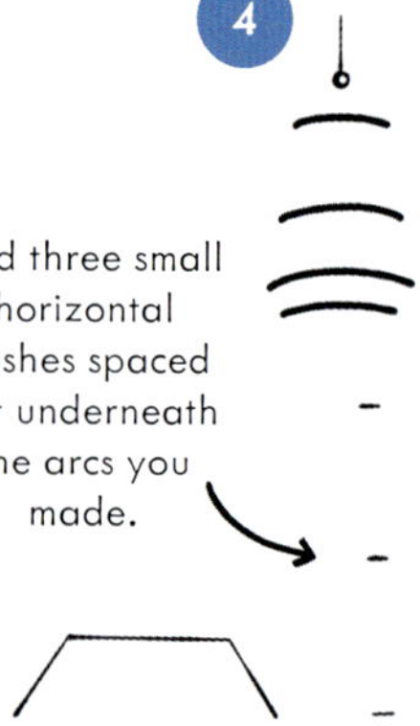

Add three small horizontal dashes spaced out underneath the arcs you made.

Make the last on the same level as the bottom of the diagonal lines.

5

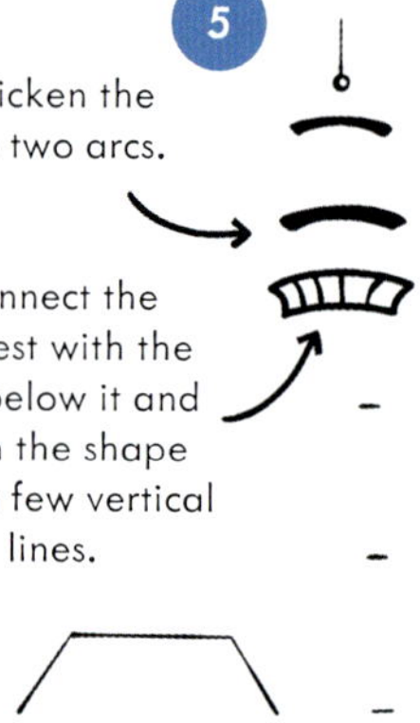

Thicken the top two arcs.

Connect the longest with the one below it and fill in the shape with a few vertical lines.

6

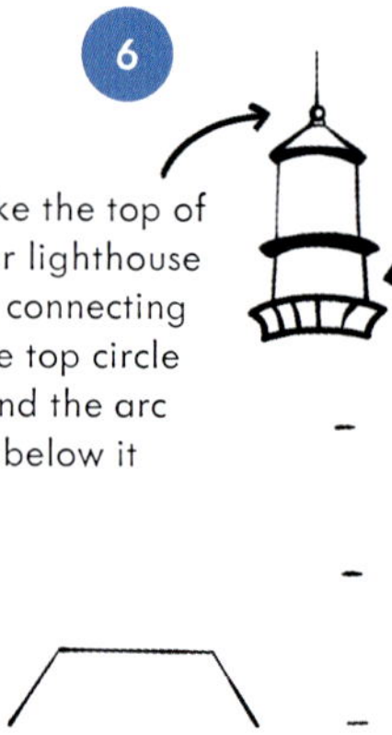

Make the top of your lighthouse by connecting the top circle and the arc below it

Draw vertical lines connecting the stack of arcs.

7

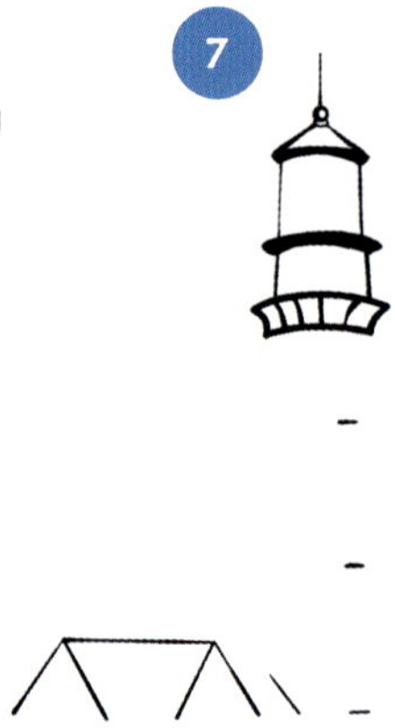

Make two upsides down Vs out of the two diagonal lines. Add a smaller diagonal line off the right side. This will be the base of your lighthouse roof.

8

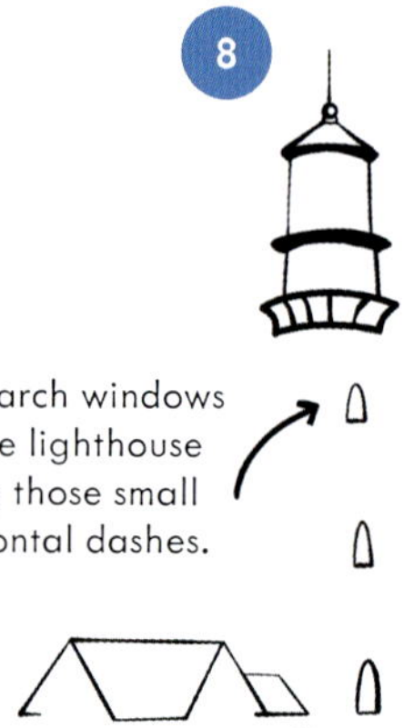

Make arch windows on the lighthouse using those small horizontal dashes.

Connect the small diagonal line to the side of the roof. Draw a horizontal line to cap its bottom and add a small horizontal line on the bottom left of the roof.

9

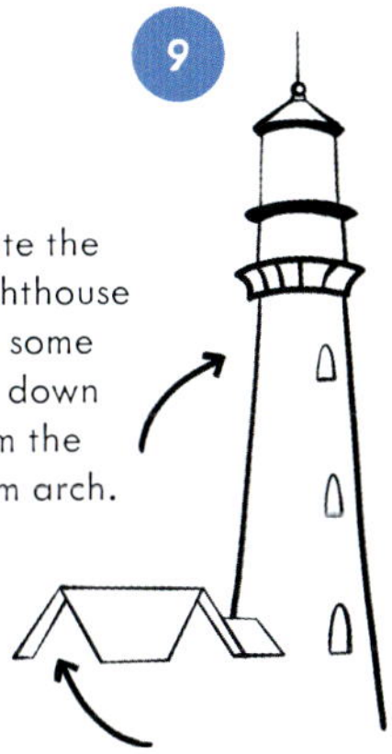

Create the tall lighthouse with some lines down from the bottom arch.

Make two more diagonal lines inside the roof to add depth.

10

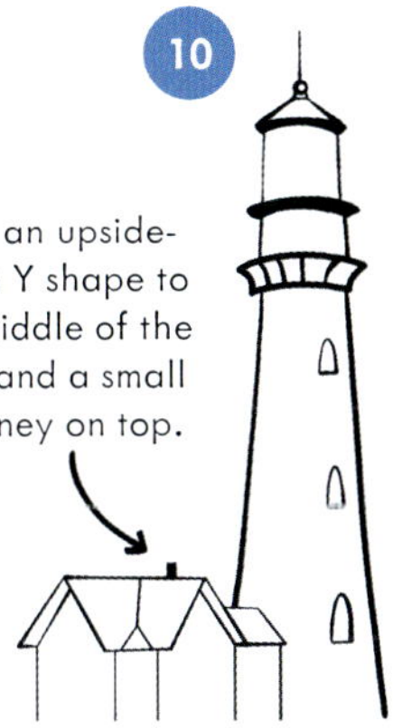

Add an upside-down Y shape to the middle of the roof and a small chimney on top.

Draw vertical lines down from the roof to make the walls. Make sure the bottom is even with the bottom of the lighthouse.

11

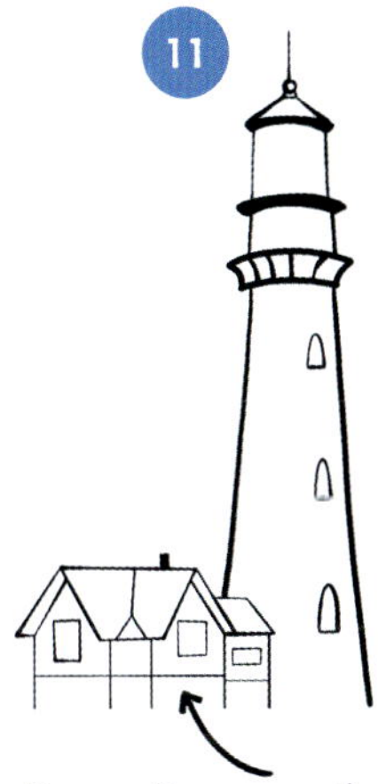

Draw a line across the middle of the house. Add some windows under each V of the roof and on the small side of the house.

12

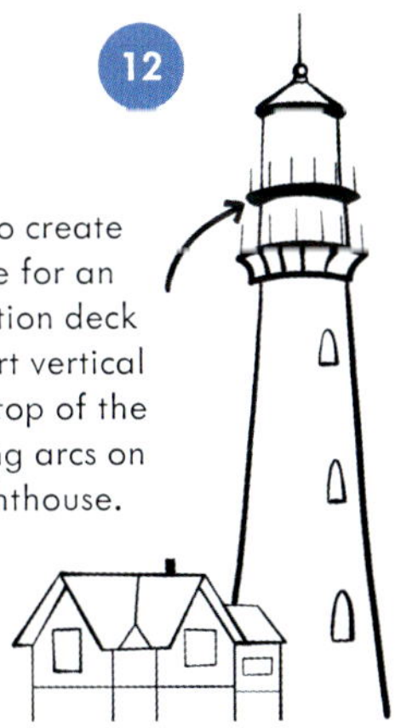

Begin to create a fence for an observation deck with short vertical lines on top of the remaining arcs on the lighthouse.

13

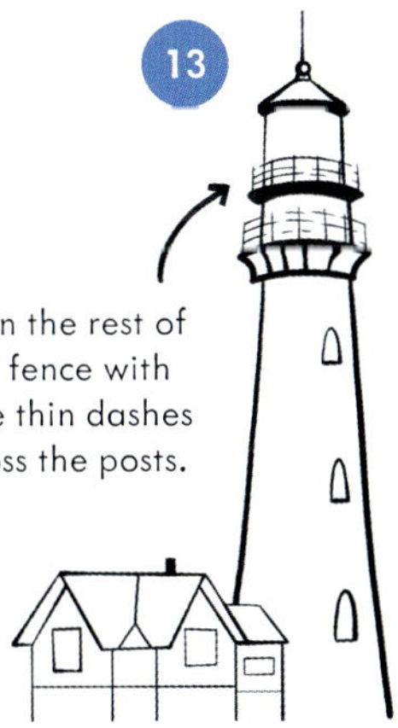

Fill in the rest of the fence with some thin dashes across the posts.

14

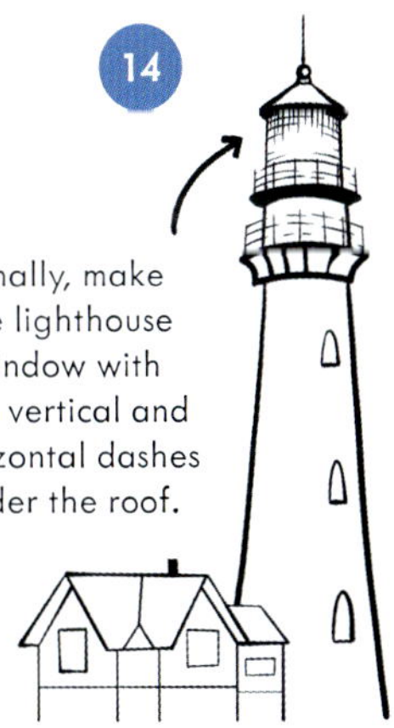

Finally, make the lighthouse window with thin vertical and horizontal dashes under the roof.

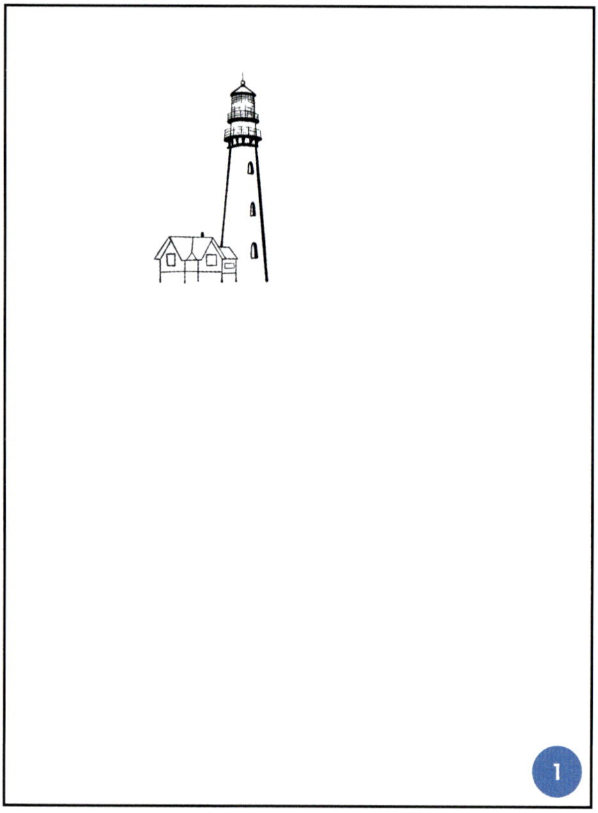
1

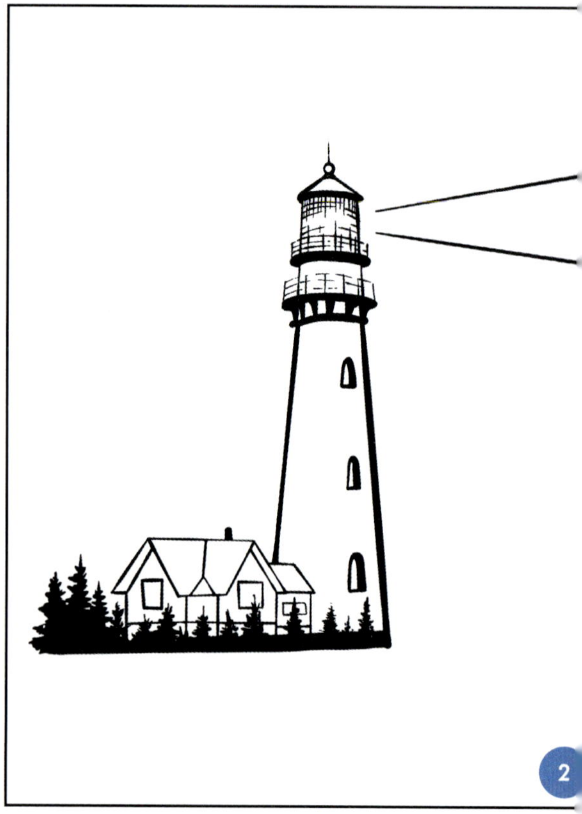
2

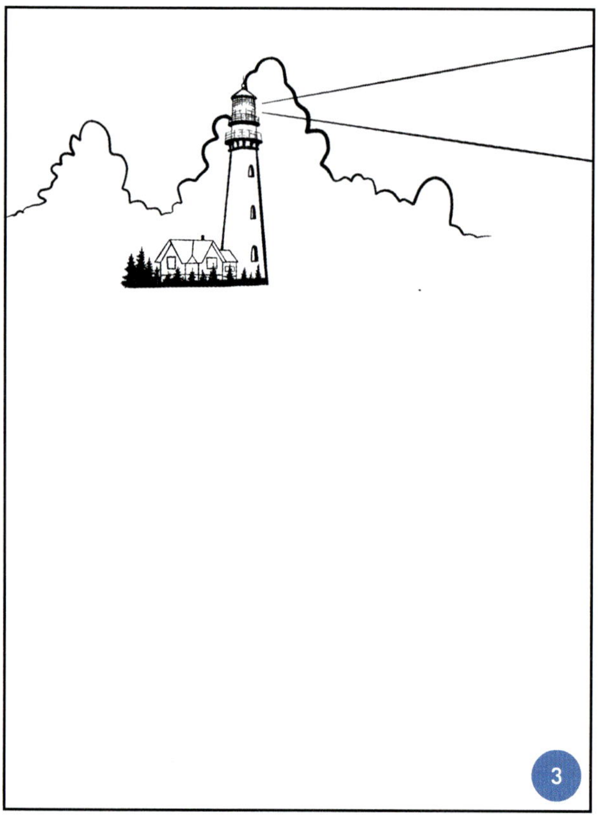
3

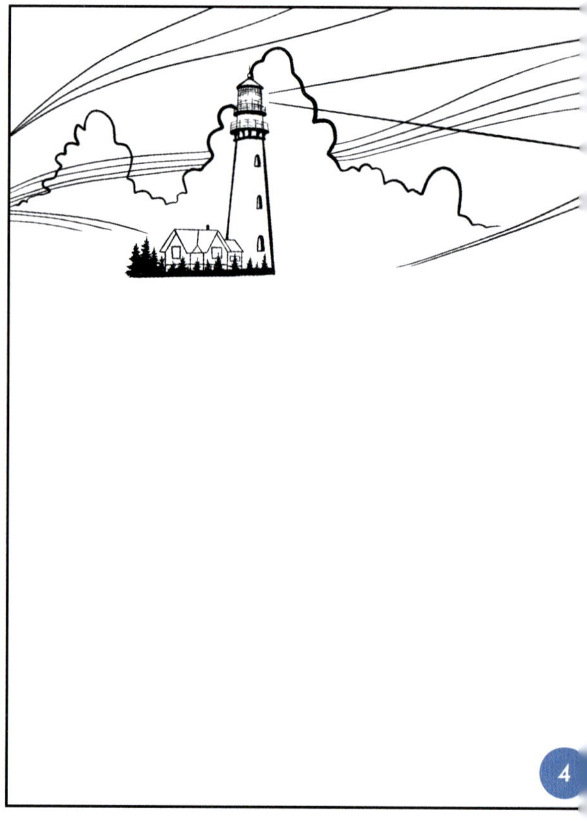
4

Now, Let's Draw the Scene

(See full image on page 124)

1. Put a Lighthouse (page 125) in the upper left side of the frame.

2. Draw a dark scribbly tree line with Simple Pine Trees (page 58) along the bottom of the lighthouse. Create a beam of light with two diagonal lines coming out of the lighthouse window, widening them as they get further away.

3. Add a large cloud shape with an irregular puffy line behind the lighthouse scene, creating peaks and valleys within.

4. Create a foggy sky by drawing waving lines coming across the scene starting from a point on the upper left of the frame. Let them overlap in front of and behind the cloud and lighthouse beam.

(continued)

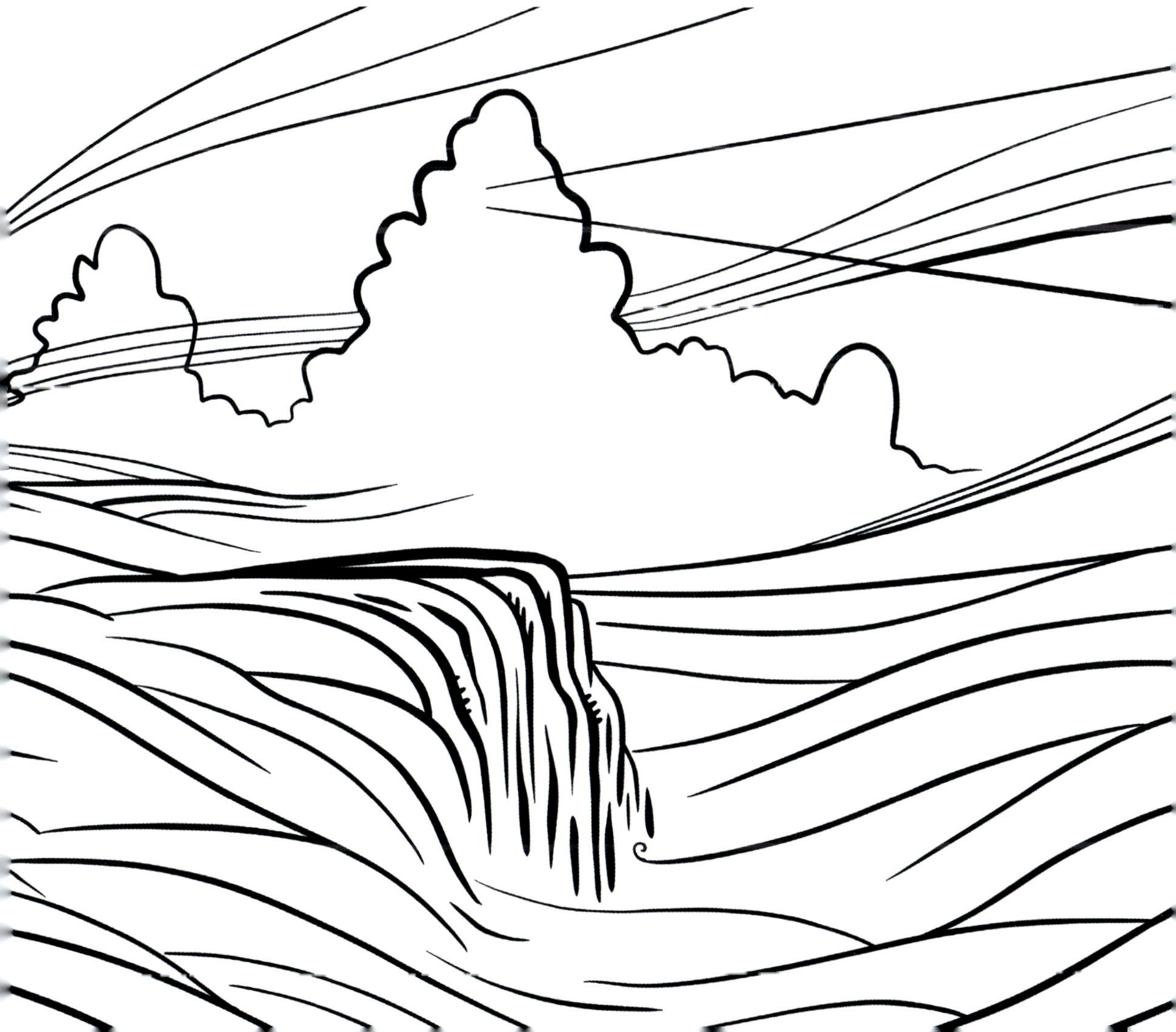

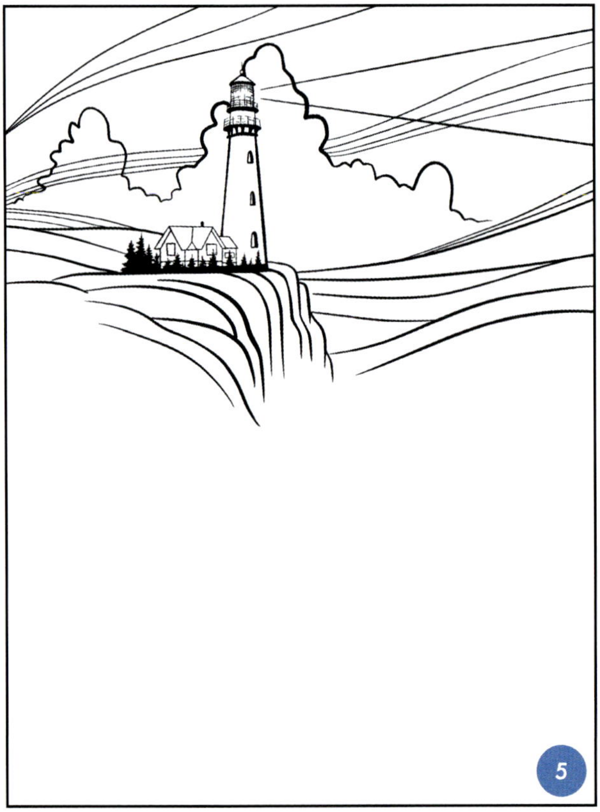
5

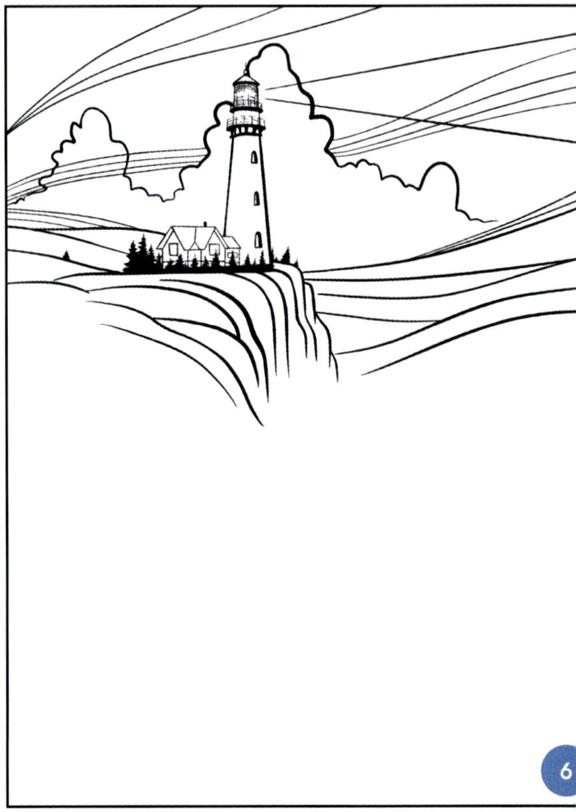
6

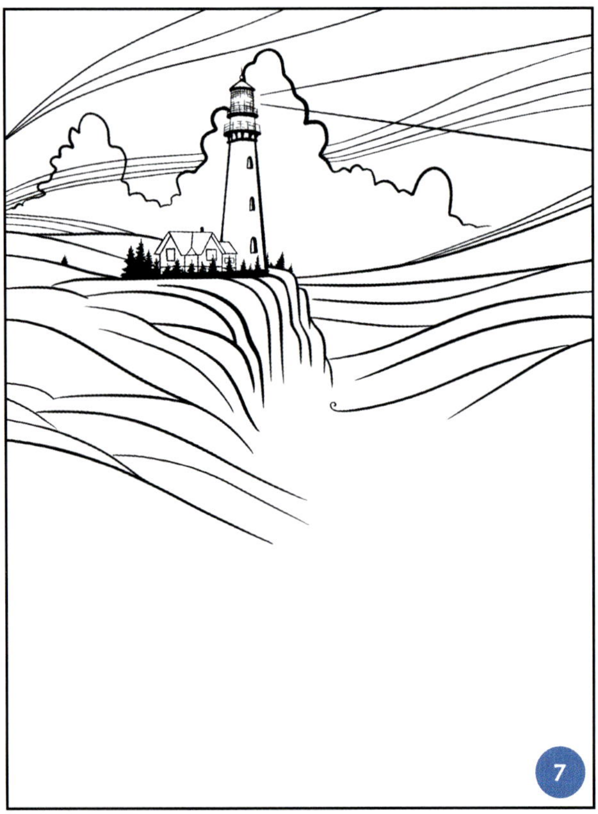
7

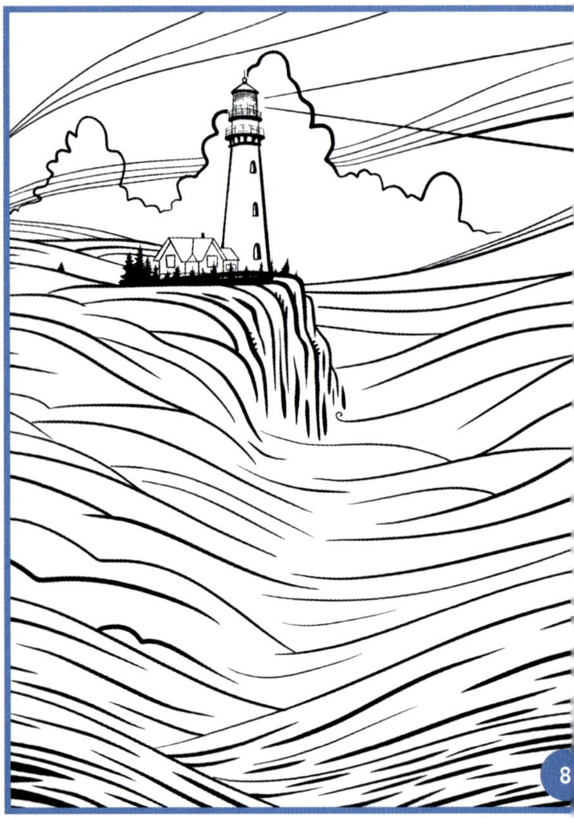
8

Now, Let's Draw the Scene (Final Steps)

5. Make a cliffside peeking out of the fog! Draw horizontal lines from the left of the page that turn sharply down just past the end of the lighthouse. Add some more foggy lines coming from behind the cliff.

6. Add a few more tiny pine trees along the cliff-side.

7. Continue to draw rolling fog banks with more lines that come in from the left and right side of the frame, dropping down the edge of the cliff into where the ocean will be. Add a small spiral or two for a swirling effect.

8. Continue this pattern of swooping lines to complete the fog bank. Let some lines on the left and right sides overlap and leave gaps in the center to indicate the shrouded ocean. This landscape is surrounded by fog so be confident with these lines to really embody its essence!

Add shading to the cliff and the bottom of your frame to add more perspective and depth.

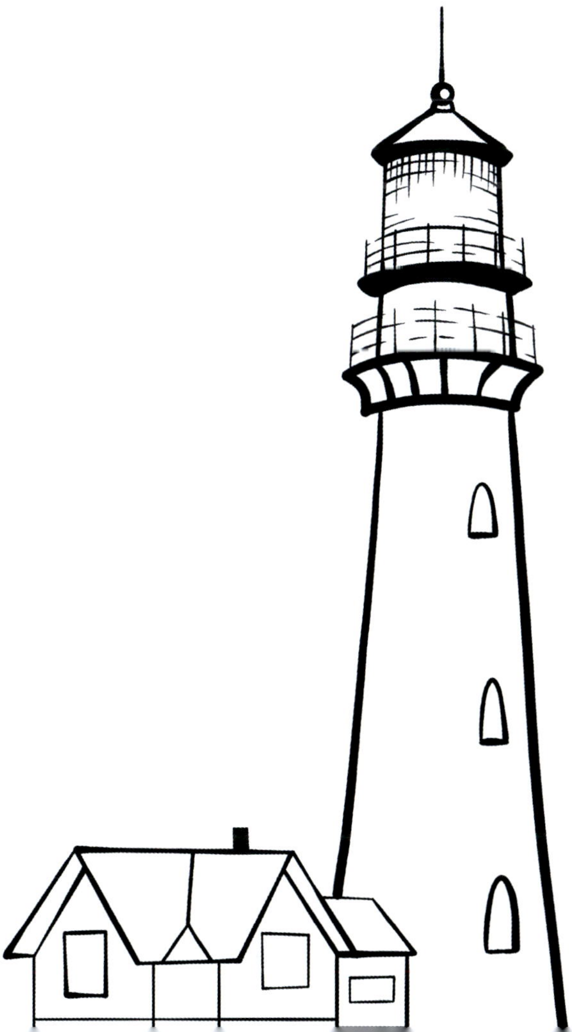

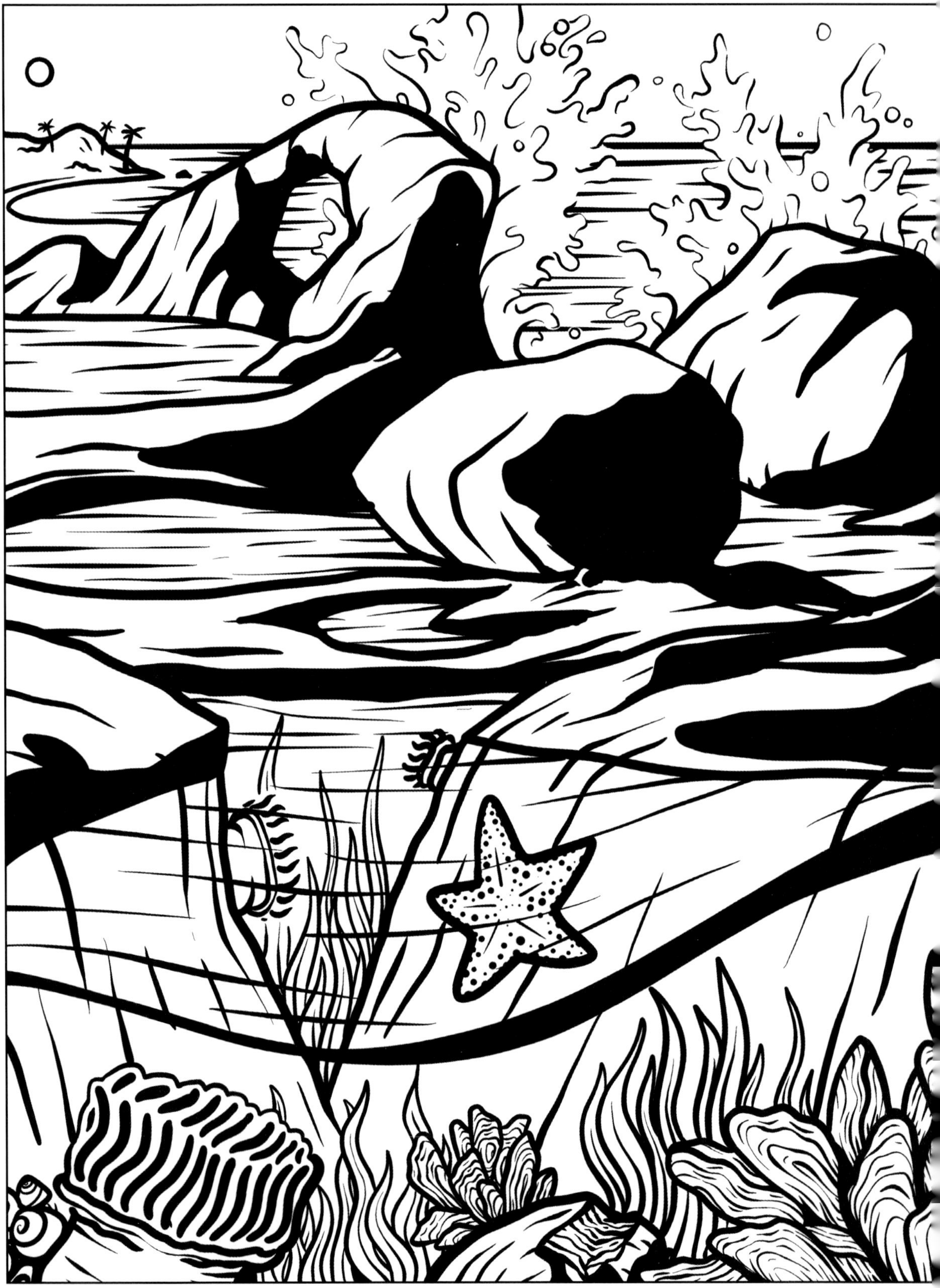

4. Otherworldly Tide Pools

As the tide recedes, the coastline undergoes a magical transformation. Where waves once crashed against the rocks, a hidden realm emerges: the tide pools. These miniature aquariums, sculpted by the rhythmic dance of the ocean, reveal a world teeming with life. Sunlight dappled pools become havens for an array of marine creatures, each clinging to life in this ever-changing environment.

Here, nestled amongst the smooth, sun-warmed rocks, you'll find curious Sea Stars (page 134), their arms reaching out like tiny suns. Sea Anemones (page 137), resembling vibrant flowers, sway gently in the currents. Timid Sea Snails peek out from their spiraled homes (page 135), while clusters of Oysters (page 136) cling stubbornly to the rocky walls. The tide pools are a symphony of textures and colors, a testament to the resilience and diversity of life found within the intertidal zone.

With a focus on capturing the unique shapes and textures of these creatures, you'll learn to recreate this hidden world on paper. So, grab your pencils and prepare to be enchanted by the mesmerizing beauty of the tide pools.

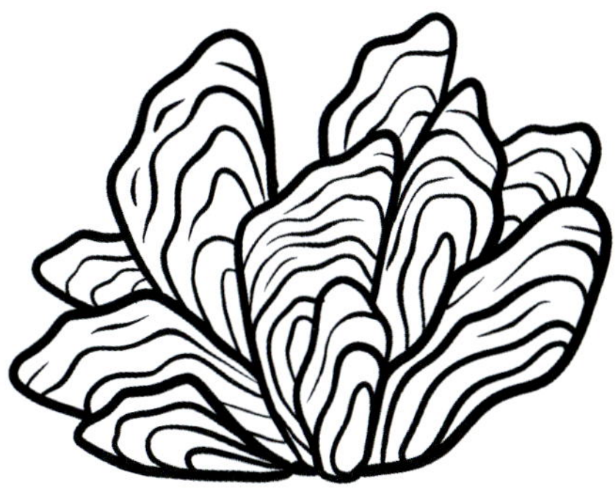

Sea Star

The tide pools teem with fascinating creatures, each playing a vital role in this miniature ecosystem. Amongst these curious inhabitants lies the sea star, an enigma with its radiating arms and star-shaped form. Often adorned with vibrant colors and intriguing textures, the sea star is a true marvel of the underwater world.

1

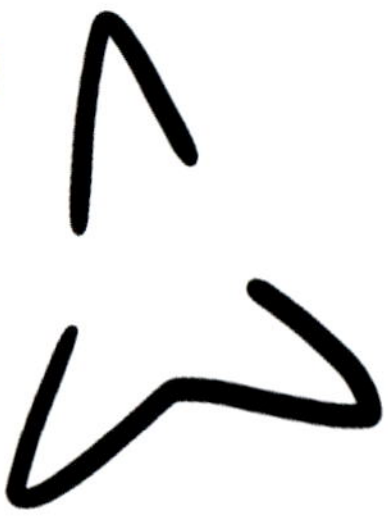

Begin with a wide W shape and an upside-down V above it.

2

Connect those two shapes with some sea star arms on each side.

3

Add five small dashes coming out from the center of the sea star that go through each arm.

4

Add a few dots throughout the sea star's center.

5

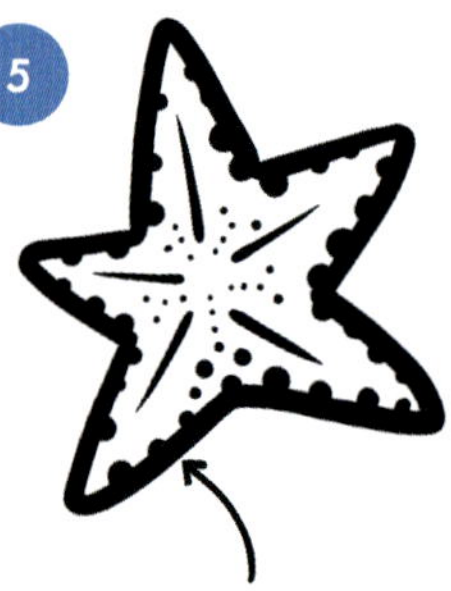

Draw bigger dots on the outline edges of the sea star.

6

Fill the rest of the space in the sea star with more small dots.

Sea Snails

The tide pools are bustling with life, not just with flamboyant creatures, but also with the unassuming sea snail. These tiny architects carrying their intricately spiraled homes on their backs, leave their mark on the rocky landscape.

1

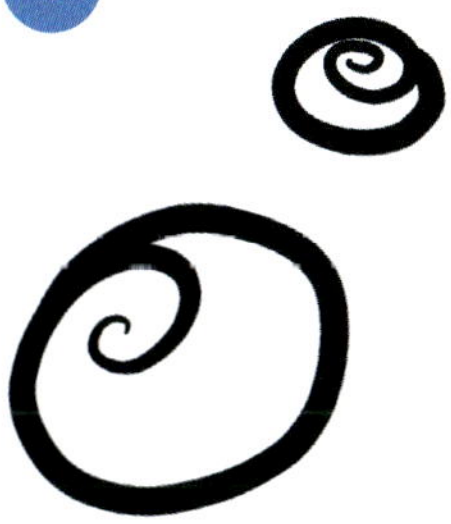

Draw a few circles with a small spiral coming from the top of each.

2

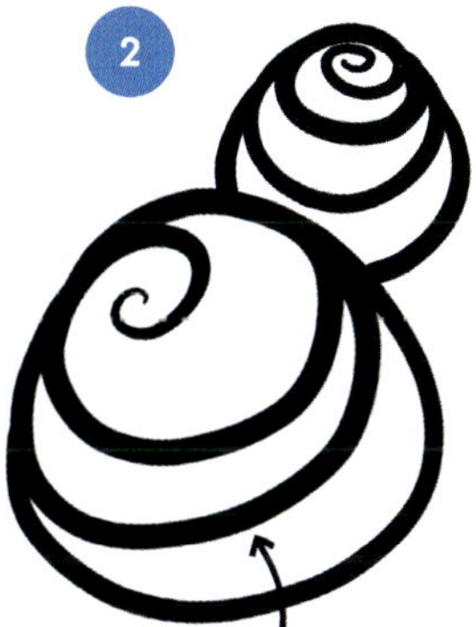

Draw a few half circles around the bottom of the initial circles.

3

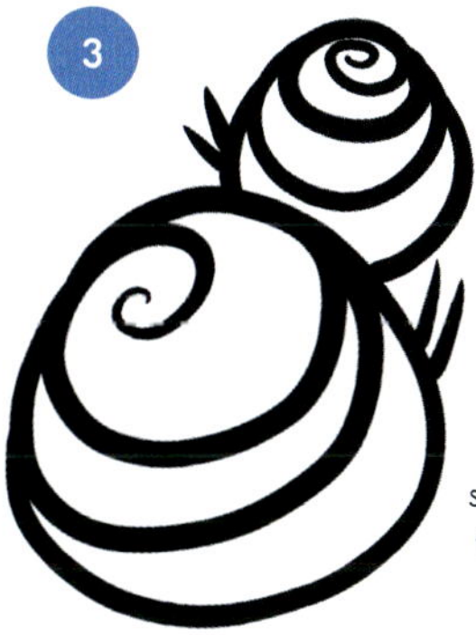

Add some small antenna to the side of each shell.

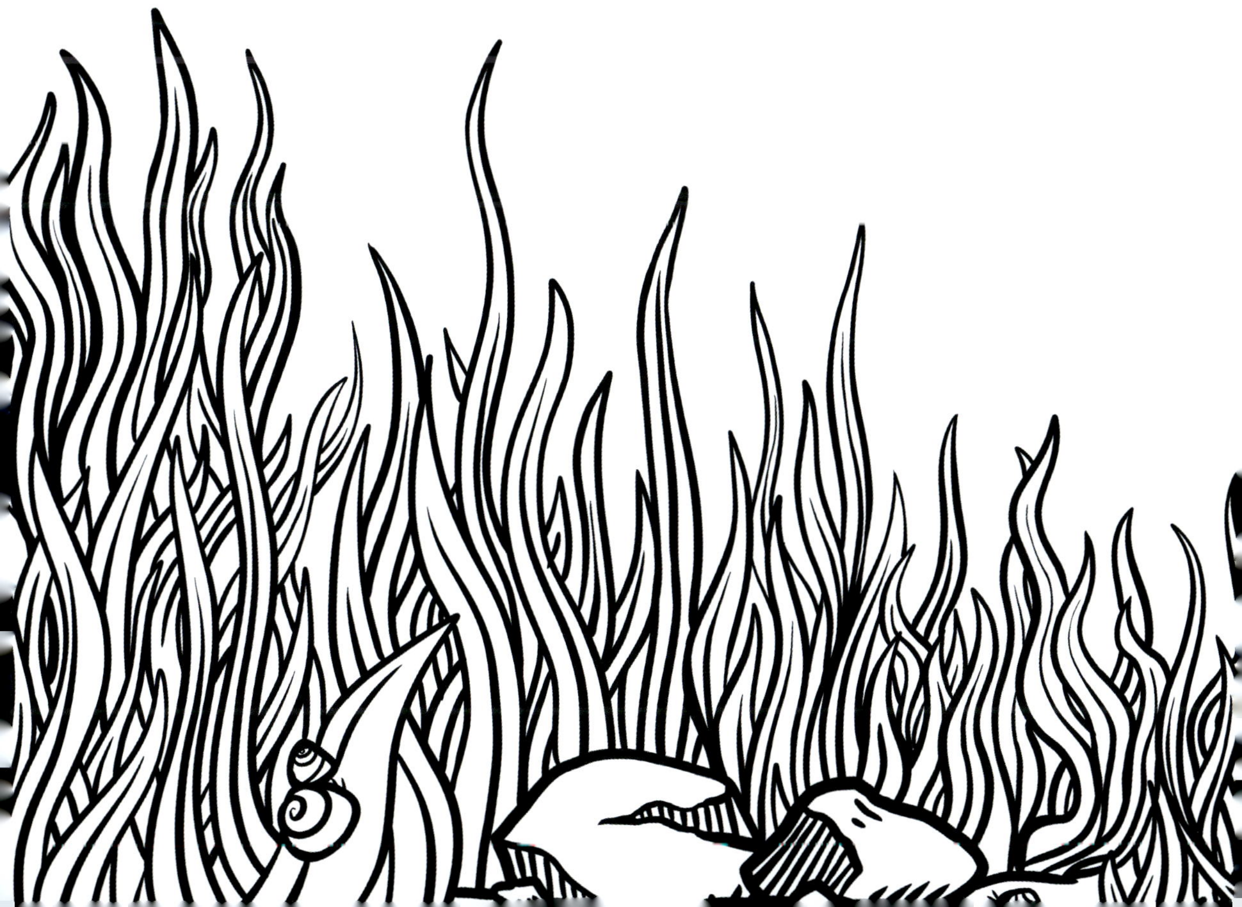

Oyster

The tide pools are a treasure trove of life, with each creature playing a part in this vibrant ecosystem. Amongst the rocks, we find the oyster, a fascinating mollusk with a uniquely textured shell. These layered homes provide protection while the oyster filters the water, keeping the tide pool healthy.

In this section, we'll focus on capturing the essence of the oyster's form. Using a combination of overlapping shapes and simple lines, you'll learn to recreate the layered effect of the oyster shell, bringing these fascinating tide pool dwellers to life on your page.

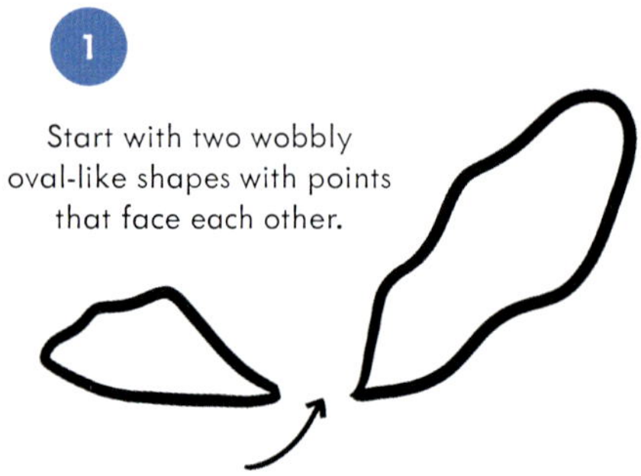

Leave some space in between the shapes.

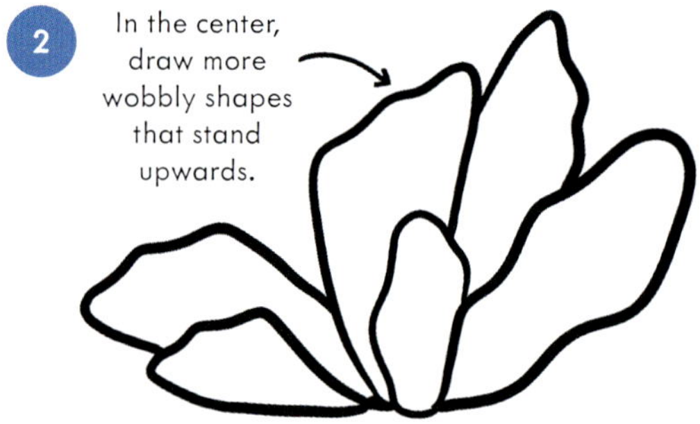

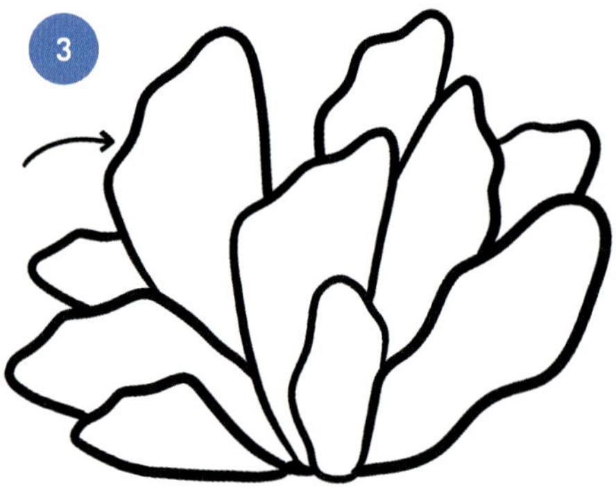

Layer more of these shapes behind and between the others, varying their size and shape.

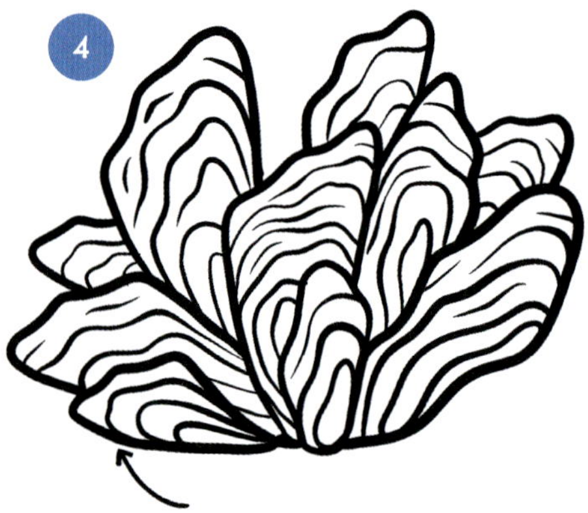

Fill in the oysters with layers of lines that organically follow their outer shape. These create the texture of growth rings on the shells.

Sea Anemone

Sea anemone are fascinating organisms, with their flowing tentacles resembling vibrant flowers swaying in the current. And they hold a surprising secret: They're not plants at all, but cunning predators! Their soft bodies and flowing tentacles can snag unsuspecting prey. In this lesson, we'll focus on capturing the deceptive beauty of the sea anemone. We'll move beyond a simple silhouette, exploring techniques to create the anemone's characteristic form—a soft, rounded body crowned with a wild array of tentacles. Prepare to be surprised as we unveil the deceptive hunter of the tide pools: the sea anemone!

1

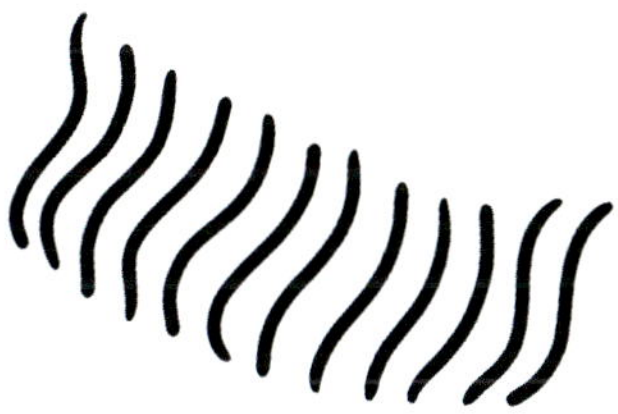

Begin with some waving S-like vertical lines that follow along a line.

2

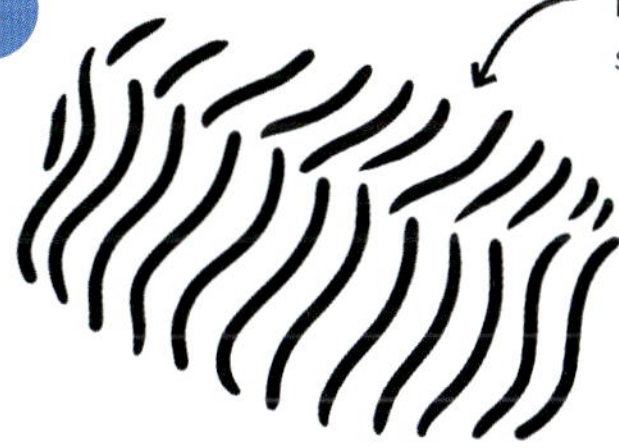

Add a few smaller wavy lines right above the first set of lines, making them form a slightly rounded shape on top.

3

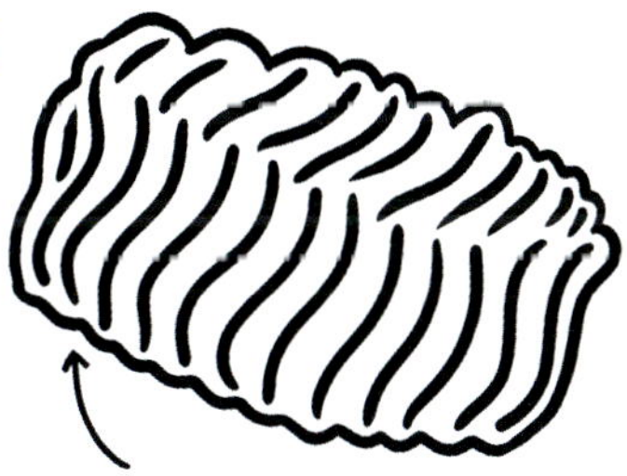

Trace an outline around all the lines you created.

4

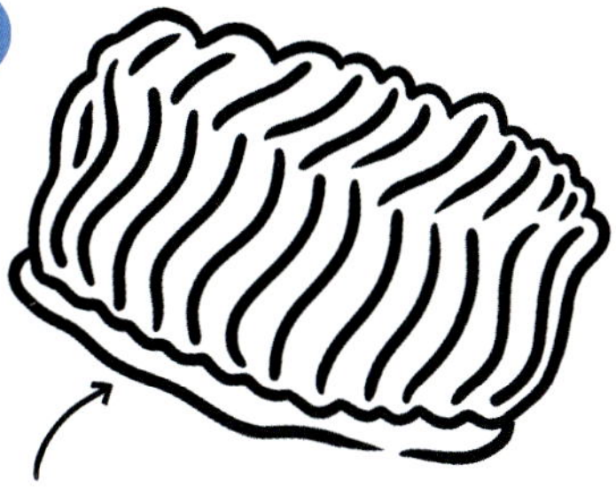

Add a narrow oval bottom to the underside of the shape.

5

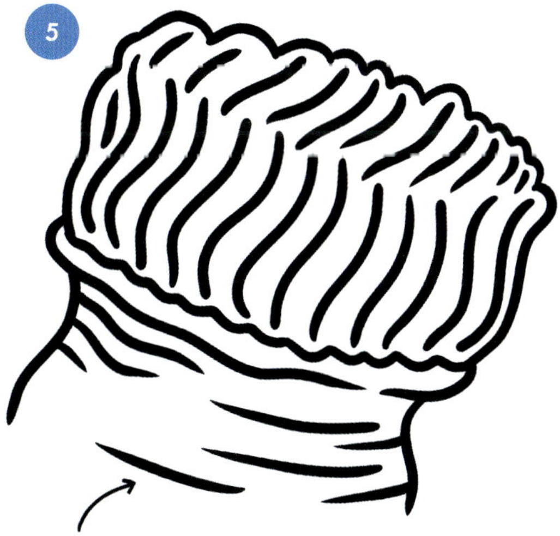

For the end, draw two lines down each side of the narrow oval then add dashes from each line toward the center.

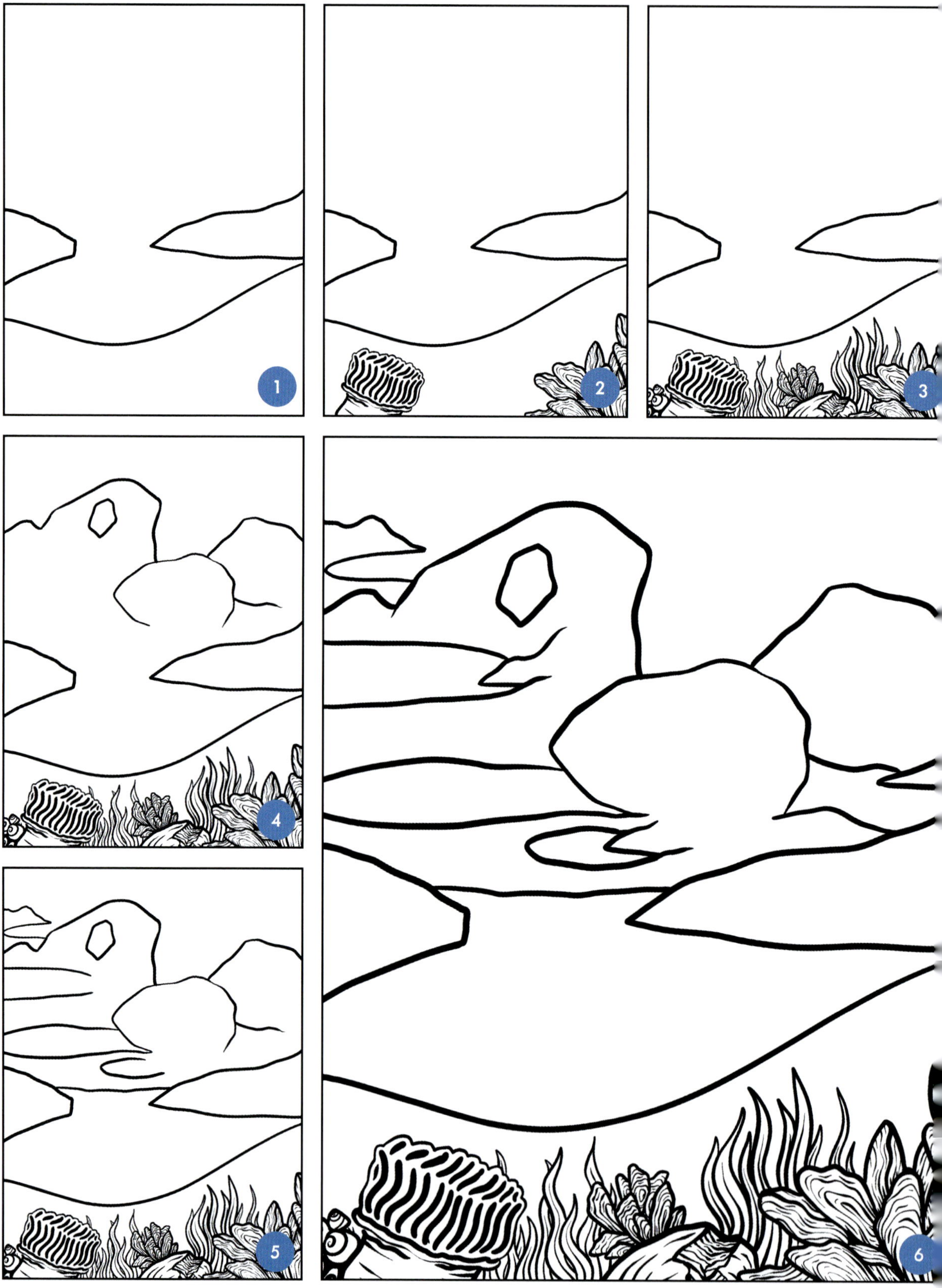
1
2
3
4
5
6

Now, Let's Draw the Scene

(See full image on page 132)

1. Start with a wavy line along the bottom third of your frame that ends higher on the right. Put an irregular sideways V pointing out from the left and right sides of your frame above the line.

2. Add a Sea Anemone (page 137) and a cluster of Oysters (page 136) along the bottom of the frame.

3. Continue to build your tidepool with some swirling Sea Snails (page 135), rocks and wavy S-shaped kelp fronds.

4. Above the horizontal V shapes, draw the beginning of three bumpy rocks with a small hole in one.

5. Add a horizontal line in between the V shapes. Draw some narrow sideways U shapes on the left side of the frame. Add a wiggling line along the top to create a faraway coastline.

6. Turn the U shapes into tidepools by drawing sideways Vs with their points facing left. Add more ground lines underneath the other rocks.

(continued)

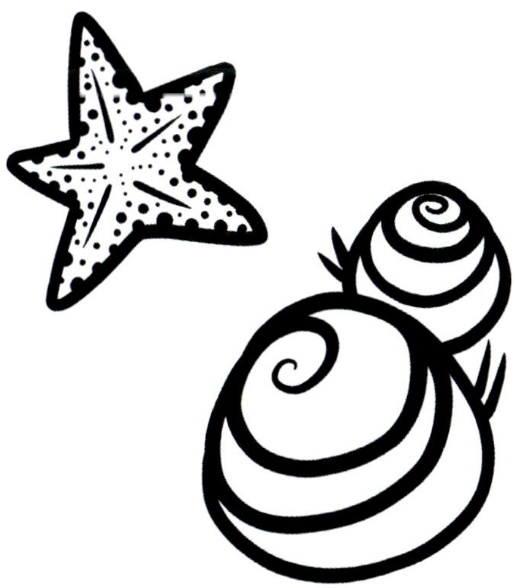

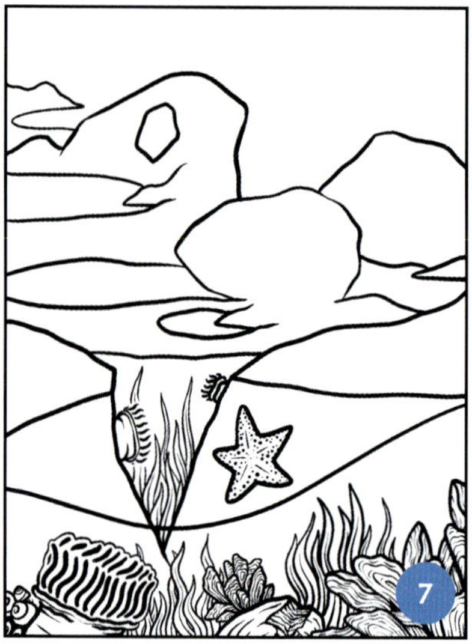
7

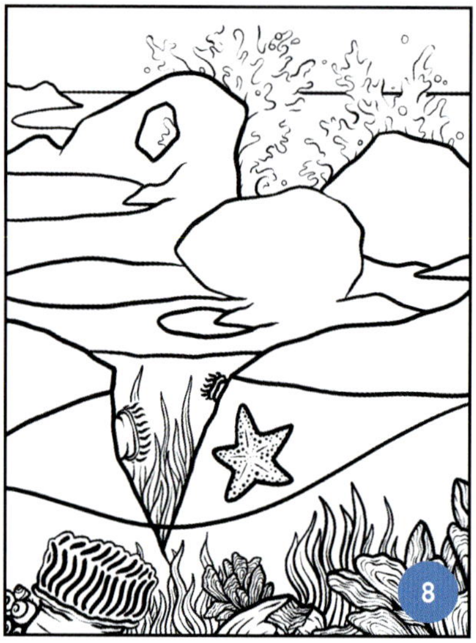
8

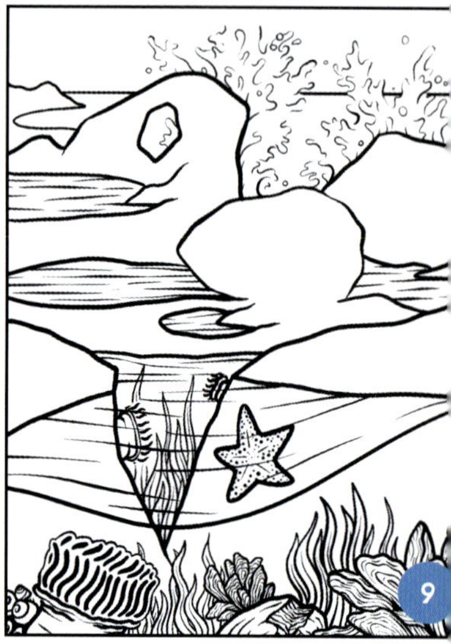
9

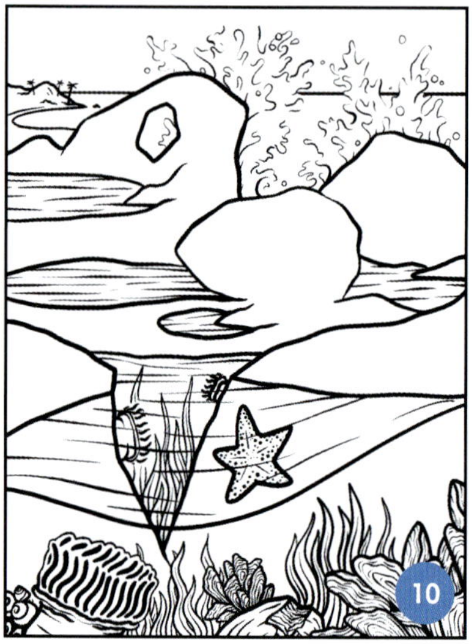
10

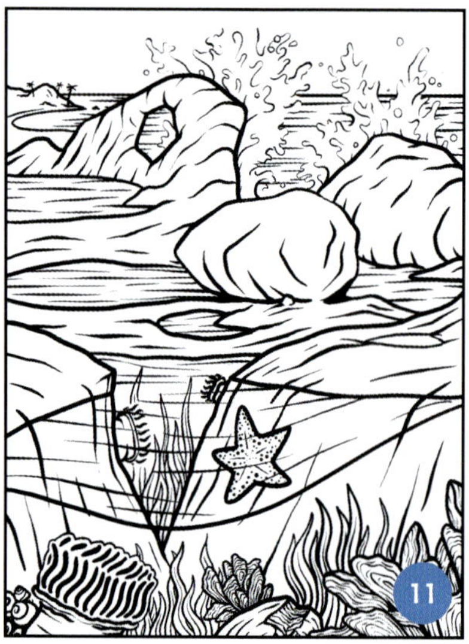
11

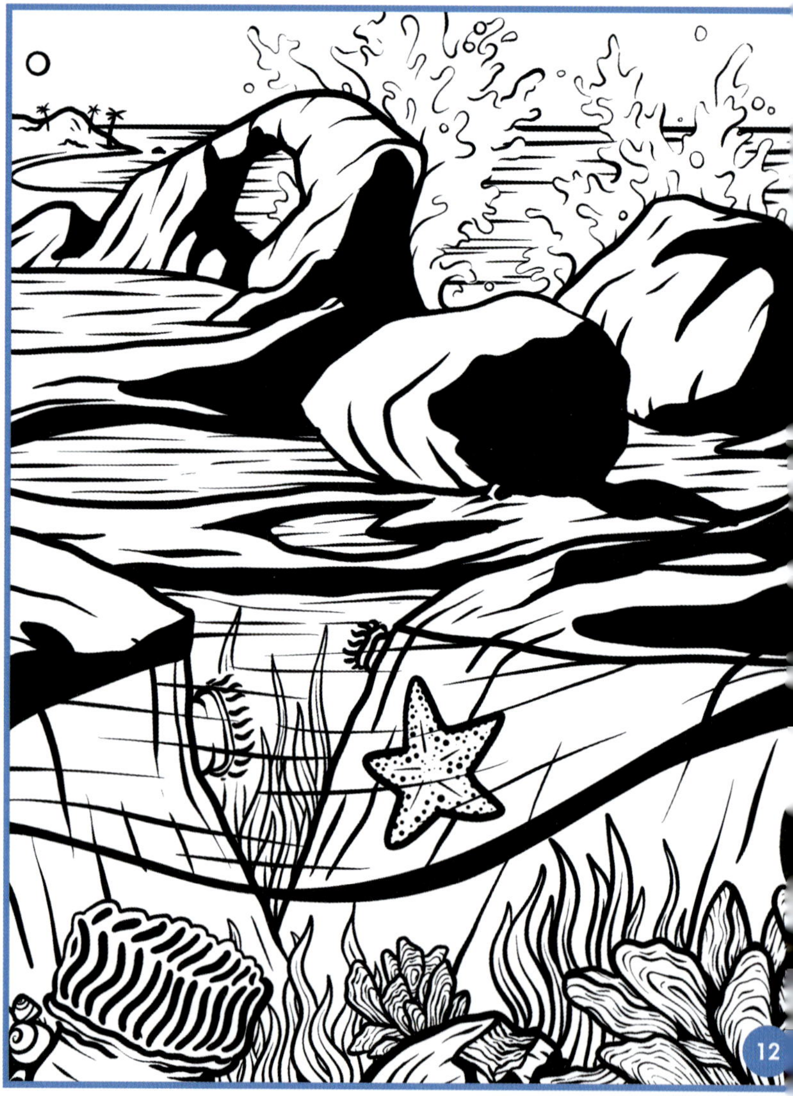
12

Now, Let's Draw the Scene (Final Steps)

7. From the two horizontal V shapes in the foreground, draw a V to make the bottom of the tidepool. Add some small anemones to these lines and some kelp in the area between. Add a happy Sea Star (page 134) to the side of one rock in the tidepool.

8. Create some splashing Waves (page 43) coming up from behind the rocks with sporadic wavy lines and small circles. Draw a horizon line behind your splashing waves.

9. Draw horizontal ripples on the top of the tidepools. Drawing these on top of the sea creatures in the closest tidepool while avoiding the area under the wavy line in the foreground will create the illusion they are submerged underwater!

10. Add a shoreline with a small line curving alongside the coastline you drew in step 5. Then add some tiny palm trees and rocks on the distant coast.

11. Build texture on your rocky surfaces with strokes following their general shapes, and add light horizontal strokes to the ocean.

12. It's finally time to add shadows! Put a circular sun in the top left of the horizon, then add shading to the bottom right sides of the rocks and the tidepool creatures. Thicken the initial wavy line you created to complete the piece.

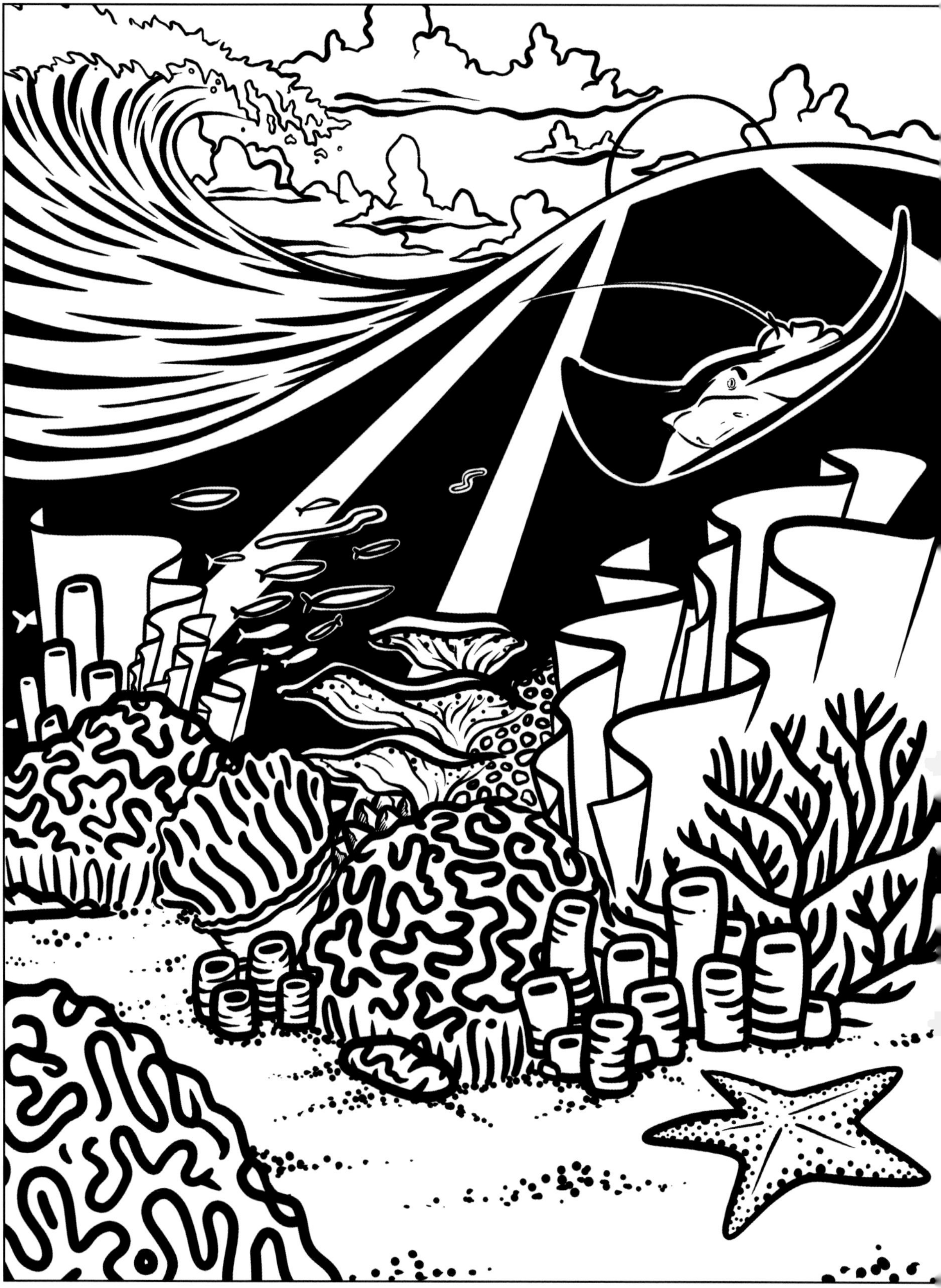

5. Thriving Shallow Reef

Sunlight dances on the water's surface, dappling the vibrant world below. Here, beneath the waves, lies a hidden city—a thriving shallow reef teeming with life. Colonies of colorful coral, sculpted by nature and life itself, rise from the seabed, creating a fascinating metropolis. Within their intricate structures, a dazzling array of creatures find sanctuary. From graceful fish darting in and out of the coral branches to majestic Manta Rays (page 149) gliding effortlessly through the water, each inhabitant plays a vital role in maintaining the delicate balance of this underwater ecosystem.

In this lesson, we'll embark on a journey to translate the wonders of the shallow reef onto paper. We'll explore techniques for drawing a variety of its fascinating residents, from the sprawling Fan Coral (page 144) with its flowing fronds to the Schools of Fish (page 148) shimmering in the sunlit water. Prepare to be amazed by the intricate beauty and vibrant tapestry of life found within this hidden city: the thriving shallow reef.

But this exploration goes beyond simply replicating the shapes we see. As you progress through this tutorial, you'll gain valuable artistic skills. You'll learn how to use complex stacking to create the illusion of depth within the coral colonies. We'll explore composition-splitting techniques to ensure your drawing balances the vibrant coral with the open water and its inhabitants. Finally, you'll master the art of depicting light and shadow underwater, capturing the unique way sunlight filters through the water and illuminates the diverse life forms of the reef. So, grab your pencils and prepare to dive into the diverse world of the shallow reef—a world waiting to be depicted on paper!

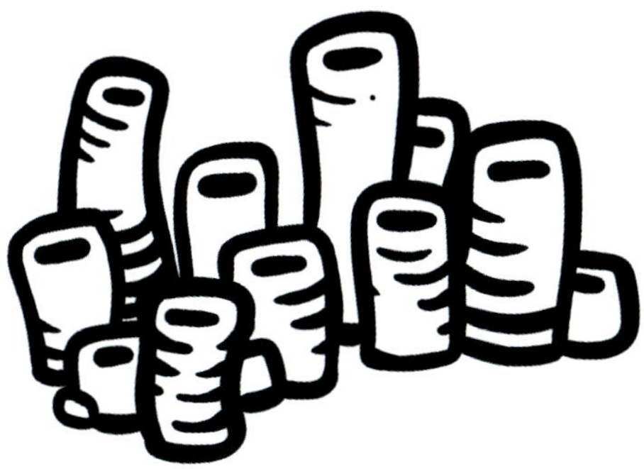

Fan Coral

Fan coral, a marvel of nature's engineering, stands out in the vibrant shallow reef. Unlike its rock-like cousins, fan coral sways gently, its countless branches forming a delicate net to ensnare tiny plankton, a vital food source. But fan coral doesn't work alone—microscopic algae live within its branches, providing the coral with nutrients through a fascinating symbiotic relationship. In this section, we'll translate this detailed design into line art, focusing on techniques to capture the strong central stalk, the multitude of branching fronds and the intricate details that make fan coral a true testament to nature's artistry.

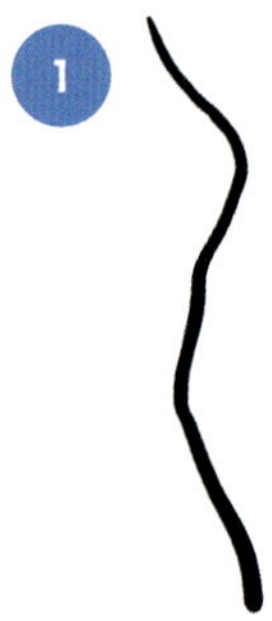

Begin with a wiggly vertical line.

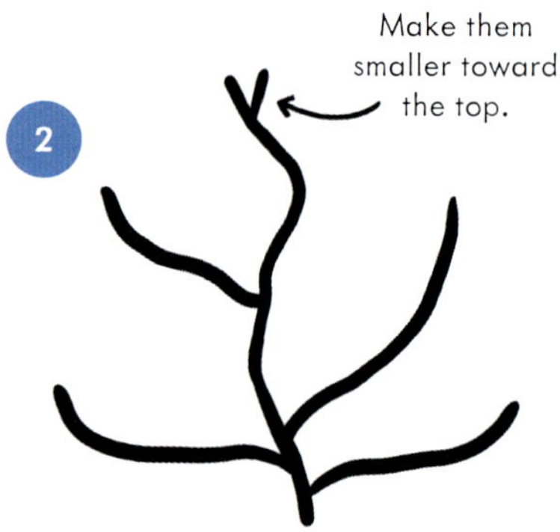

Add branching wiggly lines along the sides of the vertical line.

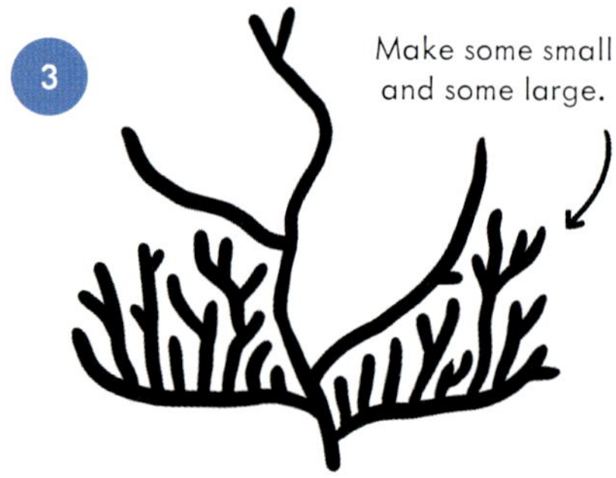

From the bottom lines, add small vertical branches coming up.

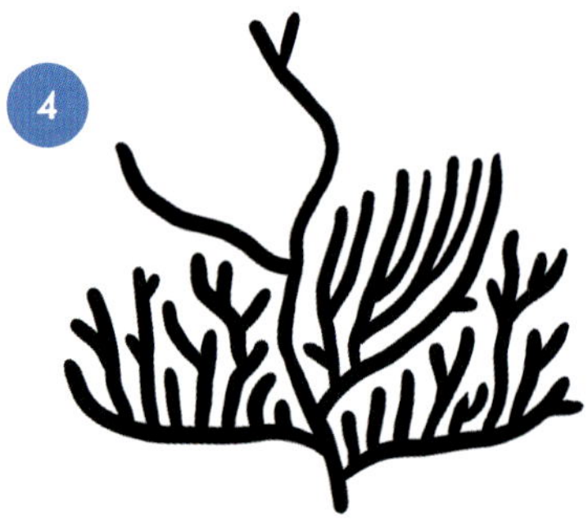

Continue this pattern with longer coral lines coming up from the next branches. Let these branches naturally fill in the shape between the center and side branches.

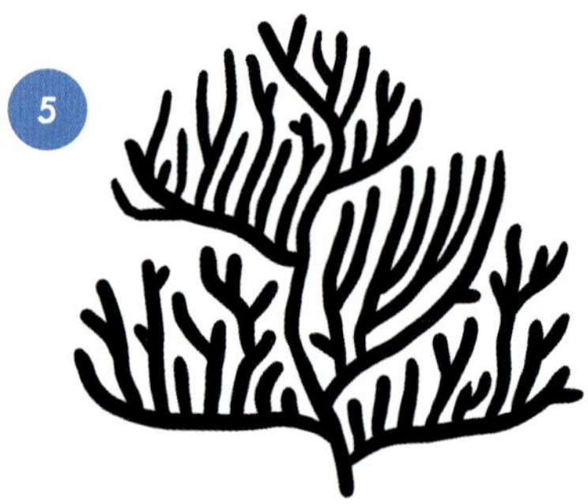

Fill the remaining space in the coral with more branches in various lengths and shapes, keeping them wiggly and natural to create a waving fan coral.

Tube Coral

The shallow reef thrives on a diversity of residents, each playing a vital role. Tube coral, unlike its fan-shaped neighbor, offers a different kind of beauty—a cluster of interconnected tubes creating a miniature underwater city. In this section, we'll explore techniques for capturing this unique form, from the initial cluster of openings to the rounded caps and textured details that make tube coral a fascinating addition to the reef's artistic landscape.

1

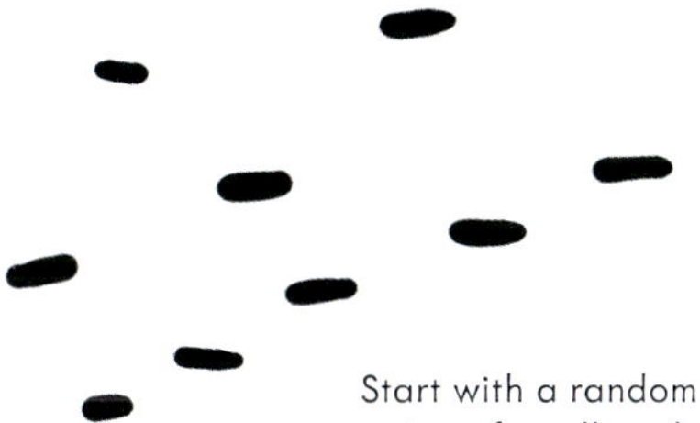

Start with a random grouping of small ovals for the tops of the tubes.

2

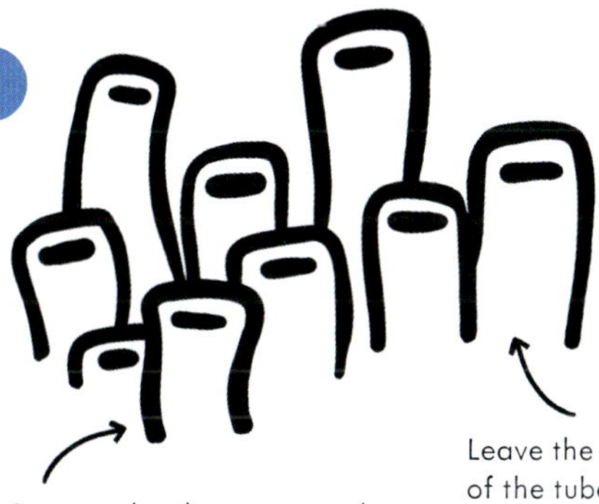

Create tube shapes around each oval that overlap and layer to make a cluster.

Leave the bottoms of the tubes open.

3

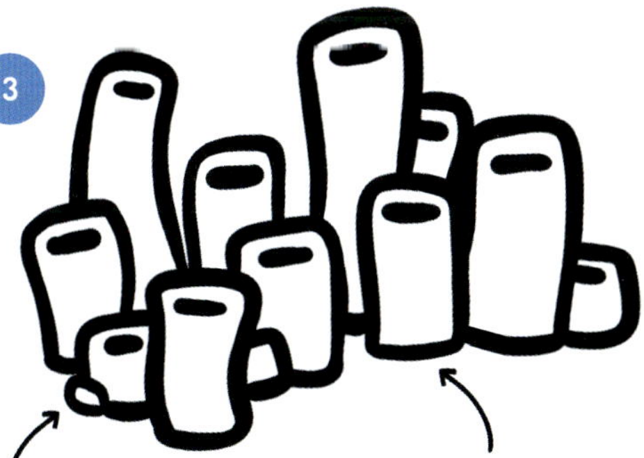

Draw small pebbles along the bottom.

Add round caps to the bottoms of the tubes.

4

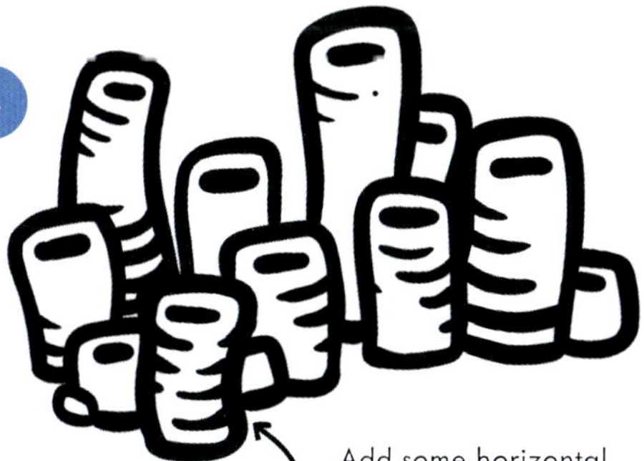

Add some horizontal dashes coming from the sides of each tube for added texture.

Lettuce Coral

The shallow reef boasts a stunning variety of coral formations, each with its own unique character. Lettuce coral, aptly named for its resemblance to leafy greens, adds a touch of whimsical texture to the underwater landscape. Unlike its smooth-branched neighbors, lettuce coral features a series of overlapping folds and cascading fronds, creating an interplay of light and shadow. In this section, we'll delve into the artistic details of lettuce coral. We'll explore techniques for capturing the layered structure, from the initial, slightly diagonal line that forms the base to the cascading downward dashes that create depth and texture. Prepare to be mesmerized by the intricate folds and flowing lines that make lettuce coral a captivating addition to your reef drawing!

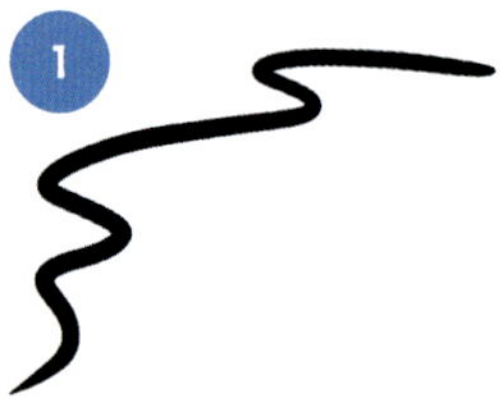

Draw a wiggly line that's slightly diagonal across your frame.

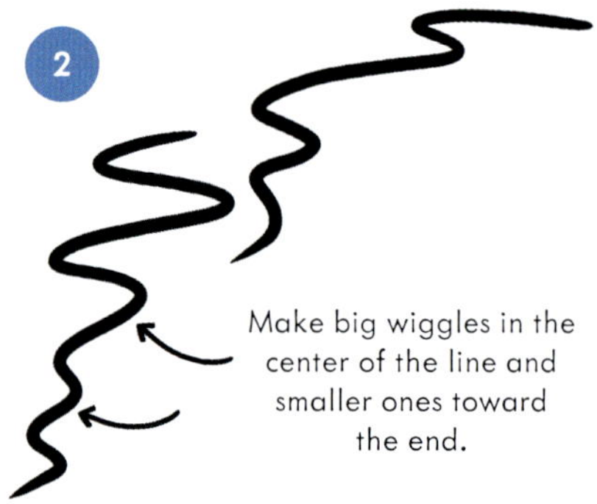

Add another wiggle underneath the first.

Make big wiggles in the center of the line and smaller ones toward the end.

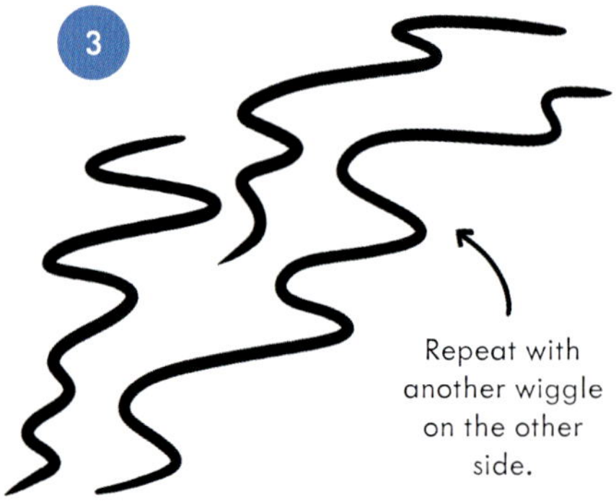

Repeat with another wiggle on the other side.

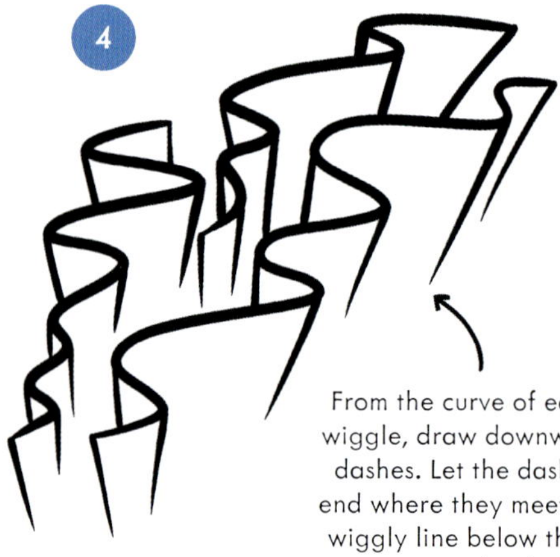

From the curve of each wiggle, draw downward dashes. Let the dashes end where they meet the wiggly line below them to create depth in your layers.

Brain Coral

The ocean depths hold a treasure trove of fascinating creatures, and brain coral is a true marvel. Unlike its soft-bodied relatives, brain coral boasts a hard, skeletal structure that resembles, you guessed it, a brain! This intricate form, covered in winding grooves and folds, provides a vital home for countless marine animals. Today's lesson will equip you with the skills to represent this underwater wonder on paper. We'll start by building the basic form and then delve into the details that make brain coral so unique. Are you ready to dive in and explore the secrets of the brain coral?

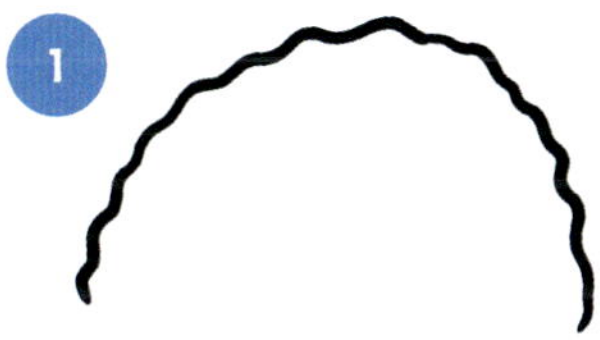

Start with an arc covered in small bumps.

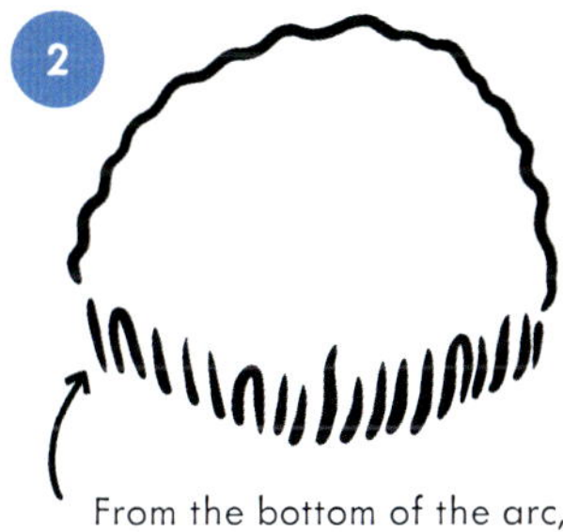

From the bottom of the arc, add small vertical dashes and some upside-down U shapes.

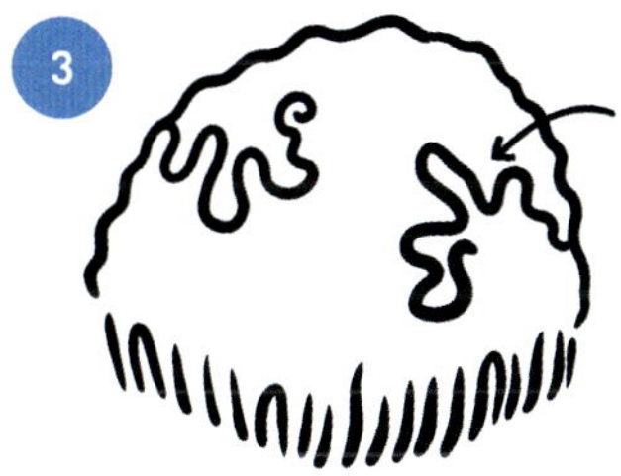

Begin your brain-like texture with two randomly wiggling lines, letting your pen go wild to create their shape.

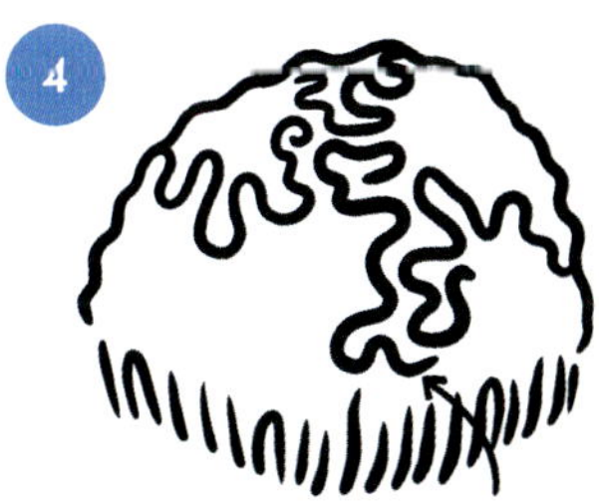

Add another wiggle in between them, making sure they don't overlap.

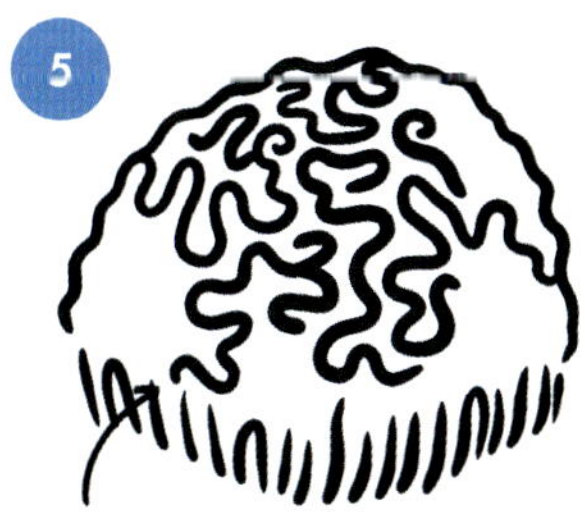

Continue with your brain-like fold with more wiggling lines throughout the shape, letting them be free and organic.

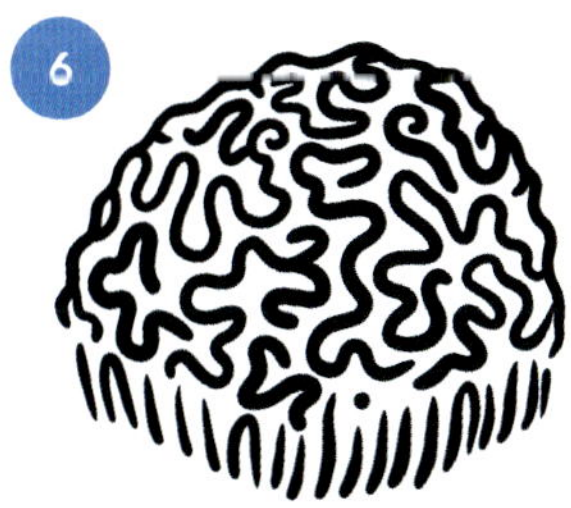

Fill in the rest of the coral with wiggles in any empty areas.

Horn Coral

The shallow reef whispers stories of the past, and horn coral stands as a testament to its rich history. Unlike its brightly colored neighbors, horn coral boasts a more subdued elegance, resembling a cluster of stacked horns. These ancient sentinels, some dating back millions of years, offer a unique architectural element to the reef.

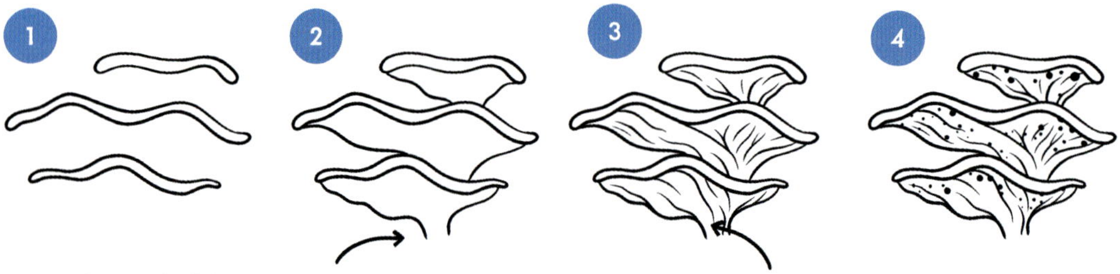

1. Begin with a stack of three worm-like shapes across the frame, leaving space in between.
2. From the ends of each worm, draw wiggly lines down to connect to the worm below. Make the bottom lines narrow and end in a slight trunk.
3. Add veiny lines to the inside of these shapes.
4. Now draw a variety of dots on these shapes to finish your coral.

School of Fish

The vibrant shallow reef teems with life, and few sights are more eye-catching than a swirling school of fish. The shimmering scales flashing in the sunlight are a testament to the collective power and beauty of these underwater creatures. In this section, we'll emulate their dynamic energy. We'll explore techniques for creating a sense of movement and flow, using a variety of shapes and sizes to bring this lively bunch to life on your page.

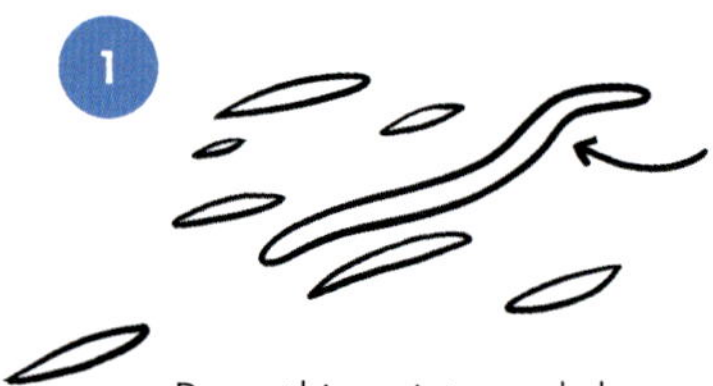

Add a wriggly worm-like shape; this could be an eel, an extra-long fish, or any other wild sea creature you could think of!

Draw thin pointy oval shapes in a random grouping, making them in a variety of sizes.

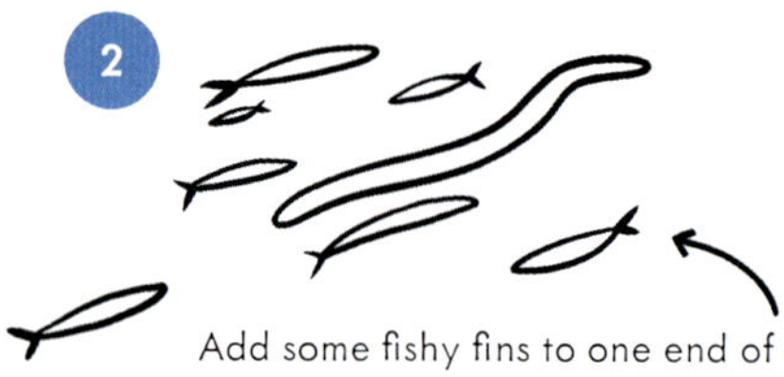

Add some fishy fins to one end of each oval shape with some small sideways Vs. Feel free to experiment with different sizes and shapes to make many different schools of fish!

Manta Ray

The shallow reef boasts a majestic resident—the manta ray. These graceful giants glide effortlessly through the water, moving with their wing-like bodies. Capturing their elegance can be approached in many ways, and this lesson offers a simplified method that integrates seamlessly into your reef scene. Remember, there's no single "right" way to draw a manta ray—feel free to experiment and personalize your creation! Here, we'll break down the manta ray's form into a series of basic shapes, allowing you to build its graceful outline and key features. We'll explore techniques for adding shading and details to bring this gentle giant to life on your page.

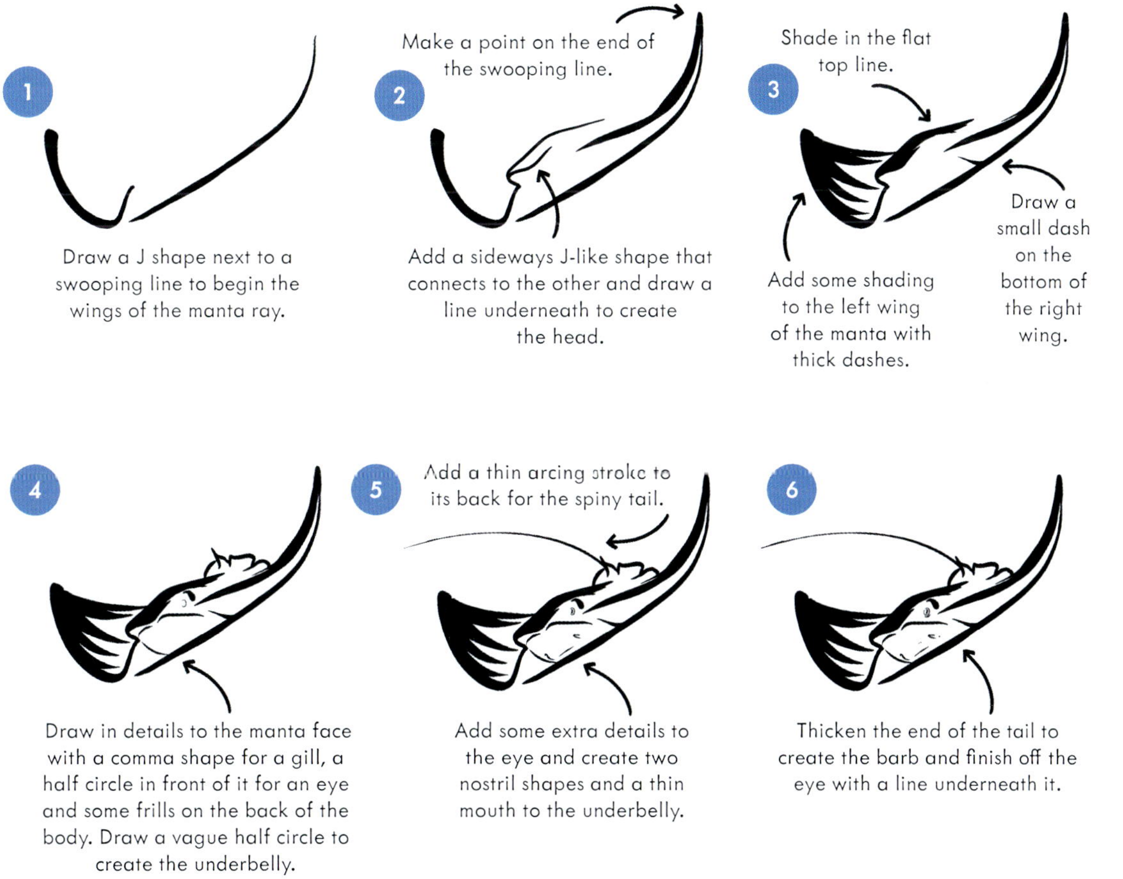

For other ideas on how to draw Manta Rays, check out the other examples given on page 151.

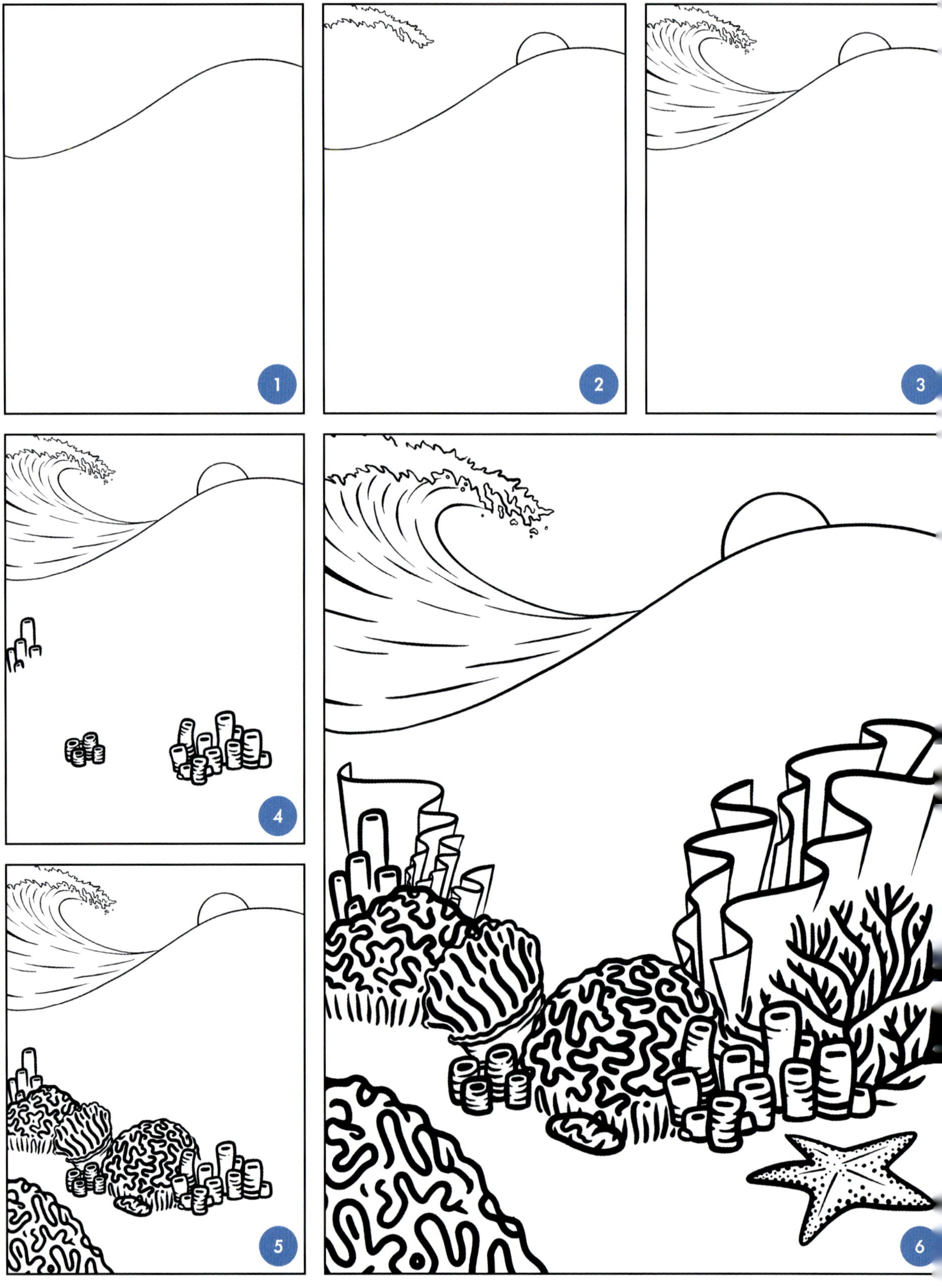
1
2
3
4
5
6

Now, Let's Draw the Scene

(See full image on page 142)

1. Start with a wavy line across the top third of the frame, with one side higher than the other.

2. Create the crest of a crashing wave in the top left corner with a scribbly arc shape. Add a sun with a semicircle on the higher part of the wave.

3. Complete your crashing wave by connecting the crest to the lower wave with an arc, then filling the arc in with strokes that follow the shape of the wave.

4. Draw a few bunches of Tube Coral (page 145) throughout the lower portion of the wave.

5. Add some Brain Coral (page 147) next to the tube coral. Throw in a Sea Anemone (page 137) between your coral families.

6. Draw a Fan Coral (page 144) on the right side of the tube corals. Put a Sea Star (page 134) in front and some Lettuce Coral (page 146) behind them.

(continued)

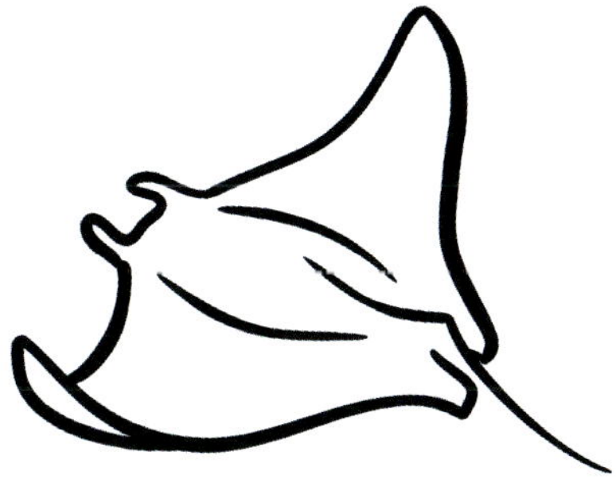

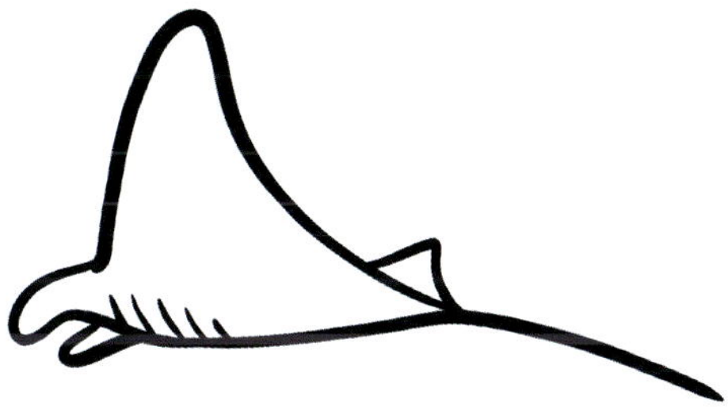

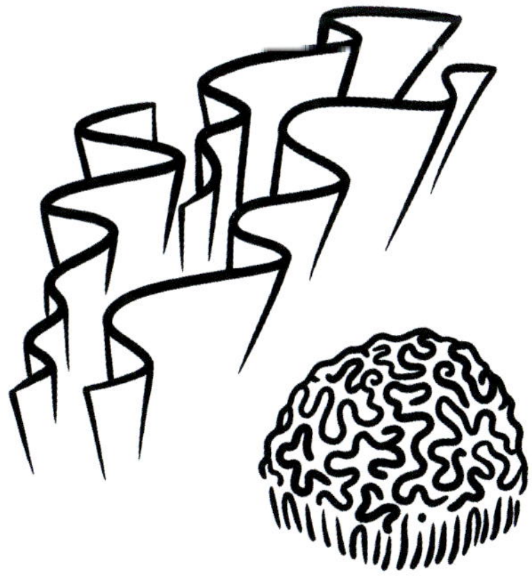

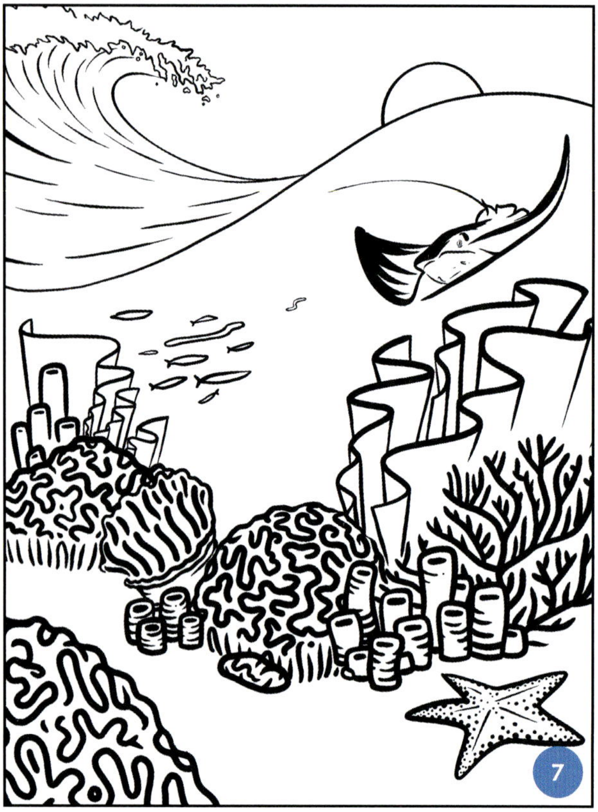
7

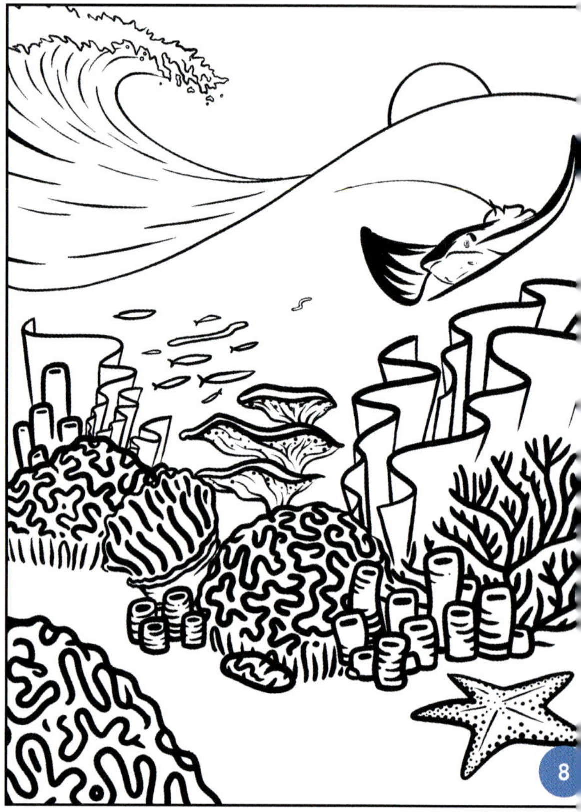
8

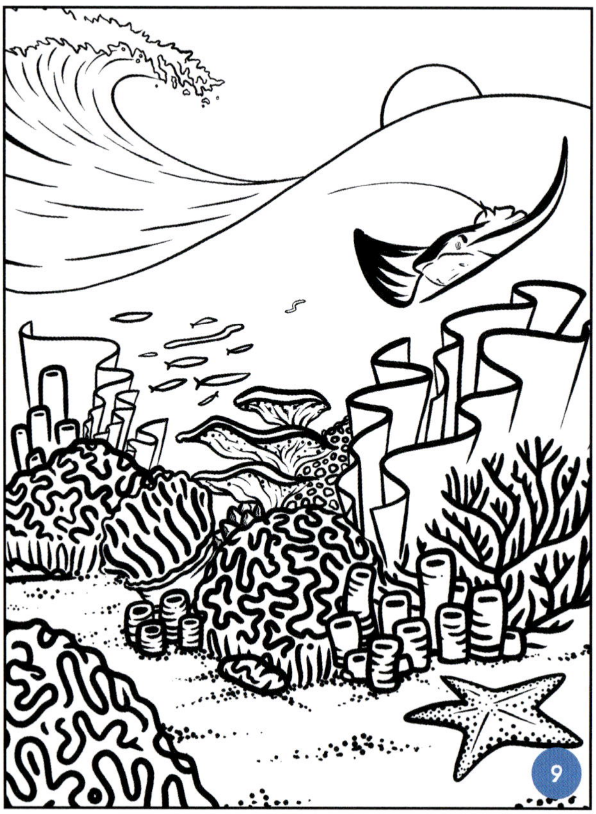
9

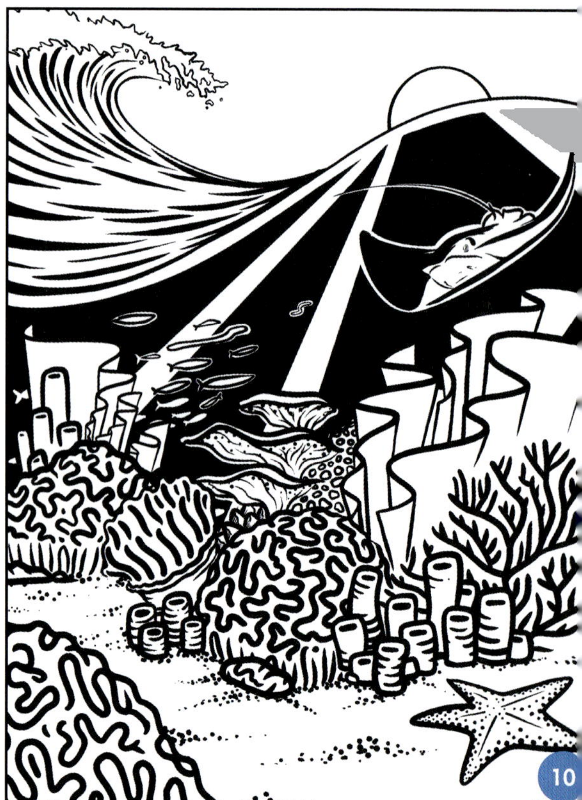
10

Now, Let's Draw the Scene (Final Steps)

7. Draw a School of Fish (page 148) and add a Manta Ray (page 149) swimming through the reef.

8. Add a Horn Coral (page 148) coming from the top of the coral reef.

9. Draw some more reeflike texture by layering small clusters of circles and rocks in the background of the reef. Make a sandy sea floor by drawing groups of small dots throughout the bottom of the reef.

10. Add sunbeams shining through the water by drawing three diagonal beams through the water underneath the wave, then shading in the surrounding areas. Thicken the rippling strokes on the top of the wave for an extra reflective surface.

11. Draw some puffy clouds in the sky, letting them overlap with the sun to create transparency.

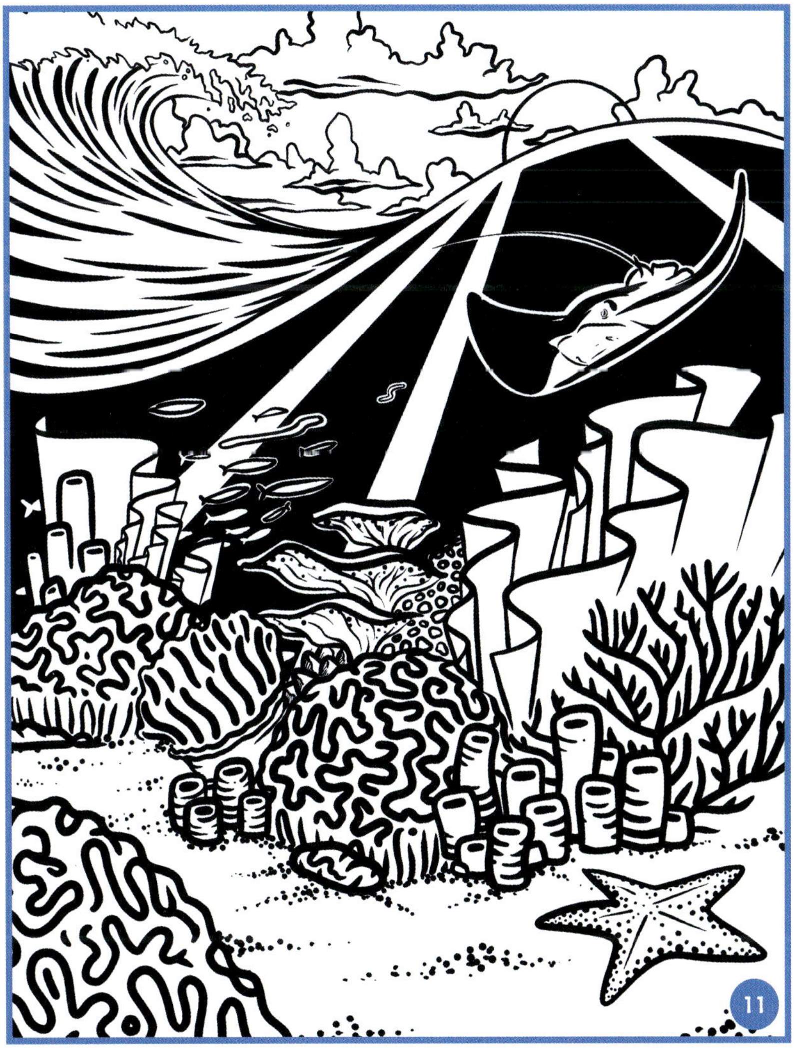

UNVEILING NATURE'S TAPESTRY
A CONCLUSION

As you've flipped through this book, you've delved into the incredible diversity of biomes—each a unique thread in the grand tapestry of our planet. But the real magic unfolds when we step outside their individual frames and witness these biomes weaving together. Lush rainforests bordering crystal-clear lakes, snow-capped mountains rising above vibrant meadows, coral reefs teeming with life alongside sandy beaches—the possibilities are endless.

This book has equipped you with the skills to capture the individual wonders of these landscapes. Now, it's time to unleash your creativity and celebrate the interconnectedness of the natural world!

Beyond the Frame: Merging Your Artistic Vision

As an artist, I'm all about pushing boundaries and finding inspiration in the unexpected. Don't be afraid to experiment and combine the techniques you've learned! Try to envision a majestic eagle soaring above a field of wildflowers, its outstretched wings mirroring the delicate veins of a nearby leaf. Picture a lone tree silhouetted against a fiery sunset, its branches echoing the intricate shapes of coral formations deep within the ocean. Let your imagination run wild!

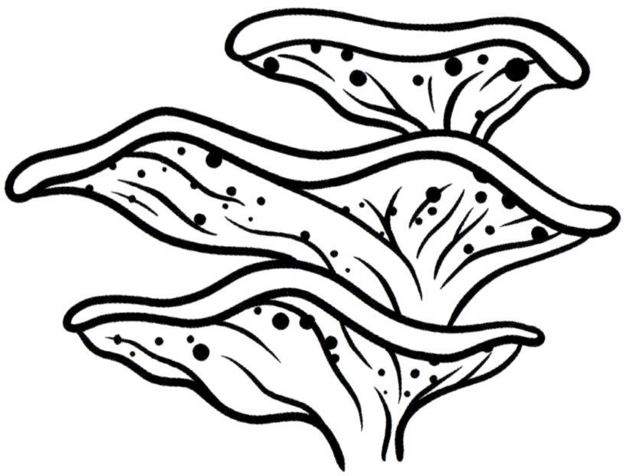

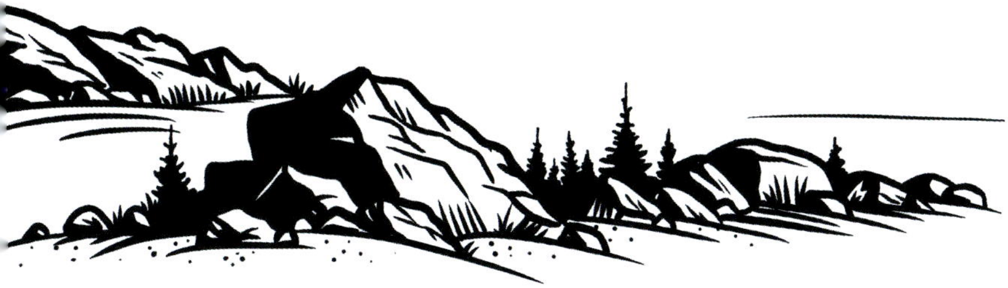

Seek Inspiration: Nature's Open Studio

The greatest inspiration lies just outside your doorstep. I often find myself sketching in local parks, exploring hidden trails or simply observing the beauty of my own backyard. You can too! Look for the intricate details—the way sunlight filters through a spiderweb, the enchanting patterns on a butterfly's wing, the way water ripples across a calm lake. These details are waiting to be translated onto your paper.

The Artistic Journey Continues

Thank you for joining me on this exploration of the natural world. Remember, drawing isn't just about capturing an image; it's about fostering a deeper connection with our planet. As you continue your artistic journey, keep these thoughts in mind:

Embrace Observation: Train your eye to see the intricate details that make each biome unique.

Draw with Passion: Let your enthusiasm for nature shine through in your artwork.

Experiment and Explore: Don't be afraid to step outside your comfort zone and try new techniques.

May your artistic adventures continue to flourish! Share your creations with the world, inspire others with your unique perspective, and remember, the greatest masterpieces are often found not in museums, but in the breathtaking landscapes that surround us.

This book is just the beginning. Now, get out there, explore, and draw the wonders of nature!

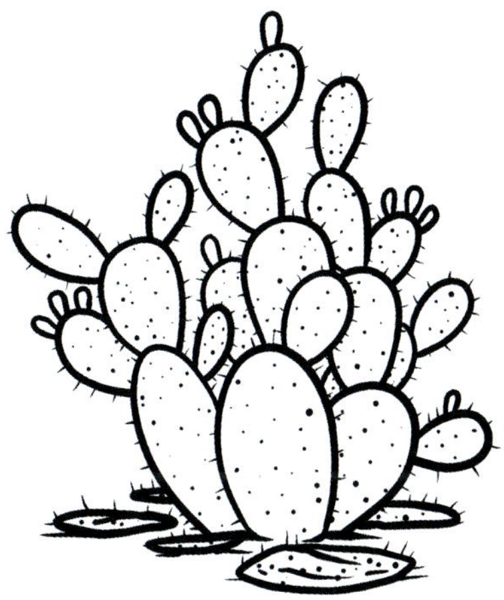

ACKNOWLEDGMENTS

I feel like the word "grateful" doesn't cover the immense gratitude I have for everyone who supported, inspired and co-created this book with me. There are so many to thank, and I hope you know if you're reading this, you're one of them.

Huge thank you to my encouraging family and all the inspiration you bring to my life.

Massive shoutout to my partner, Piper, who was with me for all the late nights, early mornings and endless hours of illustration that went into crafting each of these drawings and simplifying them to their most essential parts.

Thank you to Alexandra and the whole supportive team at Page Street. I could not do this without your guidance. Thank you for your expertise. I'm so honored and appreciative that you would choose me.

Last, but for sure not least, I'm grateful to my subscribers and followers, because without you I would have never been blessed with this opportunity!

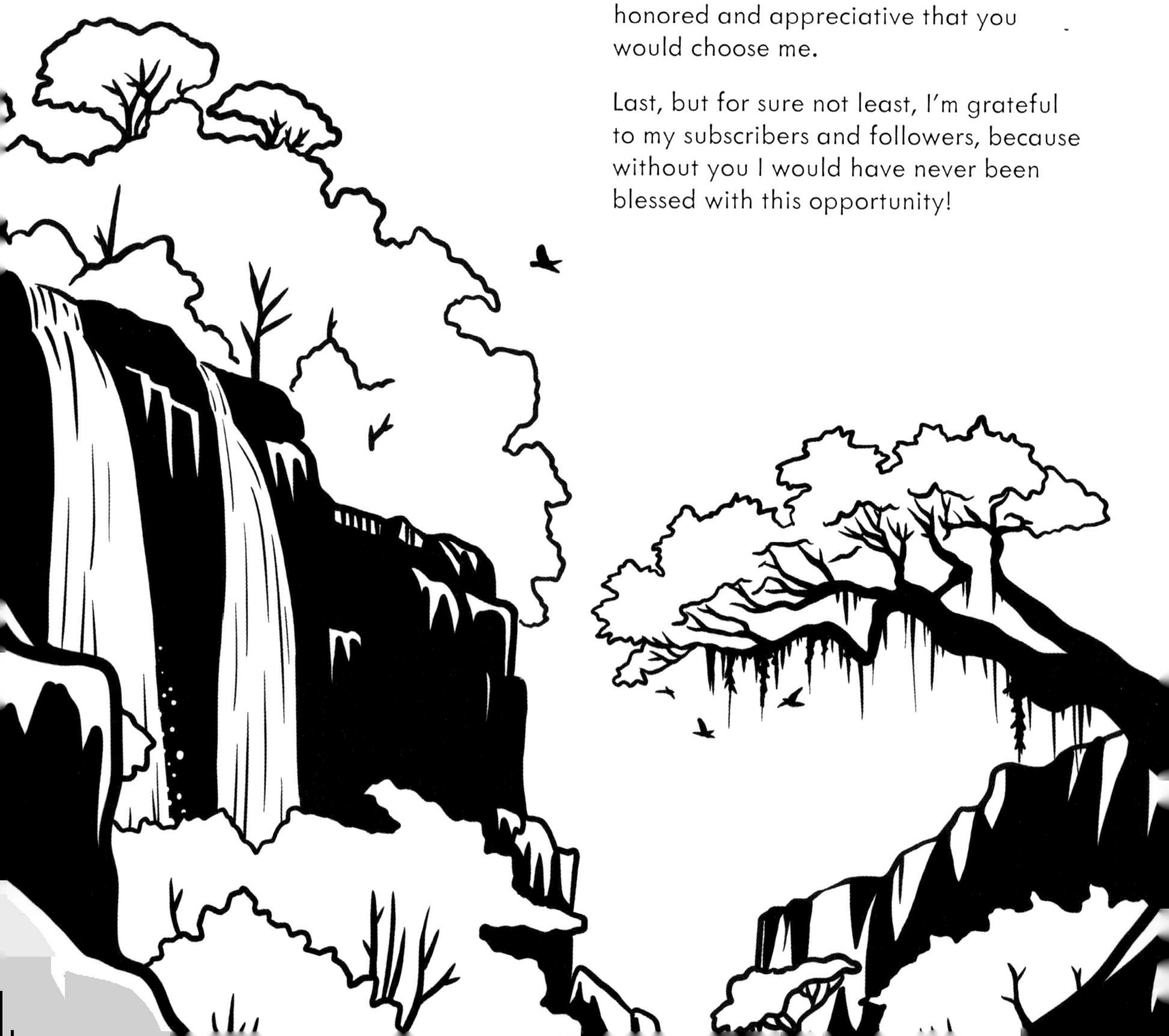

ABOUT THE AUTHOR

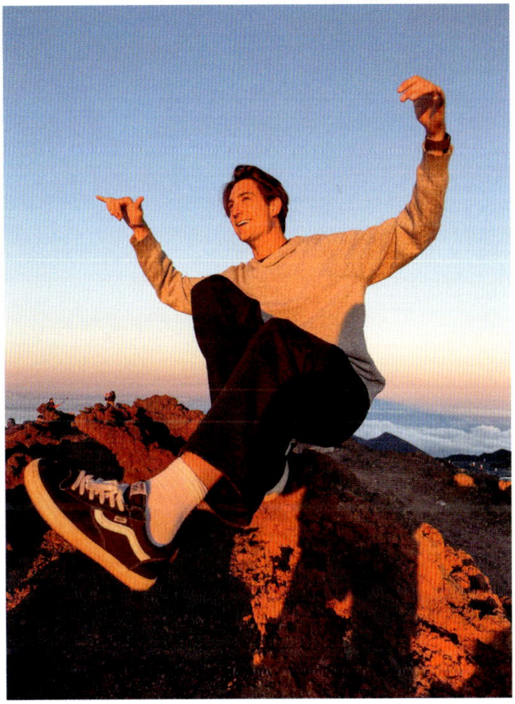

Harrison How is passionate about translating the majesty of the outdoors into attainable visuals. His love for nature bloomed during a childhood steeped in travel. Witnessing the world's diverse landscapes ignited a lifelong appreciation for the beauty that surrounds us. This deep connection spills over into his art. If you find him online as @harrisonhow, you'll discover an artist dedicated to making creativity accessible.

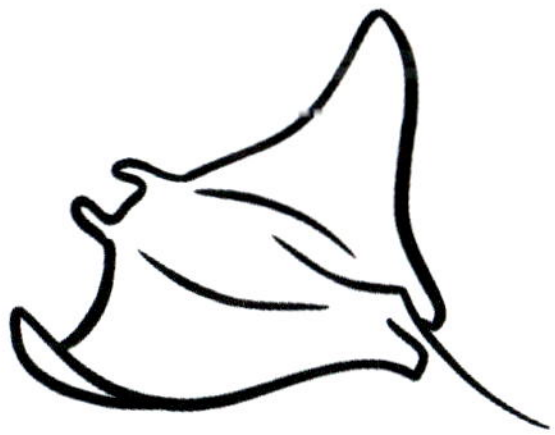

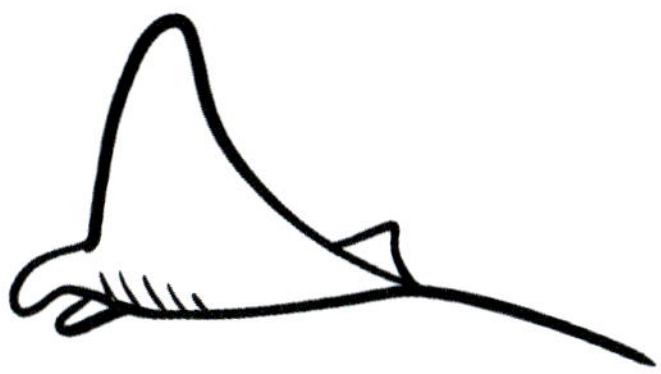

INDEX